Dear Reader

It's been an exciting and formative year for the entire team at the MICHELIN guides in North America, and it is with great pride that we present you with our 2017 edition to Chicago. Over the past year our dynamic inspectors have extended their reach to include a variety of establishments and multiplied their anonymous visits to restaurants in our selection in order to accurately reflect the rich culinary diversity this great city has to offer.

The Michelin Red Guides are an annual publication that recommends an assortment of delicious destinations and awards stars for excellence to a select few restaurants. Our company's founders, Édouard and André Michelin, published the first MICHELIN guide in 1900, to provide motorists with useful information about where they could service and repair their cars as well as find a good quality meal. Later in 1926, the star-rating system was introduced, whereby outstanding establishments are awarded for excellence in cuisine. Over the decades we have made many new enhancements to the Guide, and the local team here in Chicago eagerly carries on these traditions. As part of the Guide's historic, highly confidential, and meticulous evaluation process, our inspectors have anonymously and methodically eaten their way through the entire city with a mission to marshal the finest in each category for your enjoyment. While they are expertly trained professionals in the food industry, the Guides remain consumer-driven and provide comprehensive choices to accommodate your every comfort, taste, and budget. By dining and drinking as "everyday" customers, our inspectors are able to experience and evaluate the same level of service and cuisine as any other guest. This past year has seen some unique advancements in Chicago's dining scene. Some of these can be found in each neighborhood introduction, complete with photography depicting our favored choices.

For more information and to get our inside scoop, you may follow the Inspectors on Twitter (@MichelinGuideCH) and Instagram (@michelininspectors) as they chow their way around town and talk about unusual dining experiences, tell entertaining food stories, and detail other personal encounters. We thank you for your patronage and truly hope that the MICHELIN guide will remain your preferred reference to Chicago's restaurants.

Contents

THE MICHELIN GUIDE

CHICAGO

Michelin Travel Partner
Société par actions simplifiées au capital de 11 288 880 EUR
27 Cours de l'Ile Seguin - 92100 Boulogne Billancourt (France)
R.C.S. Nanterre 433 677 721

Dépôt légal novembre 2016

Printed in Canada - octobre 2016
Printed on paper from sustainably managed forests
Impression et Finition : Transcontinental (Canada)

Our editorial team has taken the greatest care in writing this guide and checking the information in it. However, practical information (administrative formalities, prices, addresses, telephone numbers, Internet addresses, etc) is subject to frequent change and such information should therefore be used for guidance only. It is possible that some of the information in this guide may not be accurate or exhaustive as of the date of publication. Before taking action (in particular in regard to administrative and customs regulations and procedures), you should contact the appropriate official administration. We hereby accept no liability in regard to such information.

The MICHELIN Guide

"This volume was created at the turn of the century and will last at least as long".

This foreword to the very first edition of the MICHELIN guide, written in 1900, has become famous over the years and the Guide has lived up to the prediction. It is read across the world and the key to its popularity is the consistency in its commitment to its readers, which is based on the following assurances.

→ Anonymous Inspections

Our inspectors make anonymous visits to restaurants to gauge the quality of cuisine offered to the everyday customer. They pay their own bill and make no indication of their presence. These visits are supplemented by comprehensive monitoring of information—our readers' comments are one valuable source, and are always taken into consideration.

→ Independence

Our choice of establishments is a completely independent one, made for the benefit of our readers alone. Decisions are discussed by the inspectors and editor, with the most important considered at the global level. Inclusion in the Guide is always free of charge.

→ The Selection

The Guide offers a selection of the best restaurants in each category of comfort and price. A recommendation in the Guides is an honor in itself, and defines the establishment among the "best of the best."

→ Annual Updates

All practical information, the classifications, and awards, are revised and updated every year to ensure the most reliable information possible.

→ Consistency & Classifications

The standards and criteria for the classifications are the same in all countries covered by the Michelin Guides. Our system is used worldwide and easy to apply when selecting a restaurant.

→ The Classifications

We classify our restaurants using XXXXX-X to indicate the level of comfort. A symbol in red suggests a particularly charming spot with unique décor or ambience. The ✿✿✿-✿ specifically designates an award for cuisine. They do not relate to a chef or establishment and are unique from the classification.

→ Our Aim

As part of Michelin's ongoing commitment to improving travel and mobility, we do everything possible to make vacations and eating out a pleasure.

How to Use This Guide

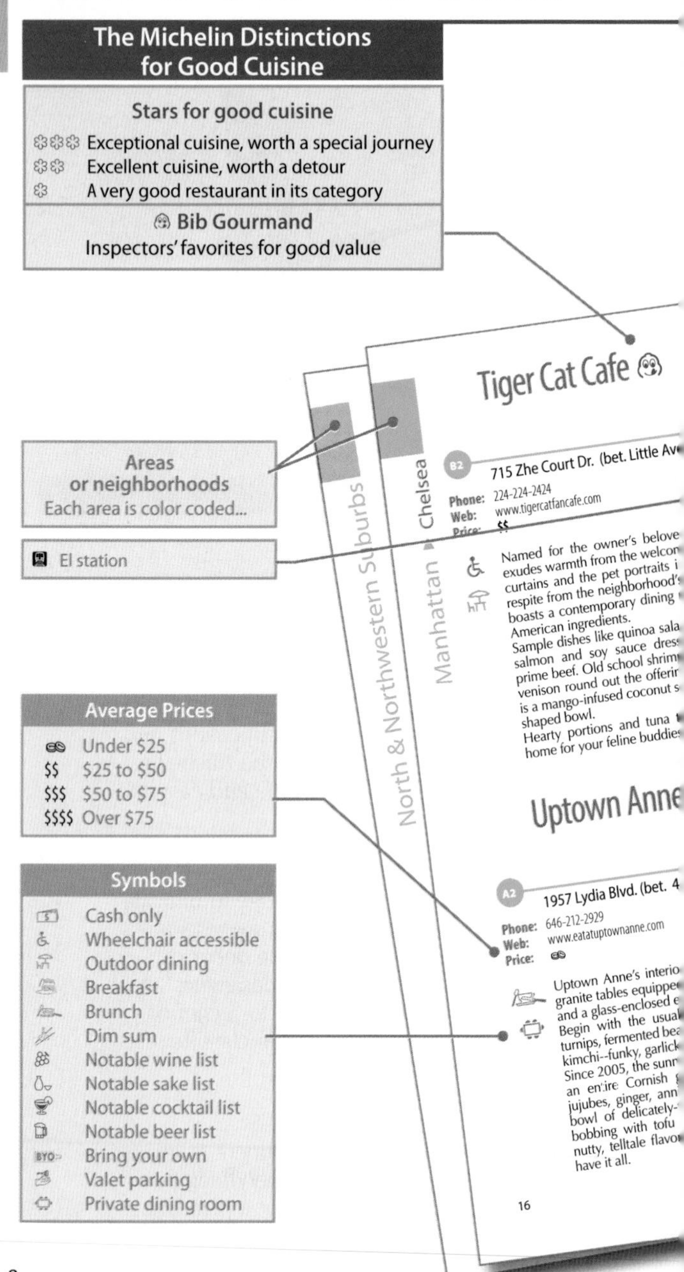

Restaurant Classifications by Comfort

More pleasant if in red

X	Comfortable
XX	Quite comfortable
XXX	Very comfortable
XXXX	Top class comfortable
XXXXX	Luxury in the traditional style
▤	Small plates

Map Coordinates

Sonya's Palace ✿

Italian XXXX

A4 100 Reuther Pl. (at 30th St.)

Dinner Mon – Sat

Subway: 23rd St (Eighth Ave.)
Phone: 917-222-1155
Web: www.sonyasfabulouspalace.com
Price: $$$$

Home cooked Italian never tasted so good as at this unpretentious palace. The decor claims no big-name designers, and while the Murano glass light fixtures are chic and the velveteen-covered chairs are comfortable, this isn't a restaurant where millions of dollars were spent on the interior.

Instead, food is the focus here. The restaurant's name may not be Italian, but it nonetheless serves some of the best pasta in the city, made fresh in-house. Dishes follow the seasons, thus ravioli may be stuffed with fresh ricotta and herbs in summer, and with pumpkin in fall. Most everything is liberally dusted with Parmigiano Reggiano, a favorite ingredient of the chef. Start meals with an immaculately fresh caprese salad, then sample a crisp pie from the Neapolitan wood-burning pizza oven. One bite of the lasagna, rich with creamy ricotta and hearty Bolognese, will have you cheering "Mamma mia," while oversized portions have some crying "basta!"

For Dessert, you'll have to deliberate between the likes of creamy tiramisu, ricotta cheesecake, and the homemade gelato. One thing's for sure: you'll never miss your nonna's cooking when you eat at Sonya's.

17

Manhattan ▸ Chelsea

Where to Eat

Chicago

Andersonville, Edgewater & Uptown

LINCOLN SQUARE · RAVENSWOOD

A walk through Chicago's North side, rich with culinary traditions from centuries of immigrant settlers, is like globe-trotting. A number of local businesses, specialty stores, row houses, and hotels populate the quaint streets of Andersonville, and architecture buffs never grow weary of the numerous art deco buildings set along Bryn Mawr Avenue and Lake Michigan's beaches.

HOW SWEDE IT IS

A water tower emblazoned with the blue-and-yellow Swedish flag rises above Clark Street, proudly representing Andersonville's Nordic roots. Step inside the Swedish-American Museum for a history lesson. Then head to one of the last Swedish emporiums in the area—**Wikstrom's Gourmet Foods'** online-only gift shop—to take home a bag of red fish or even meatballs and herring among other packaged goods. While some early birds line up for cinnamon-streusel coffee cake at the **Swedish Bakery**, others may be found perched at their counter for an individually sized treat and complimentary cup of coffee. For the heartiest appetites, a Viking breakfast at **Svea Restaurant** complete with Swedish-style pancakes, sausages, and toasted limpa bread fits the bill. Beyond the well-represented Scandinavian community, Andersonville brings the world to its doorstep thanks to those amply stocked shelves at **Middle East Bakery & Grocery**. Their deli selection features a spectrum of spreads, breads, olives, and hummus making it entirely feasible to throw a meze feast in minutes. But, if your tastes run further south (of the border), then **Isabella Bakery** is a gem for all things Guatemalan—and turns out a host of tamales to die for. Adventurous foodies depend on the grocery section to keep their pantries stocked with fresh spices, dried fruits, rosewater, nuts, teas, and more.

AN ASIAN AFFAIR

Across town, the pagoda-style roof of the Argyle El stop on the Red Line serves as another visual clue to the plethora of eats available here. Imagine an East Asian lineup of Chinese, Thai, and Vietnamese restaurants, noodle shops, delis, bakeries, and herbalists. Platters of lacquered, bronzed duck and pork make **Sun Wah BBQ** an inviting and popular spot for Cantonese cuisine, while **dak Korean** is always a cult favorite for spicy chicken wings and rice bowls served from a counter. However, sushi lovers will need to content themselves with just one, very delicious maki. And for those less inclined to cook for themselves, a genesis of casual eateries is prospering along these streets. **BopNgrill** for instance specializes in fusion food like *loco moco* or fantastically messy burgers including the "Umami" which is typically packed with truffled mushrooms. Finally, make sure to stop by **Little Vietnam** on Bryn Mawr for affordable salads, sandwiches, and that divine bowl of steaming *pho*.

MEAT, POTATOES —AND MORE

Chicagoans can't resist a good sausage, so find them giving thanks regularly to the German immigrants who helped develop Lincoln Square and whose appreciation for fine meats still resonates in this neighborhood. Old World-inspired butchers ply their trade, stuffing wursts and offering specialty meats and deli items at **Gene's Sausage Shop**. For a more refined selection of chops, steaks and free-range poultry,

head to **Lincoln Quality Meat Market**. And speaking of meat treats, **Wolfy's** serves one of the best red-hots in Uptown, piling its dogs with piccalilli, pickles, peppers, and other rainbow-colored condiments. Its iconic neon sign (a crimson frankfurter jauntily pierced by a pitchfork) only intensifies the urge to stop here.

Andersonville's charming tap room and restaurant **Acre** specializes in farm-fresh ingredients and local, organic meats to produce a hearty menu of soups, sausages and pasta. But for dinner party essentials (think veggies, fruits and flowers), there is a farmer's market in most areas, most days of the week. The **Andersonville Farmer's Market** (held on Wednesdays) hosts a number of bakeries and an orchard's worth of Asian fruit. Then there's the **Lincoln Square Farmer's Market**, which throws its doors open on Tuesdays and hosts live music during market hours every Thursday evening. Also in Lincoln Square, **HarvesTime Foods** wears its sustainability on its sleeve, with a solar-paneled roof and array of regionally sourced produce. A collaboration between beloved artisans Co-op Sauce and Crumb Chicago, Edgewater's **Sauce and Bread Kitchen** brings two of the city's favorite local products together at one café. Made-to-order breakfast and lunch sandwiches filled with maple sausage or applewood-smoked turkey are lavished with house-made condiments like tomato sauce (a fan fave for a fitting reason), while other party treats like hot sauce have a cult-ish following.

RAISE A GLASS

Critically acclaimed as one of the country's best boutique coffee shops, **The Coffee Studio** pours a mean cup of joe. Their locally roasted brews pair perfectly with a box of the "glazed & infused" doughnuts, which may need to be ordered in advance. In Edgewater, the creative community convenes at **The Metropolis Café**, an offshoot of Chicago's own **Metropolis Coffee Company**. Searching for something stronger than caffeine to bring to your next reservation? As the name suggests, family-owned producers and small-batch offerings are the focus at **Independent Spirits Inc.**, a wine and liquor shop replete with global selections.

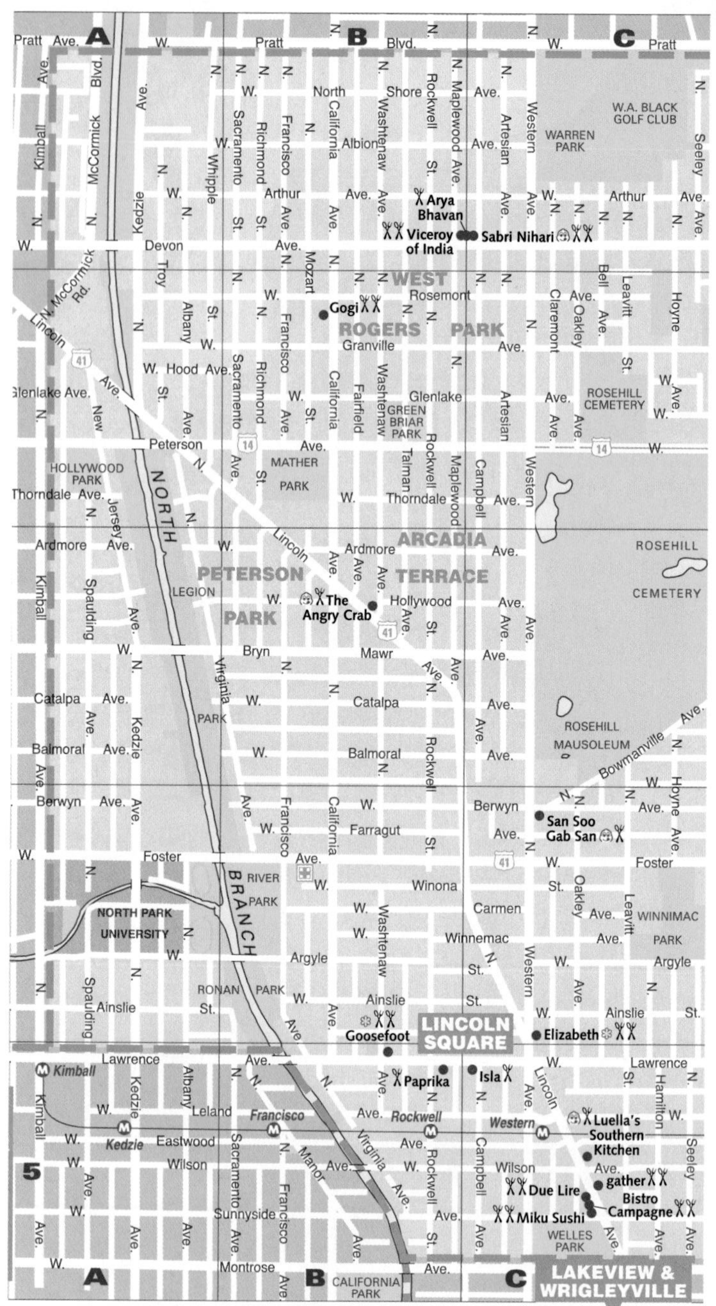
A
B
C
5
Pratt Ave.
W. Pratt Blvd.
North Shore Ave.
Albion Ave.
Arthur Ave.
Devon Ave.
Rosemont Ave.
Granville Ave.
W. Hood Ave.
Glenlake Ave.
Peterson Ave.
Thorndale Ave.
Ardmore Ave.
Hollywood Ave.
Bryn Mawr Ave.
Catalpa Ave.
Balmoral Ave.
Berwyn Ave.
Farragut Ave.
Foster Ave.
Winona St.
Carmen Ave.
Winnemac Ave.
Argyle St.
Ainslie St.
Lawrence Ave.
Leland Ave.
Eastwood Ave.
Wilson Ave.
Sunnyside Ave.
Montrose Ave.
Bowmanville Ave.
Lincoln Ave.
Virginia Ave.
Manor Ave.
N. McCormick Rd.
Kimball Ave.
McCormick Blvd.
Kedzie Ave.
Troy St.
Albany Ave.
Whipple St.
Sacramento Ave.
Richmond St.
Francisco Ave.
Mozart St.
California Ave.
Fairfield Ave.
Washtenaw Ave.
Talman Ave.
Rockwell St.
Maplewood Ave.
Campbell Ave.
Artesian Ave.
Western Ave.
Claremont Ave.
Oakley Ave.
Bell Ave.
Leavitt St.
Hoyne Ave.
Hamilton Ave.
Seeley Ave.
Jersey Ave.
Spaulding Ave.
New Ave.
W.A. BLACK GOLF CLUB
WARREN PARK
WEST ROGERS PARK
ROSEHILL CEMETERY
GREEN BRIAR PARK
MATHER PARK
HOLLYWOOD PARK
ARCADIA TERRACE
PETERSON PARK
LEGION PARK
ROSEHILL MAUSOLEUM
NORTH BRANCH
NORTH PARK UNIVERSITY
RIVER PARK
RONAN PARK
WINNIMAC PARK
LINCOLN SQUARE
WELLES PARK
CALIFORNIA PARK
Kimball
Kedzie
Francisco
Rockwell
Western
41
14
Arya Bhavan
Viceroy of India
Sabri Nihari
Gogi
The Angry Crab
San Soo Gab San
Goosefoot
Elizabeth
Paprika
Isla
Luella's Southern Kitchen
gather
Due Lire
Bistro Campagne
Miku Sushi
LAKEVIEW & WRIGLEYVILLE

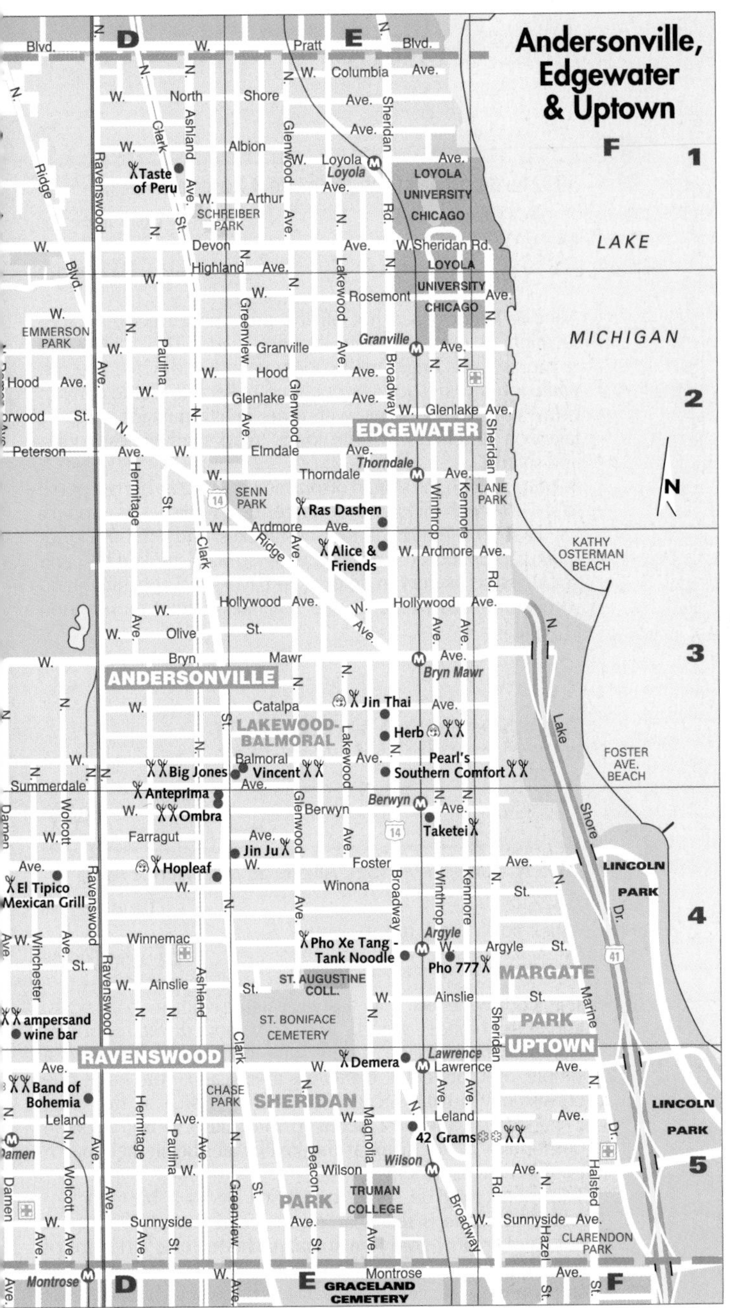

Andersonville, Edgewater & Uptown
LAKE
MICHIGAN
EDGEWATER
ANDERSONVILLE
LAKEWOOD-BALMORAL
RAVENSWOOD
SHERIDAN PARK
MARGATE PARK
UPTOWN
LOYOLA UNIVERSITY CHICAGO
SCHREIBER PARK
EMMERSON PARK
SENN PARK
LANE PARK
KATHY OSTERMAN BEACH
FOSTER AVE. BEACH
LINCOLN PARK
ST. AUGUSTINE COLL.
ST. BONIFACE CEMETERY
CHASE PARK
TRUMAN COLLEGE
CLARENDON PARK
GRACELAND CEMETERY
Taste of Peru
Ras Dashen
Alice & Friends
Jin Thai
Herb
Pearl's Southern Comfort
Big Jones
Vincent
Anteprima
Ombra
Taketei
Jin Ju
Hopleaf
El Tipico Mexican Grill
Pho Xe Tang - Tank Noodle
Pho 777
ampersand wine bar
Demera
Band of Bohemia
42 Grams
Loyola
Granville
Thorndale
Bryn Mawr
Berwyn
Argyle
Lawrence
Wilson
Damen
Montrose

Alice & Friends

5812 N. Broadway (bet. Ardmore & Rosedale Aves.)

Phone: 773-275-8797 — Dinner Wed – Mon
Web: N/A
Price: ⊛ — Thorndale

Alice & Friends' is a hot off the press vegan gem, set in a location as unusual as its kitchen's carte. This multi-room restaurant feels bright with canary yellow and white accents, while the mood is forever cool and collected. Come early or risk waiting in line along with other health-nuts for guilt-free takes on America's favorite foods (read sandwiches, soups, and salads).

In keeping with the slogan displayed on its walls, bring a posse to share in such inexpensive and restorative dishes as peppery winter soup with Korean radish, shiitakes, and kombu. *Dolsot bibimbap* or "burnt" brown rice tossed with smoked tofu and *gochujang* is as fiery in color as in flavor; and zucchini bread with walnuts as well as raisins feels just right at morn, noon or night.

ampersand wine bar

American 

D4

4845 N. Damen Ave. (bet. Ainslie St. & Lawrence Ave.)

Phone: 773-728-0031 — Dinner Tue – Sun
Web: www.ampersandchicago.com
Price: **$$** — Damen (Brown)

This cool wine bar cuts a stylish figure with its pale walls, gorgeous blonde wood, and sun-flooded dining room. Combine that urbane setting with polished service and a simple, but perfectly executed menu and you have one consistently great Chicago spot. Grab a seat at the long, L-shaped bar, the best perch in the house to ask a zillion questions—or just dig in as the small plates begin their march from behind the counter.

The menu may be small, but it still packs a big punch—what's available is seasonal, diverse, and extremely fresh. A cold and creamy gold tomato gazpacho features tart strips of roasted eggplant and cool cucumber; while a deconstructed strawberry shortcake arrives in layers of luscious basil caramel and sweet berries.

The Angry Crab

Seafood

B3

5665 N. Lincoln Ave. (bet. Fairfield & Washtenaw Aves.)

Phone: 773-784-6848
Web: N/A
Price: $$

Lunch Sat – Sun
Dinner nightly

BYO

Don't be shellfish—bring friends, beer, and wine to dinner at The Angry Crab for a messy, more-the-merrier experience. Lines form nightly for the chance to fill up on a Cajun-style spread shot through with Vietnamese flavors that reflect the owners' heritage.

Order from the laminated menus or the large overhead chalkboard for a seafood feast with options like whole head-on shrimp or enormous snow crab legs. Pick from a choice of lemon, garlic, or spicy sauces, stake your claim on a roll of paper towels and a seat at the communal tables, and then rip open the plastic bags in which the seafood arrives and dig in with your claws. Still hungry? Make it a true crab boil and add sausage, corn on the cob, and red bliss potatoes to round out the meal.

Anteprima

Italian

D4

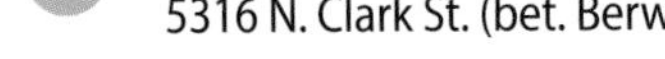

5316 N. Clark St. (bet. Berwyn & Summerdale Aves.)

Phone: 773-506-9990
Web: www.anteprimachicago.net
Price: $$

Dinner nightly
Berwyn

Nestled into a vibrant strip of shops and eateries, this family-friendly gem is set apart by smart plate-glass windows and olive green-tinted woodwork. Inside, rusticity rules the roost with pressed-tin ceilings and wood paneling. It's the kind of place where even solo diners feel welcome—perched at the bar, ogling a copper vat full of *grissini* or the chef's knife swishing through a loaf of bread.

Peek at the list of starters (or have them all on one plate), before diving into treats like grilled sardines with sweet fennel and fragrant herbs. Pasta is made fresh and ranges from tubular *paccheri* to ravioli filled with crushed peas and mint—finished in a light, parmesan-flecked sauce. For dessert, a well-made panna cotta wobbles with lemon syrup and zest.

Arya Bhavan

Indian X

B1

2508 W. Devon Ave. (bet. Campbell & Maplewood Aves.)

Phone: 773-274-5800 Lunch Sat – Sun
Web: www.aryabhavan.com Dinner Wed – Mon
Price: ⊜

This stretch of Devon teems with spots to sate Indo-Pakistani cravings, including dozens of longtime restaurants, catering halls, and markets serving curry, kebabs, and tandoori chicken. But Arya Bhavan stands out with personal, family-friendly service and fresh, carefully prepared Indian cuisine that also just happens to boast a few buzzwords (namely, vegan, organic, and gluten-free),

Even omnivores won't be able to resist the mixed basket appetizer, a substantial platter of tasty street snacks like tamarind-stuffed *mirch pakora* and spicy lemon-kissed potato *vada*. A classic rendition of garlicky, gingery *palak dal* blends hearty yellow lentils and fresh spinach. To finish the meal, take the plunge and reward your palate with outstanding avocado ice cream.

Big Jones

Southern XX

E3

5347 N. Clark St. (bet. Balmoral & Summerdale Aves.)

Phone: 773-275-5725 Lunch & dinner daily
Web: www.bigjoneschicago.com
Price: **$$** Berwyn

At Big Jones, guests are greeted with a "Guide to Good Drinking": a menu that includes barrel-aged punch selections and an impressive lineup of Bourbon and whiskey. Between that, the high bar tables, and plush velvet touches, this is a guaranteed good time. Yes, it's no front porch in Louisiana, but it's certainly close.

The menu is filled with dishes that reach back in Southern history and the service staff loves to dive into ancient detail. But this does not mean that the delicious cuisine doesn't explain itself: one may look forward to the likes of homemade pimento cheese with out-of-this-world Tasso ham cured in-house; or spot-on crawfish étouffee swimming with butter and wine and served atop a fluffy mound of spicy, smoky Braggadocio rice.

Band of Bohemia ✿

Gastropub XX

4710 N. Ravenswood Ave. (bet. Lawrence & Leland Aves.)

Phone: 773-271-4710
Web: www.bandofbohemia.com
Price: $$

Lunch Sat – Sun
Dinner nightly
Damen (Brown)

So much more than a working brewery with a talented kitchen, Band of Bohemia is in fact a truly inspired gastropub that produces its own utterly unique creations both in the glass and on the plate.

Located in a repurposed brick building across from the Metra tracks, the look is understandably industrial, with an open layout that unwinds into a series of seating options, inviting bar, and an open kitchen with another small bar set against pretty blue tiles. Curved, high-backed booths lend intimacy to counter the room's sheer size.

Stainless steel tanks displayed in the back hold the culinary-minded handiwork of their head brewer. On tap, expect a handful of rotating beers like the Coconut ESB, a copper-hued ale brewed with toasted fennel, coriander seeds, and coconut sugar.

Those rich brews are matched seamlessly to the kitchen's boundless small and large plates, which defy expectations with delicious success. Change is a virtue of the menu, but hits have included fresh pasta tinted green from nettles and tossed with aged goat cheese, toasted hazelnuts, and charred allium. The banana curry is a wonder of spicy and sweet notes from roasted cauliflower, smoky eggplant, goat's milk caramel, and peanuts.

Bistro Campagne

C5 French XX

4518 N. Lincoln Ave. (bet. Sunnyside & Wilson Aves.)

Phone: 773-271-6100 Lunch Sun
Web: www.bistrocampagne.com Dinner nightly
Price: $$ Western (Brown)

The romantic ideal of a French bistro is alive and well at quaint Bistro Campagne, where a tiny bar by the entrance is ready with your aperitif. Light slants through wooden Venetian blinds, bouncing off cream-and-brick walls in the welcoming dining room. Choose a white cloth-covered table inside or go outside under the garden's twinkling lights and green tree branches.

Inspired accompaniments make for memorable versions of rustic French standards. Start with a large, savory bowl of *soupe à l'oignon gratinée* capped with a thick layer of melting Gruyère. Then, discover their pitch-perfect duck *pithiviers,* wild mushroom duxelles and hazelnuts in puff pastry with a Madeira reduction. Brown butter *pain perdu* tucked with black figs is moist and delicious.

Demera

E5 Ethiopian X

4801 N. Broadway (at Lawrence Ave.)

Phone: 773-334-8787 Lunch & dinner daily
Web: www.demeraethiopian.com
Price: $$ Lawrence

Demera's well-lit corner location welcomes hungry Uptown residents looking to immerse themselves in Ethiopian cuisine. Colorful wicker seating at the dining room's communal table gives groups an authentic dining experience, while picture windows offer plenty of people-watching for everyone.

Vegetarian and omnivorous offerings abound on the menu, which features a small glossary of terms to help newcomers. Pleasantly spicy *yesiga wot* combines tender chunks of beef with onions and ginger in a rich *berbere* sauce. Served with turmeric-infused split peas and jalapeño-laced collard greens, this stew is a hearty pleasure. Sop up extra sauce with piles of tangy and soft *injera,* presented in the traditional Ethiopian manner in lieu of silverware.

Due Lire

Italian XX

4520 N. Lincoln Ave. (bet. Sunnyside & Wilson Aves.)

Phone: 773-275-7878 Dinner Tue – Sun
Web: www.due-lire.com
Price: $$ Western (Brown)

Naples native and gentleman's gentleman Massimo Di Vuolo welcomes guests from near and far to charming Due Lire. Smartly situated near the Old Town School of Folk Music, the dining room is often dotted with locals enjoying a pre-show dinner or lingering on the back patio with a glass of *falanghina*. Abstract art brings bright color and energy to the otherwise understated décor.

Comforting but refined modern Italian dishes offer hearty satisfaction: creamy polenta sops up *agnello*, a slow-simmered stew featuring braised lamb shank and tender root vegetables. Then strands of freshly made spaghetti are bathed in a rich, porky *amatriciana*-style ragù. For a refreshing finish, bite-sized ricotta *ciambelle* (doughnuts)—topped with *limoncello*-orange *crema*—keep things light.

El Tipico Mexican Grill

D4

1905 W. Foster Ave. (at Wolcott Ave.)

Phone: 773-754-8962 Lunch & dinner daily
Web: www.eltipicomexicangrill.com
Price: ⓢ Damen (Brown)

This sweet, hacienda-like spot has a lot heart—from the embracing family vibe to the bright and cozy interior. Rich, saturated walls and bright mural-like paintings set the mood; while thick, rustic wood chairs and a small service bar in the back offer a welcome reprieve for the weary.

The dishes at El Tipico are straightforward, plentiful and affordable—prepared with ultra-fresh ingredients and a careful eye. If they're not reinventing the wheel, they're certainly making sure it's crafted with love. Witness a warm, savory *sopa de tortilla* laced with bright green avocado, thick tortilla strips and gooey cheese; or the flavorful Azteca combo featuring a cheese-and-refried bean burrito, chicken tostada and soft enchilada with ranchero sauce.

Elizabeth ✿

Contemporary XX

C4

4835 N. Western, Unit D (bet. Ainslie St. & Lawrence Ave.)

Phone: 773-681-0651 Dinner Tue – Sat
Web: www.elizabeth-restaurant.com
Price: **$$$$** Western (Brown)

Elizabeth is a restaurant that endeavors to tell a story—one that explores land and sea through contemporary American cuisine.

The diminutive interior has only a handful of tables, each with views of the brightly lit kitchen. The whitewashed-tin ceiling and shelves stocked with everything from Dutch ovens to jars of pickles make it seem like we're all dining in Chef Iliana Regan's cottage-chic underground restaurant. You might even see her refilling your water glass; this is a humble place where dedication trumps attitude.

The nightly multi-course menu is a clear treatise on local, organic and foraged cuisine. Don't be surprised to be served a gnarled log, laden with wild mushrooms and grains stuffed into cabbage leaves, or a quail's nest containing crusty rye, fromage blanc, and topped with a soft-cooked egg. House breads can be an extraordinary highlight, including sourdough with tallow-enriched butter and walnut bitters, as well as nori bread served with bonito-infused butter and topped with caviar. Desserts may be inspired by the sea, as in the glass terrarium of dense pistachio sponge cake, dots of birch-flavored ice cream, blueberry sorbet, foraged herbs, and seashell-shaped kefir gummies.

42 Grams 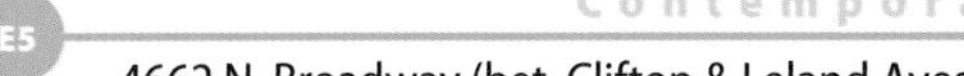

Contemporary XX

E5

4662 N. Broadway (bet. Clifton & Leland Aves.)

Phone: N/A — Dinner Wed – Sun
Web: www.42gramschicago.com
Price: $$$$ — Wilson

BYO

To know the name refers to the supposed weight of two souls is to also know that this is not your usual restaurant. In fact, it's hardly a restaurant at all and more like a dinner party with strangers—you even need to arrive with a bottle or two of wine under your arms. There are two seatings: the first is at the counter where you watch Chef/owner Jake Bickelhaupt and his two colleagues in action; for 8.30 P.M. arrivals, it's the large communal table. For both, you'll be sharing your dinner with people you don't know, but the ice is usually broken by someone asking where their fellow diners have eaten recently.

The set menu offers no choice but any allergies are discussed during the bothersome flurry of e-mails that follow the initial impersonal booking process. Then it's over to Jake's smiling wife, Alexa, to guide diners through the parade of dishes. The cooking is clever and contemporary and the ingredients superlative, whether that's the peekytoe crab "dumpling" or *mojama de atún* (air-dried, salt-cured tuna) plated on black slate and perched above a light green pea gelato. Dishes are wonderfully well-balanced and modern techniques are used to great effect to deliver superb flavors.

A coffee "spuma" flavored with cardamom and whipped cream is an ideal way to cap off this exceptional meal.

gather

C5

4539 N. Lincoln Ave. (bet. Sunnyside & Wilson Aves.)

Phone: 773-506-9300 — Lunch Sun
Web: www.gatherchicago.com — Dinner nightly
Price: $$ — Western (Brown)

A chic, cozy space lets guests get up close and personal at gather. Diners seeking dinner and a show take front row seats at barstools lining the open kitchen's polished granite counter, while tall communal tables fill with patrons enjoying bites from the menu's "gather and share" section. A rear dining room offers more solitude and romance.

Family-style Sunday dinners are a local draw, but the à la carte menu showcases flavorful options nightly. Slice into a single large *uovo raviolo* to mingle poached egg and ricotta with white truffle butter, jalapeño slivers, and chopped chives, or share a crock of Pernod-splashed mussels. Fragrant and garlicky, they're served with sourdough toast points for soaking up every last drop of the white wine-cream sauce.

Gogi

B2

6240 N.California Ave. (bet. Granville & Rosemont Aves.)

Phone: 773-274-6669 — Lunch Sun
Web: www.gogichicago.com — Dinner nightly
Price: $$

The surging popularity of Korean food continues to flourish along these shores of Lake Michigan. And as foodies would have you know, Gogi is one of the best places in the city to experience it. With its hip, industrial décor, imposing exhaust fans over each table (a clear sign that there's a ton of grilling going on), and lively blend of sweet, spicy, and sour flavors, dinner here promises to be a sensory explosion like no other. One could feast on the abundant pre-meal *banchan* alone—a stunning selection of kimchi, mirin-soaked fish cakes, sake-steamed black beans, and more. But, that would mean missing out on delicate slices of sirloin *bulgogi* smothered in a sweet, gingery marinade; or restorative, spicy *sundubu jjigae* bubbling away in an iron pot.

Goosefoot ✿

Contemporary XX

B5

2656 W. Lawrence Ave. (bet. Talman & Washtenaw Aves.)

Phone: 773-942-7547 Dinner Wed – Sat
Web: www.goosefoot.net
Price: $$$$ Rockwell

BYO

This understated plate-glass façade may seem lost in a sea of mediocrity, but the restaurant it houses is truly distinct. The soothing décor appears minimal, with splashes of orange banquettes, bare tables, and Rodin replicas to fashion a space that is instantly likeable. Menus are made of planting seed paper that guests are encouraged to take home, soak, and use to grow their own wildflowers. Dishes are intricate and take time for the well-versed staff to describe, which may explain the relatively slow pace of dining here.

The menu showcases noteworthy Chef Chris Nugent's classical edge and contemporary artistry. Start with a plump, butter-poached scallop seared until golden, set in a lobster-rich and coconutty sauce with maitake mushrooms and curry spices, surrounded by edible flower petals placed in gels redolent of lemongrass. This may be followed by a unique egg and shell presentation of black garlic custard dotted with shrimp, tucked with an enticingly sharp sprout purée. Superb cheese and dessert courses are a consistent highlight.

Goosefoot is still BYO, but an attached wine shop ensures that no one is caught empty-handed. Pay attention to the chocolate lab and market, too.

Herb

Thai

E3

5424 N. Broadway (bet. Balmoral & Catalpa Aves.)

Phone: 773-944-9050 Dinner Thu – Sun
Web: www.herbrestaurant.com
Price: $$ Bryn Mawr

BYO

In the sea of Thai restaurants that flank this area, elegant Herb stands out for its lovely wood and stone décor; and service staff friendly enough to use your name. This is killer Thai, elevated and prepared with care.

Herb offers both a three- and six-course prix-fixe dinner at tremendous value, but Chef/owner Patty Neumson's cooking is light (and delicious) enough to go the distance. A sample menu might begin with a cool pile of crunchy green papaya, carrot, and cucumber, laced in a beautifully balanced lime dressing with crispy vermicelli noodles and peanuts. Then move on to tofu and kabocha in a deliciously complex coconut curry full of wilted basil and heat. Soft glass noodles find their match in sautéed onions, fresh crab, and crunchy shrimp.

Hopleaf

Gastropub

D4

5148 N. Clark St. (bet. Foster Ave. & Winona St.)

Phone: 773-334-9851 Lunch & dinner daily
Web: www.hopleaf.com
Price: $$ Berwyn

There are so many things to love about Chicago's taverns: their complete lack of attitude; their undying hospitality; their downright delicious cooking.

Hopleaf is a classic example of all that and more, still packing the house almost 25 years after opening. A traditional bar graces the front, but the glassed-in kitchen is where the magic happens. Named after a pale ale brewed in Malta, Hopleaf fittingly flaunts a beer list so long that it's been called "a novel."

It's hard to go wrong at this beloved gastropub, but don't miss the mussels if they're available. Another gem: the wood-grilled Duroc pork chop—a thick, juicy chop in a red wine glaze, set over white grits with smoky Gouda, and accompanied by roasted cauliflower and broccoli salsify.

Isla

2501 W. Lawrence Ave., Unit D (bet. Campbell & Maplewood Aves.)

Phone: 773-271-2988 — Lunch & dinner Tue – Sun
Web: www.islapilipina.com
Price: — Rockwell

BYO

Don't let Isla's plain-Jane décor dissuade you—despite the flimsy curtains and bare-bones dining room, the space is practically bursting with Filipino pride. From the convivial owners and servers to the bantering patrons getting their fix of Filipino cable TV as they eat, the warmth and love for this Southeast Asian country is clear here.

Traditional dishes populate a menu that offers a whirlwind tour of the islands' bold flavors. *Tinolang manok*, a refreshing take on chicken soup, is redolent with ginger and punctuated by green papaya. Dried taro leaves in *laing sa gata* lend smokiness to tender, coconut milk-simmered pork and shrimp, and a side of Isla's famous adobo rice, spooned with the classic tart and garlicky pork stew, goes with everything.

Jin Ju

5203 N. Clark St. (at Foster Ave.)

Phone: 773-334-6377 — Dinner Tue – Sun
Web: www.jinjurestaurant.com
Price: $$ — Berwyn

A sexy spot on a bustling stretch of North Clark, Jin Ju spins out luscious Korean classics with aplomb. Inside, dim lighting, dark wood furnishings, and luxuriant fuchsia-red walls create a sophisticated coziness, while servers are gracious and attentive.

A simply named house salad showcases the restaurant's modern, accessible Korean ethos, combining meaty pan-seared portobello strips atop delicately bitter green leaf lettuce, torn sesame leaves, cucumbers, and scallions in a funky garlic-soy sauce. Without tableside barbecue grills, fatty pork slabs are sautéed in the kitchen for sweetly caramelized *samgyupsal*. Wrapped in sesame leaves with Brussels sprouts, beets, crispy leeks, and a smear of kicky miso paste, the package provides instant gratification.

Jin Thai

E3

5458 N. Broadway (at Catalpa Ave.)

Phone: 773-681-0555 — Lunch & dinner Wed – Mon
Web: www.jinthaicuisine.com
Price: — Bryn Mawr

BYO

In-the-know locals fill up on tasty Thai at this sleek corner hot spot, whose curving glass windows beckon many a passerby with views of and aromas from vibrant curries and spicy *laab*. Inside, a row of splashy pillows lends color and comfort to a wooden banquette, and woven placemats dress up dark wood tables.

Start a meal with zingy *miang kham*, a chopped mix of dried shrimp, fresh ginger, lime, peanuts, and coconut, all wrapped in a betel leaf. From there, move on to hot curry catfish or *Sukothai* noodle soup teeming with minced pork and steaming broth (add pinches of warm spices from the accompanying condiment tray for an even more soul-satisfying slurp). For dessert, pick from either roti ice cream, wonton bananas, or warm Thai custard.

Luella's Southern Kitchen

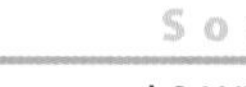

C5

4609 N. Lincoln Ave. (bet. Eastwood & Wilson Aves.)

Phone: 773-961-8196 — Lunch Tue – Sun
Web: www.luellassouthernkitchen.com — Dinner nightly
Price: $$ — Western (Brown)

BYO

Luella's is named for Chef Darnell Reed's Southern-born great-grandmother, and for good reason: one bite of its soul-infused fare will transport you to her hometown of Morgan City, Mississippi, a place she left behind for Chicago many years ago—and one that lives on in her grandson's cooking. The no-frills, order-at-the-counter spot is simply adorned, with genuinely welcoming service that only adds to the charm.

Every spoonful of Luella's andouille and chicken gumbo is one to remember, thanks to a roux that's been cooked for five (count 'em) hours. The hot, sugary beignets are a pastry wonder, and chicken and waffles drizzled with Bourbon syrup are Southern by way of Brussels, featuring thick, eggy Liège waffles standing in for the usual rounds.

Miku Sushi

4514 N. Lincoln Ave. (bet. Sunnyside & Wilson Aves.)

Phone: 773-654-1277 — Lunch & dinner daily
Web: www.mikuchicago.com
Price: $$ — Western (Brown)

Miku Sushi piles on the style in a spacious location with a polished, airy room featuring a 12-seat counter plus a full bar for cocktail hounds. More than a simple sushi spot, the menu boasts artfully presented and inventive maki, ramen, *yakitori*, and small plates that make for a festive night of sharing with fellow food lovers.

Snack on the *robusuta* roll, surely to become a "Lincoln Square classic" pairing lobster and fried banana; or for a more traditionally savory but still modern option, the Miya maki combines white tuna, snow crab, and avocado with grilled asparagus. Warm up with a bowl of springy, correctly spicy ramen teeming with fresh mushrooms, soft-boiled egg, and tender pork belly in a cloudy, miso-rich broth spiked with garlic and sesame oil.

Ombra

D4

5310 N. Clark St. (bet. Berwyn & Summerdale Aves.)

Phone: 773-506-8600 — Dinner nightly
Web: www.barombra.com
Price: $$ — Berwyn

Though it shares a kitchen with next-door gastropub Acre, Ombra is a destination in its own right. Booths patched with recycled leather jackets and "wallpaper" of vintage Italian newspapers give the cozy dining room a unique sense of place, and the Italian-inspired cuisine is just as interesting.

Diners make quick work of dishes like toothsome farro and mushroom "arancini," deviled eggs kissed with lemon aïoli, or parmesan-dusted meatballs in a chunky tomato sauce. Crispy skin-on whitefish is paired with buttery potatoes and takes a heavenly swim in caper-lemon sauce. Pizzas arrive charred from the wood oven, their dough flavorful and chewy, and creative cocktails like the Chicagroni—modernized with IPA and tea—keep the bar hopping.

Paprika

Indian

2547 W. Lawrence Ave. (bet. Maplewood Ave. & Rockwell St.)

Phone: 773-338-4906 — Dinner Tue – Sun
Web: www.paprikachicago.com
Price: $$ — Rockwell

Chef Shah Kabir and his family know hospitality. Prepare to be swept up in their warmth and care (with maybe a splash of kitsch) the minute you enter this richly colored space, adorned with artifacts. Even the chef himself is at the door welcoming guests to sit and sip a cool, refreshing *lassi*.
From aromatic, homemade curries to tasty twists on *dahls* (*turka dahl ki shabzi* is a revelation), everything is fresh and fragrant. Bengali fish curry is a notable attraction—its flavors mild yet lively with mustard seeds, firm and fresh green beans, and silky-sweet onions. A very nice selection of vegetarian dishes might include the veggie samosa: its soft, light shell is stuffed with spiced potatoes, peas, cauliflower, and served with a trio of tangy chutneys.

Pearl's Southern Comfort

Southern

E3

5352 N. Broadway (bet. Balmoral & Berwyn Aves.)

Phone: 773-754-7419 — Lunch Sat – Sun
Web: www.pearlschicago.com — Dinner Mon – Sat
Price: $$ — Berwyn

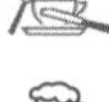

Chicago's been on a Southern food kick of late, and this sparkling Andersonville charmer is a straight up hepcat. Its enormous arched windows open up to a completely revamped 100 year-old room, featuring long exposed ceiling beams, whitewashed brick, dark slate walls, and soft leather chairs.
But even with all that design swag, the main draw at Pearl's Southern Comfort is still the food. For starters, there's the ace barbecue, but guests should hardly stop there. Try the enormous double cut pork chop, grilled to supple perfection and paired with "dirty" farro salad, Cajun slaw, and pork jus. Another staple, the Louisiana jambalaya, is served decadently dark and spicy, brimming with tender chicken, Andouille sausage, and Crystal hot sauce.

Pho 777

E4

1063-65 W. Argyle St. (bet. Kenmore & Winthrop Aves.)

Phone: 773-561-9909 Lunch & dinner Tue – Sun
Web: N/A
Price: ₲ Argyle

A market's worth of fresh ingredients allows Pho 777 to stand out in a neighborhood where Vietnamese restaurants—and their signature soup—seem to populate every storefront. Bottles of hot sauce, jars of fiery condiments, and canisters of spoons and chopsticks clustered on each table make it easy for regulars to sit down and start slurping.

Add choices like meatballs, tendon, flank steak, and tofu to the cardamom- ginger- and clove-spiced beef broth, which fills a vat large enough to sate a lumberjack-sized appetite. Then throw in jalapeños, Thai basil, and mint to your liking. If you're not feeling like *pho* this time around, snack on spring rolls with house-made roasted peanut sauce; or a stack of lacy *bánh xèo* stuffed with pork, chili sauce and sprouts.

Pho Xe Tang - Tank Noodle

Vietnamese 

E4

4953-55 N. Broadway (at Argyle St.)

Phone: 773-878-2253 Lunch & dinner Thu – Tue
Web: www.tank-noodle.com
Price: ₲ Argyle

BYO

A stone's throw from the Little Saigon EL, this simple corner spot keeps *pho* enthusiasts coming back for more. Communal cafeteria-style tables, crowded during prime meal times, are stocked with all the necessary funky and spicy condiments. Efficient service keeps the joint humming and lets the patrons focus on slurping.

Pho is the definitive draw here, and this fragrant, five-spiced, rice noodle- and beef-filled broth is accompanied by sprouts, lime wedges, and plenty of basil. Other delights on the massive menu include shrimp- and pork-stuffed rice flour rolls with addictive spicy and sour *nuoc cham*. Follow that with a fiery catfish soup simmered with an intriguing combination of okra, pineapple, and bamboo shoots drizzled with garlic oil.

Ras Dashen

E2

5846 N. Broadway (bet. Ardmore & Thorndale Aves.)

Phone: 773-506-9601 — Lunch & dinner Wed – Mon
Web: www.rasdashenchicago.com
Price: $$ — Thorndale

If you're lucky, grab a stool at one of the *mossab* tables to relish this Ethiopian kitchen's authentic cooking. Walls splashed with rust-orange and rattan chairs further elevate the faithful appeal, while a bar pouring honey wine and African beers keeps the local community happy.

Collective trays with delicacies speed out of the kitchen, so those who wish to immerse themselves in this nation's culinary culture should begin—on a light note—with Zenash's salad tossing chickpeas and crispy shallots with a touch of vinegar and tons of toasty spices. *Gored gored* highlights brisket marinated with *awaze*; and *yebeg alicha* is an aromatic lamb stew complete with spicy veggies. Sides of spongy and tart *injera* are ideal for cooling the palate from the creeping heat.

Sabri Nihari

Indian 

C1

2500-2502 W. Devon Ave. (at Campbell Ave.)

Phone: 773-465-3272 — Lunch & dinner daily
Web: www.sabrinihari.com
Price:

Sabri Nihari outshines the restaurant competition on this crowded stretch of West Devon Avenue. A recent expansion has doubled the size of the posh Indo-Pakistani spot, where crystal chandeliers make gold-hued walls gleam more brightly.

As with many Southeast Asian restaurants, vegetarian dishes abound—but that's only the beginning of the expansive menu. Whole okra pods add a grassy, peppery bite to beefy *bhindi gosht*, and delightful chicken *charga*, an entire spatchcocked bird marinated in yogurt and lime, is rubbed generously with spices before crisping up in the deep fryer. No alcohol is served in deference to many of the abstaining clientele, but you won't miss it; buttery naan and creamy lassi with homemade yogurt help to balance out the spice-fest.

San Soo Gab San

5247 N. Western Ave. (at Berwyn Ave.)

Phone: 773-334-1589 — Lunch & dinner daily
Web: www.sansoogabsan.com
Price: $$ — Western (Brown)

Tucked into a tiny strip mall in the West Edgewater-Upper Andersonville area, San Soo Gab San has generated quite a buzz among serious Korean food fans. Inside, you'll find a warm, welcoming space with large tabletop grills to cook your own meats.

Most excitingly, the authentic, traditional dishes turned out of the kitchen don't bow or cater to Western sensibilities—to wit, an incredibly flavorful bowl of piping hot goat meat soup arrives with wild sesame green leaves and a flutter of seeds. Among the many popular casseroles and stews, don't miss the *beo seot danjan zigae*, choc-a-block with tender tofu, savory mushrooms, beef and veggies. The delicious barbecue is perfect for a group feast or those looking to have some fun with their food.

Taketei

1111 W. Berwyn Ave. (bet. Broadway & Winthrop Ave.)

Phone: 773-769-9292 — Dinner Mon – Sat
Web: N/A
Price: ⊜ — Berwyn

BYO

Though it's a mere sliver of a space, Taketei's Japanese temple to fresh fish makes a bold statement in this neighborhood, noted for its Vietnamese joints. The wee room, so small there's not even a true sushi counter, remains serenely bright but minimal, filled with a handful of white tables and chairs.

A limited menu makes the most of shiny pieces of fish. With a good number of nigiri available for less than $3 each, regulars know to load up. Or, go all out with a sashimi platter featuring a wide selection of generously sliced seafood like mackerel, octopus, and *maguro* with a bowl of rice.

Manageably sized, non-gimmicky rolls along with appetizers like pert, crunchy *hiyashi wakame* salad or spinach with sweet sesame sauce supplement this appealing array.

Taste of Peru

Peruvian 

D1

6545 N. Clark St. (bet. Albion & Arthur Aves.)

Phone: 773-381-4540 Lunch & dinner daily
Web: www.tasteofperu.com
Price: ⓢⓢ

BYO

Tucked inside a strip mall and entirely plain-Jane in appearance, foodies trek to this *caliente* fave for a formidable meal of authentic dishes. The owner is chatty and tunes groovy, all of which make for a wonderful precursor to such peppery items as *aji de gallina* (shredded chicken in a walnut sauce, enriched with parmesan) or *chupe de camarones* (a hot, spicy, bright bowl of shrimp and rice). This is clearly not the place for a pisco sour, but feels like Sundays *con la familia* where *papa a la huancaina* doused in *amarillo chile*, and *arroz chaufa* with veggies and beef jerky-like strips are merely some of the items on offer.

It's worth noting though that while the food is decidedly traditional, mysteriously there's no pork to be found anywhere on the menu.

Viceroy of India

Indian 

B1

2520 W. Devon Ave. (bet. Campbell & Maplewood Aves.)

Phone: 773-743-4100 Lunch & dinner daily
Web: www.viceroyofindia.com
Price: ⓢⓢ

Solid cooking, an "upscale" setting and a full bar all set this South Asian spot in a league of its own. A visible highlight on Devon Avenue, this quaintly christened restaurant features steely blue walls, tables dressed with linen, arches, and dramatic chandeliers. The spacious dining room is perfect for large parties; and in the front vestibule, there's even a small café to pick up sweets to go.

Sit back, relax, and enjoy the fragrant curries with spices like cardamom and cumin that fill the air. Much of the menu is delicious, but the flaky samosa served with coconut chutney is a notable highlight. Other picks include tamarind rice studded with nuts and herbs; or *paneer makhani*—homemade cottage cheese cooked with tomato sauce, butter and cream.

Vincent

Belgian 

1475 W. Balmoral Ave. (bet. Clark St. & Glenwood Ave.)

Phone: 773-334-7168
Web: www.vincentchicago.com
Price: **$$**

Lunch Sun
Dinner Tue – Sun
Berwyn

Go Dutch at Vincent, where innovative yet approachable cooking meets a tried-and-true European bistro menu, boasting enough cheese to satisfy even the pickiest turophile. Adding to the romance, high-top marble tables and brocade-papered walls make for a warm, intimate ambience that's accented by tall votive candles.

Got an appetite? An overflowing pot of P.E.I. mussels is a decadent meal on its own, brimming with bits of pork belly, chilies, scallions, and cilantro, accompanied by a big bowl of traditional frites with mayonnaise. Basil and lemon balsam perk up risotto with charred purple cauliflower and braised fennel. Also, you'll want to hold on to your fork for slices of lemon butter cake with Chantilly cream and blueberry compote.

Look for our symbol, spotlighting restaurants with a notable beer list.

Bucktown & Wicker Park

UKRANIAN VILLAGE · WEST TOWN

A CAVE OF COOL

Like many of the Windy City's neighborhoods, Bucktown and Wicker Park have seen their residents shift from waves of Polish immigrants and wealthy businessmen who've erected stately mansions on Hoyne and Pierce avenues, to those young, hip crowds introducing modern taquerias and craft breweries to these streets. Still, the neighborhood knows how to retain its trendsetting rep, and continues to draw those who crave to be on the cutting edge of all things creative, contemporary, and culinary. Far from the internationally known boutiques along Magnificent Mile, indie shops and artisan producers of Milwaukee and Damen avenues offer one-of-a-kind treasures for all the five senses. Get a taste of Wicker Park's vast underground music scene at Reckless Records or at some of the city's largest music events, including the Wicker Park Fest, which is held each July and features no less than 28 bands. Likewise, the annual Green Music Fest draws every

eco-minded resident around. Snap up funky home accessories and original works at flea market-chic Penguin Foot Pottery, or wear art on your sleeve by designing your own Tee at the appropriately named T-shirt Deli.

HOT DOGS AND HAUTE TREATS

It's a well-known saying that you don't want to know how the sausage is made, but the person who coined this phrase clearly never tasted the bounty from **Vienna Beef Factory**. Their popular workshop tour leaves visitors yearning for a 1/3-pound Mike Ditka Polish sausage at the café, or even a make-your-own-Chicago-dog kit with celery salt, sport peppers, and electric-green pickle relish from the gift shop. For more Eastern European fun, **Rich's Deli** is Ukrainian Village's go-to market for copious cuts of smoked pork as well as *kabanosy*, *pasztet*, Polish vodka, and Slavic mustard among other terrific stuff.

Unlike many local markets, the staff here is fluent in English, so don't be afraid to make your inquiries. All other lingering questions on meat may be answered after talking with husband-and-wife team, Rob and Allie Levitt, the brains (and stomachs) behind Noble Square's **The Butcher & Larder**. Combining the growing interest in whole animal butchery and a desire to support local farmers, the Levitts showcase sausages, terrines, and house-cured bacon; while also conducting demos on how to break down a side of beef. If God is indeed in the details, then marketplace extraordinaire, **Goddess & Grocer**, brings to life this turn of phrase. While

its vast selection of items may be the stuff of dreams among snooty gourmands and top chefs, even novices can be found here, stocking up on soups, salads, and chili—better than what Mom used to make back in the day. They also cater, so go ahead and pretend like you crafted those delicate dinner party hors d'oeuvres all on your own!

SUGAR RUSH

A world of hand-crafted goodies make this neighborhood a rewarding destination for anyone addicted to sweet. For nearly a century, family-run **Margie's Candies** has been hand-dipping its chocolate bonbons and serving towering scoops of homemade ice cream to those Logan Square denizens and dons (including Al Capone, that old softy). Equally retro in attitude, the lip-smacking seasonal slices and small-town vibe of **Hoosier Mama Pie Company** brings old-timey charm to this stretch of Ashland Avenue. From tiered wedding cakes to replicas of Wrigley Field recreated in batter and frosting, a tempting selection

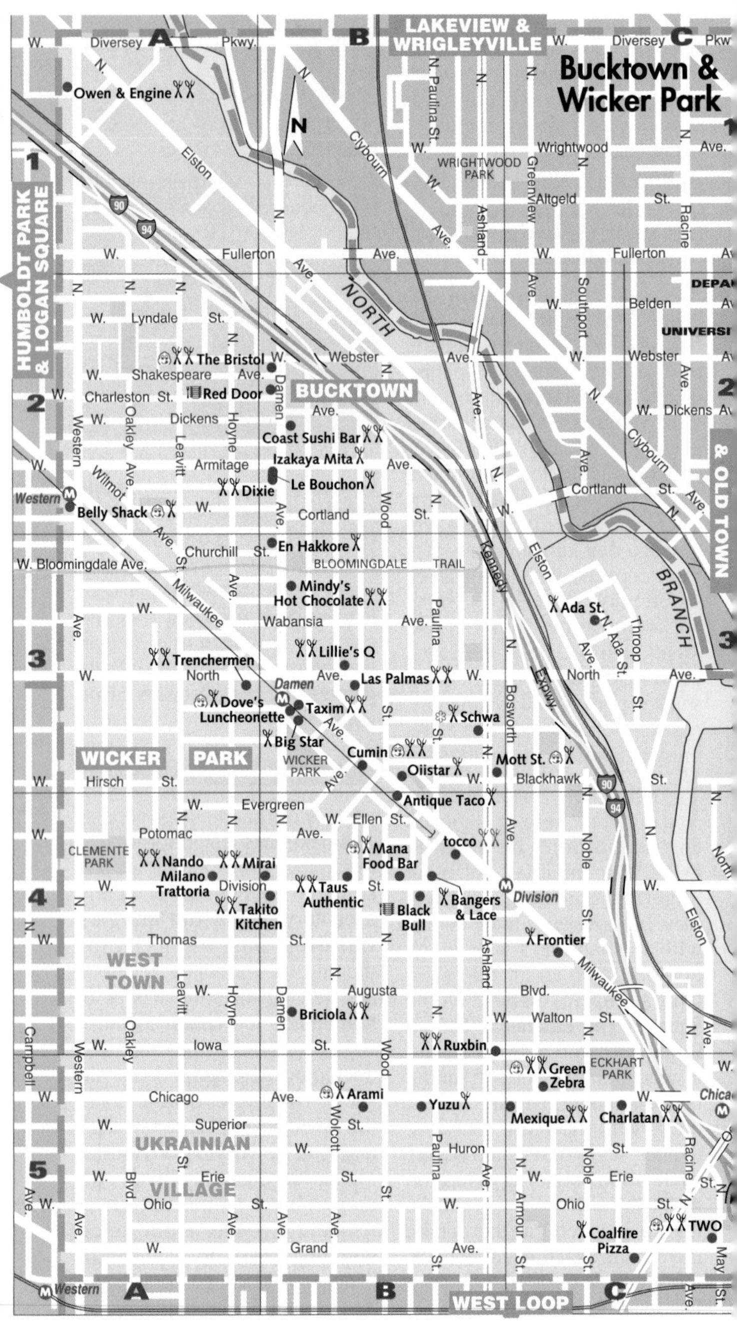

Bucktown & Wicker Park
LAKEVIEW & WRIGLEYVILLE
HUMBOLDT PARK & LOGAN SQUARE
& OLD TOWN
WEST LOOP
BUCKTOWN
WICKER PARK
WEST TOWN
UKRAINIAN VILLAGE
Owen & Engine
The Bristol
Red Door
Coast Sushi Bar
Izakaya Mita
Le Bouchon
Dixie
Belly Shack
En Hakkore
Mindy's Hot Chocolate
Ada St.
Lillie's Q
Trenchermen
Las Palmas
Dove's Luncheonette
Taxim
Big Star
Schwa
Cumin
Mott St.
Oiistar
Antique Taco
tocco
Mana Food Bar
Nando Milano Trattoria
Mirai
Taus Authentic
Takito Kitchen
Black Bull
Bangers & Lace
Frontier
Briciola
Ruxbin
Green Zebra
Arami
Yuzu
Mexique
Charlatan
Coalfire Pizza
TWO

of desserts is displayed in the window at **Alliance Bakery** and would make even Willy Wonka green with envy. But, if you're looking for something a little less traditional, unusual combinations are the norm at **Black Dog Gelato**, where goat cheese, cashew, and caramel come together for a uniquely satisfying scoop.

SUDS AND SPUDS

The craft beer movement has been brewing in Chicagoland for some time now, where lovers of quality suds and superlative bar snacks find an impressive listing of both in Bucktown and Wicker Park. Regulars at Logan Square's **Revolution Brewing** snack on bacon-fat popcorn and sweet potato cakes while sipping on the in-house Double Fist Pale Ale or Anti-Hero IPA. This holy union between food and beer is always reaching epic heights at **Piece**, which not only serves up one of Chicagoland's most popular hand-tossed pizzas but also produces a roster of award-winning beers to accompany its crusty New Haven-style pies. And, for a master class on the wide and wonderful world of craft brews, the noted beer school at Wicker Park's **Map Room** gives students a greater appreciation for the art—though a self-taught tour of the bar's worldwide selection is quite educational and perhaps more enjoyable?

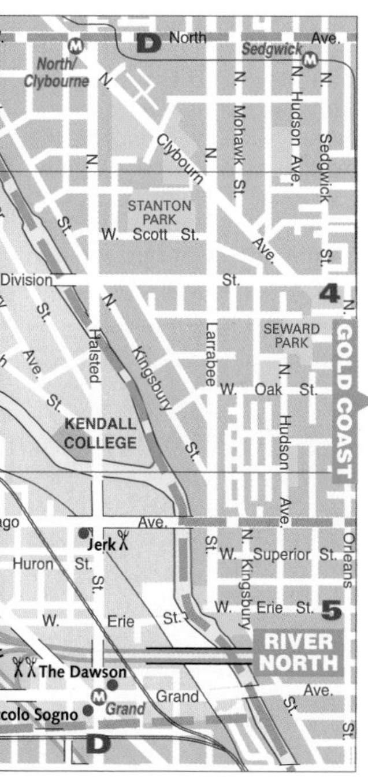

THE LUSH LIFE

Considering its dramatic role in the era of Prohibition, it's no surprise that speakeasy-inspired spots go over like gangbusters in Chicago. **The Violet Hour**, one of the pioneers of the bespoke cocktail trend, still shakes things up late into the night at its no-reservations temple—pair your updated Old Fashioned with frites and aïoli for a truly appetizing experience. The subterranean vaults of a former bank are now home to **The Bedford** whose heavy steel doors, walls of shining safe deposit boxes, and marble-limestone accents lead the way to a warren of lounge-y areas and dining dens. But, if that's not your speed and spicy, south-of-the-border flavor is what you really need, then make a beeline for **Taco Burrito Express #3** on North Ashland. This fast, family-run, and cash-only favorite doles out *al pastor* and chorizo tacos until the party winds down—at 11:00 P.M. For those who prefer their Mexican food brought to them by *luchadores* donning wrestling masks, cool and quirky **Tamale Spaceship** truck has touched down in these parts in the form of a brick and mortar storefront. Sports of another sort grab the spotlight at **Emporium Arcade Bar** where rows of video games and pinball machines from the 1980s bring back memories for those who grew up hitting the arcade. And this of course becomes even more fun when paired with a craft beer or whiskey shot.

KITCHEN SKILLS

Meals at **Kendall College Dining Room** let you brag about knowing future Michelin-starred chefs before they've hit it big. As one of Chicago's premierw culinary institutions, this college gives its chef trainees real-world guidance by way of elegant lunch and dinner service. Floor-to-ceiling windows overlook the professional kitchen, where instructors can be seen helping students fine-tune their fine-dining skills. Reservations are required, but the experience is a must for home cooks looking to be inspired. For a more hands-on affair, classes at **Cooking Fools** lets aspiring Food Network stars hone their knife skills or prepare a batch of tamales from scratch. Feeling the need to flaunt your culinary credentials over a dinner party at home? Simply swing by the **Wicker Park & Bucktown Farmer's Market** (open on Sundays) and stock your pantry with an impressive fleet of fresh produce, artisanal cheeses, and much, much more. Afterwards, you can always peruse the shelves of **Olivia's Market** for painstakingly sourced specialty items, as well as a massive wine and beer selection.Then **LocalFolksFood** is a family-run enterprise whose chief mission is to develop natural gourmet condiments (mustard and hot sauce anyone?) for slathering over hearty burgers or dogs. You may also purchase these same delightful treats from the lauded **Green Grocer** and make your next cookout the envy of everyone on the block. Finally, feel ready to grow your own vegetables? Sign up for a plot at **Frankie Machine Community Garden** and see if you've got a green thumb!

CHICAGO
STARZ 1ST AMENDMENT
COMEDY SHOW MAY 13-16
DIANA ROSS MAY 27

Ada St.

C3

1664 N. Ada St. (bet. Concord Pl. & Wabansia Ave.)

Phone: 773-697-7069 — Dinner Tue – Sun
Web: www.adastreetchicago.com
Price: $$

Despite its obscure location among the industrial warehouses of far-east Wicker Park, adventurous diners have no trouble seeking out Ada St. Reservations aren't accepted after 6:30 P.M., so the cozy, brick-walled lounge quickly becomes a party space where patrons peruse the wooden cubbies of vinyl to create their own soundtrack.

The menu of small plates is influenced by both hearty gastropub dishes and lighter Mediterranean bites. Tabasco mash ketchup heats up a plate of charred, tender octopus, while a poached egg gilds rich duck confit tossed with *cavatelli*. Even the snappy green beans need nothing more than Dijon butter to shine. Before you take off, show your appreciation by choosing the last item on the menu: a six-pack of beer for the kitchen staff.

Antique Taco

Mexican

B4

1360 N. Milwaukee Ave. (at Wood St.)

Phone: 773-687-8697 — Lunch & dinner Tue – Sun
Web: www.antiquetaco.com
Price: ¢¢ — Damen (Blue)

No reservations and walk-up counter service lead to a frenetic pace at Antique Taco. Place your order, then browse the well-curated racks of knick-knacks (thrown together by the wife of Chef/owner Rick Ortiz) before finding a seat at a boxy plank table and digging into your feast of market-fresh Mexican fare—all of it piled onto mix-and-match china plates.

The superior corn tortillas are loaded with substantial and delicious fillings: local lamb roasted with cumin is joined by cabbage slaw, pickled jalapeños, and peppercorn yogurt for a unique bite; while the delightful chorizo chile is thick and rich, highly seasoned, and cooled with avocado *crema*. To wash it all down, vodka-spiked *agua frescas* are nice, but the *horchata* milkshake is unmissable.

Arami

Japanese

1829 W. Chicago Ave. (bet. Wolcott Ave & Wood St.)

Phone: 312-243-1535 — Lunch Sun
Web: www.aramichicago.com — Dinner nightly
Price: $$ — Division

Come to this bamboo-clad *izakaya*, with its comfortable sushi bar and soaring skylights, for impressively rendered small plates and specialty cocktails featuring Japanese spirits. The night's *tsukemono* can reveal spicy okra, crisp hearts of palm, and sweet burdock root. The nigiri selection might showcase New Zealand King salmon topped with pickled wasabi root. The *robata* produces grilled maitakes with Japanese sea salt and black garlic purée; and *gani korroke*, a crunchy-creamy crab croquette, is plated with *togarashi*-spiked mayonnaise. Don't turn down the all-ice cream dessert menu, which includes enticing flavors like coconut-cinnamon-banana. It comes nestled in granola-like bits of miso-graham cracker crumble for a finish as sweet as it is unique.

Bangers & Lace

Gastropub

1670 W. Division St. (at Paulina St.)

Phone: 773-252-6499 — Lunch & dinner daily
Web: www.bangersandlacechicago.com
Price: $$ — Damen (Blue)

Despite the frilly connotations, this sausage-and-beer mecca's name refers not to doilies, but to the delicate layers of foam that remain in the glass after your craft brew has been quaffed. You'll also have lots of opportunity to study the lace curtains as you plow through their extensive draft beer menu, noted on blackboards in the comfortably worn-in front bar room.

Decadent foie gras corn dogs (actually French garlic sausage wrapped with soft-sweet brioche cornbread) and veal brats with melted Gouda elevate the humble sausage; while a slew of sandwiches suit simpler tastes. Grilled cheese gilds the lily with taleggio, raclette, and Irish cheddar; and dreamy house-made chips drizzled with truffle oil and malt vinegar are more than a bar snack.

Belly Shack

Fusion

A2

1912 N. Western Ave. (at Milwaukee Ave.)

Phone: 773-252-1414 Lunch & dinner Tue – Sun
Web: www.bellyshack.com
Price: ⊜ Western (Blue)

Like its patrons, Belly Shack's menu is an eclectic mash-up that reflects the Korean and Puerto Rican backgrounds of Chef Bill Kim and his wife, Yvonne. Place your order, take a number (which is basically a metal stand that looks like it was made by a high school shop class), and wait for your dishes to arrive.

Korean barbecued beef is still a thrill, but regulars know to enjoy new and inventive offerings, like the hot and sour tortilla soup. This fusion of the classics from Mexico and China features a sumptuous dashi and chicken broth base laced with cubes of tender chicken and tortilla strips. For a more filling treat, get the all-beef hot dog garnished with crispy egg noodles, pickled green papaya, and served with *togarashi nagami*-seasoned shoestring fries.

Big Star

Mexican

B3

1531 N. Damen Ave. (bet. Milwaukee & Wicker Park Aves.)

Phone: 773-235-4039 Lunch & dinner daily
Web: www.bigstarchicago.com
Price: ⊜ Damen (Blue)

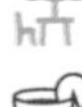

Bucktown's favorite taqueria has all the fixings for a fiesta. Craft beers, custom-bottled Bourbons, and pitchers of margaritas wash down the affordable abundance. And, despite the grungy décor, the vibe is as intoxicating as the aroma of the *taco de chorizo verde*. The patio is even more of a party, and sun-starved Chicagoans can be spotted out there soon after the groundhog has (or hasn't) seen his shadow.

Tacos are served individually, thus allowing ample opportunity to graze on the likes of the *pollo pibil*—achiote- and citrus-marinated chicken thighs steamed in banana leaves, topped with pickled onion slices and cilantro. Save room for the *salsa de frijole con queso*, a crock of pinto bean dip accompanied by lime salt-sprinkled tortilla chips.

Black Bull

B4

1721 W. Division St. (bet. Hermitage Ave. & Paulina St.)

Phone: 773-227-8600 — Lunch Sun
Web: www.blackbullchicago.com — Dinner Tue – Sun
Price: $$ — Division

Like bulls, hungry foodies are drawn to the color red—at least that's what the thinking must be at this chic tapas spot dominated by a neon bull and candy-apple exterior. Inside, glasses of crimson and rosé sangria are in everyone's hands, helping the noise skyrocket as the night wears on.

Look at the colorful chalk-drawn mural above the kitchen, depicting Spanish scenes, products, and food terms, to get a sense of what's on offer. Shareable plates mix tradition with contemporary twists, like crispy hollowed-out *patatas bravas* filled with ketchup and aïoli. A half-dozen pickled mussels arrive in a tin beneath a layer of creamy potato foam; while an excellent consommé poured over a farm egg yolk and truffles is brightened by a dash of manzanilla sherry.

Briciola

Italian

B4

937 N. Damen Ave. (bet. Augusta Blvd. & Iowa St.)

Phone: 773-772-0889 — Dinner Tue – Sun
Web: www.briciolachicago.com
Price: $$ — Division

After decades of cooking and traveling, Chef/owner Mario Maggi was ready to open a small place—just a crumb, or "una briciola," of a restaurant. Thus the birth of Briciola, which is a tiny trattoria nestled between Ukrainian Village's brick buildings. Upon entry, find that this space is indeed a speck of warmth and charm, festooned with party lights on the patio and mustard-toned walls inside.

Traditional Italian cuisine gets personalized tweaks from the chef. *Carpacci* may include paper-thin octopus, beets, or beef; *macaroncini alla Briciola* folds diced Tuscan sausage into a spicy garlic-sage sauce; and a hefty bone-in pork chop, pounded thin, breaded, and pan-fried until golden, is a house classic dressed with arugula and shaved parmesan.

The Bristol

American

2152 N. Damen Ave. (bet. Shakespeare & Webster Aves.)

Phone: 773-862-5555 — Lunch Sat – Sun
Web: www.thebristolchicago.com — Dinner nightly
Price: $$

Get to know your neighbors a little better at this dim, bustling haunt boasting seasonal American fare with a Mediterranean twist. Regulars sit shoulder-to-shoulder at the concrete bar, squinting under filament bulbs to see the constantly changing menu's latest additions on chalkboards throughout the room. Start with a Moscow Mule in a frosty copper mug to go with your head-on prawns *a la plancha* with anchovy butter and tarragon, or smoked whitefish dip with horseradish and saltines. Large plates sing with comfort, especially the Amish half-chicken with mustard-dill spaetzle and chicken jus.
Weekend brunch is mighty popular, whether for the hangover-curing noodle bowl or plump cinnamon rolls. Homemade nutter butters remain an iconic finale.

Charlatan

Mediterranean

C5

1329 W. Chicago Ave. (at Throop St.)

Phone: 312-818-2073 — Lunch Sun
Web: www.charlatanchicago.com — Dinner Tue – Sun
Price: $$ — Chicago (Blue)

Despite what its moniker might suggest, Charlatan is in fact a genuine and authentic show of talent. Hip and comfortable, this gastropub boasts whimsical toile and velvet details, a trio of mounted animal heads, and quality fare that puts pub grub to shame.
The menu is anchored by a number of inventive pastas prepared in-house, like charred fennel-stuffed tortellini bobbing in a boldly seasoned porchetta *brodo* hit with fennel pollen and garlic-mustard oil. Unbelievably tender grilled octopus is plated with beef-braised carrots and fried bone marrow-enriched romesco; and the honeycomb-topped chocolate tart tastes as silky as a bowl of pudding. To make the most of your meal, wash it all down with a local brew or wine from a small producer.

Coalfire Pizza

Pizza

1321 W. Grand Ave. (bet. Ada & Elizabeth Sts.)

Phone: 312-226-2625 — Lunch Fri – Sun
Web: www.coalfirechicago.com — Dinner Tue – Sun
Price: ⊜ — Chicago (Blue)

Sure, you could come for a salad, but the focus here is on pizza—and yours should be, too. The cozy room features an open kitchen where pie production is on display for all to see. And in a playful bit of recycling, empty tomato sauce cans on each table become stands for sizzling pizzas churned straight from the 800-degree coal oven.

This hot spot has its ratio down to a fine art and knows not to burden its thin, crispy crust that's blackened and blistered in all the right places. The mortadella is a delight, with chopped garlic and gossamer slices of peppercorn-flecked sausage. Care to go your own way? Build the perfect pie with toppings that run the gamut from Gorgonzola to goat cheese.

A second location in Lakeview continues to thrive.

Coast Sushi Bar

Japanese

2045 N. Damen Ave. (bet. Dickens & McLean Aves.)

Phone: 773-235-5775 — Lunch Sat – Sun
Web: www.coastsushibar.com — Dinner nightly
Price: $$

Dimly lit but lively, this high-volume sushi bar cranks out a remarkable variety of rolls to keep up with demand especially on weekends from noon till night. Two spacious dining rooms and a narrow sushi counter armed with wood-framed chairs accommodate the chatty crowds. Bring your own sake, wine, and bottle opener to make the wait more tolerable.

The broad selection of Japanese dishes ranges from signature maki and nigiri to innovative appetizers like fried soft-shell crab with mango-shallot salsa. Miso soup spiked with jalapeño is served in a coffee cup for easy sipping. A deep bowl of boatman *chirashi* is laden with orange *tobiko*, pickled veggies, shiso leaves, and an array of sashimi. Dig right in or grab a sheet of toasted nori for a custom-wrapped hand roll.

Cumin

Indian XX

B3

1414 N. Milwaukee Ave. (bet. Evergreen & Wolcott Aves.)

Phone: 773-342-1414 — Lunch Tue – Sun
Web: www.cumin-chicago.com — Dinner nightly
Price: — Damen (Blue)

This proudly-run blend of Nepalese and Indian eats sits among a plethora of bars, coffee shops, and vintage stores in boho-centric Bucktown. While fans of the sub-continent love Cumin for its clean and modern surrounds, linen-lined tables struggle to contain the myriad plates that pile up during its ubiquitous lunch buffet.

Paintings of mountain scenes decorate crimson-red walls and prep diners for an authentic range of flavorful food hailing from the Northeast. Get gnawing on *namche sekuwa* or *tandoori* goat flecked with spices and paired with crunchy green peppers. Then soak up pieces of buttery naan in a hearty vegetarian stew (*aalu tama bodi*) combining potatoes, bamboo shoots and black eyed peas. Cool things down with sweet and milky mango *kulfi*.

The Dawson

Gastropub XX

D5

730 W. Grand Ave. (at Halsted St.)

Phone: 312-243-8955 — Lunch Sat – Sun
Web: www.the-dawson.com — Dinner nightly
Price: $$ — Chicago (Blue)

The Dawson has everything you can ask for in a gastropub—a convivial vibe, clever bites, and great libations. The Surfer Rosa for instance (with tequila, mezcal, blood orange and chilies) serves to loosen up diners jonesing for big flavors. Inside, globe lights shine like beacons through the façade's lofty windows. And, a wraparound bar attracts spirited guests like moths to a flame. A communal table and open kitchen with counter offer multiple opportunities for meeting, greeting, and eating.

When hunger strikes, caramelized onion sabayon, potato confit, and garlicky pea shoots add depth to Arctic char. And lest you forget dessert, Bourbon-pecan bread pudding with flash-frozen vanilla cream and sea salt-butterscotch sauce, is meant for sharing—or not.

Dixie

Southern 

B2

1952 N. Damen Ave. (bet. Armitage Ave. & Homer St.)

Phone: 773-688-4466 Dinner Tue – Sun
Web: www.dixiechicago.com
Price: $$ Damen (Blue)

From the brightly whitewashed exterior to the freshly installed porch area complete with rocking chairs, the Southern-styled redo of the old Takashi space is everything you'd expect from Chef—and South Carolina native—Charlie McKenna (also of Lillie's Q). Despite the somewhat curious absence of antebellum style and slow drawls, this cozily arranged interior is luminous, chic, and charming. And then there's the bar of course, which proffers a great Bourbon listing and impressive cocktails that may include a vintage Boulevardier.
The glassed-in kitchen, where the team is sharply accented with indigo-hued aprons, turns out a roster of updated down-home cooking. And while the flavors are familiar, the execution here is actually quite modern—envision pan-seared catfish with succotash and foamy harissa nage.

Dove's Luncheonette 

American

B3

1545 N. Damen Ave. (bet. Milwaukee & Pierce Aves.)

Phone: 773-645-4060 Lunch & dinner daily
Web: www.doveschicago.com
Price: $$ Damen (Blue)

With a chill, throwback vibe, all-day breakfast, and a drink list with more than 70 labels of agave spirits, this One Off Hospitality roadhouse is a Wicker Park hipster's dream come true. To drive the point home, the diner features wood-paneled walls, counter seating, a record player spinning the blues, and of course, Tex-Mex fare listed on a wall-mounted letter board. The daily special may be a blueberry quinoa pancake, while savory favorites include crunchy buttermilk fried chicken with chorizo verde gravy or the farmer's cheese-stuffed Anaheim *chile relleno*, served in a pool of tomato-serrano sauce with pasilla chiles and pickled chayote slices.
Pies from Hoosier Mama Pie Co. are a grand finale; try the lemony Atlantic Beach with a saltine crust.

En Hakkore

1840 N. Damen Ave. (bet. Churchill & Moffat Sts.)

Phone: 773-772-9880 — Lunch & dinner Mon – Sat
Web: N/A
Price: ꝏ — Damen (Blue)

Healthy doesn't have to be humdrum. This simple little Korean eatery, run by a husband-and-wife team and decorated with more than a hint of whimsy, specializes in big bowls of *bibimbap*. You choose your rice and protein, be it pork or barbecue beef, decide on the heat level and then dive straight in—up to 16 different vegetables are used and they're as tasty as they are colorful. Also worth trying are the steamed *mandoo* (pork dumplings) and the curiously addictive tacos made with *paratha*.

Simply place your order at the counter, grab a plastic fork and, if you're with friends, commandeer the large communal table. There's no alcohol (and it's not BYOB) so instead take advantage of an invigorating soft drink from the fridge. You'll feel so virtuous.

Frontier

1072 N. Milwaukee Ave. (bet. Noble & Thomas Sts.)

Phone: 773-772-4322 — Lunch Sat – Sun
Web: www.thefrontierchicago.com — Dinner nightly
Price: $$ — Division

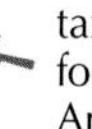

If Davy Crockett is king of the wild frontier, then chances are he'd be smitten by this stylish, modern-day saloon. To start, a taxidermied grizzly bear, wolf, and bison head hang among football-flaunting flat-screens behind the 40 foot-long bar. And even Frontier's menu drives home the hunt-and-gather theme, with dishes divided into three sections: "Fried," "Foraged," and "Whole Animal Service."

Carnivores revel in the chef's signature duck tacos juiced with salsa verde, while pescetarians beg for crab Benedict—a superb staple of toasted muffins with sweet crabmeat, soft poached eggs, and spicy Hollandaise. Calorie-counters love the well-dressed house salad, but for dessert, there is no passing up on crispy sugar doughnuts—gently caressed with a rum-apple sauce in true Crockett fashion.

Green Zebra

Vegetarian

1460 W. Chicago Ave. (at Greenview Ave.)

Phone: 312-243-7100 — Dinner Tue – Sun
Web: www.greenzebrachicago.com
Price: $$ — Chicago (Blue)

Named after the popular heirloom tomato, Chef/owner Shawn McClain's vegetarian standby is beloved among Chicagoans looking for an upscale meat-free experience. The dining room's minimalist décor is sleek and soothing, all earthy brown hues and potted greenery. The kitchen's offerings keep the omnivore palate interesting by weaving in a world of influences, while the small plates conceit allows diners to freely explore a variety of this skillful cuisine.

Tomato rasam soup is a nod to India frilled with roasted eggplant and lentils, just as kimchi-and-tofu potstickers with black garlic soy sauce display influences farther east. The highly satisfying za'atar-roasted acorn squash is composed with a black kale- and chickpea-flour cobbler.

Izakaya Mita

Japanese

1960 N. Damen Ave. (at Armitage Ave.)

Phone: 773-799-8677 — Dinner nightly
Web: www.izakayamita.com
Price: — Western (Blue)

This Bucktown addition is a family-run tavern worth seeking out for its homespun take on *izakaya* eats and gracious hospitality.

Start with single-serve sake in a jar so cute you'll want to smuggle it home, or a cocktail inspired by Japanese literature (the Norwegian Wood, a delicious interpretation of the Haruki Murakami novel blends whiskey, Luxurdo, sweet vermouth, and orange bitters). The array of small plates brims with creativity and flavor: *tsukune* are coarse-ground, delightfully chewy, and achieve a mouthwateringly charred exterior from having been grilled over *bincho-tan*; while *tako-yaki* are as delicious as any found on a Tokyo street cart. *Korroke*, a panko-crusted potato croquette, comes with *tonkatsu* sauce for delicious dunking.

Jerk

Jamaican

D5

811 W. Chicago Ave. (at Halsted St.)

Phone: 312-763-2870 — Lunch & dinner daily
Web: www.jerkgrill.com
Price: — Chicago (Blue)

The jerk chicken prepared by Jamaica-born Chef/co-owner Dion Solano rose to fame from behind the window of a food truck, and now it's being plated up in a tidy and inviting brick and mortar locale. The upgraded digs rock a vibe that's more barbecue joint than kitschy beach shack, but pale blue-painted wooden-window shutters soften the industrial sway, and appropriately themed reggae reigns supreme on the playlist.

Hungry diners line up at the counter and make their choice among succulently marinated and slow-grilled chicken, pork shoulder, or beef brisket. The platters include a slice of dense Jamaican-style hard dough bread, "festival" (a cornbread fritter), as well as sides likes rice and peas, creamy coleslaw, or sweet potato-and-yuca mash.

Las Palmas

Mexican

B3

1835 W. North Ave. (at Honore St.)

Phone: 773-289-4991 — Lunch Sat – Sun
Web: www.laspalmaschicago.com — Dinner nightly
Price: $$ — Damen (Blue)

Vivid décor complements the spirited flavors on the menu at Las Palmas, from the colorful Mexican artwork on adobe-style walls to exposed ductwork welded to resemble a scaly dragon winding through the deceptively large space. If the weather suits, the outdoor garden or glassed-in atrium beckon; if not, a cozy fireplace in the front room keeps things intimate.

The cocktail menu draws inspiration from both South and Central America, featuring a variety of capirinhas and mojitos alongside inventive cucumber-lime and pineapple margaritas. Vibrant and modern Mexican dishes like crispy *taquitos* with chicken *barbacoa*, pickled red onion, and tangy salsa *cruda*; as well as seafood-filled cornmeal empanadas with peanut-jalapeño relish showcase the kitchen's flair.

Le Bouchon

French

1958 N. Damen Ave. (at Armitage Ave.)

Phone: 773-862-6600 Lunch & dinner Mon – Sat
Web: www.lebouchonofchicago.com
Price: $$ Damen (Blue)

Pressed-tin ceilings? Check. Brick-and-Dijon color scheme? Of course. Le Bouchon proffers the quintessential bistro experience, where straightforward French cooking never goes out of style and the regulars keep returning for more. The informal atmosphere gets convivially raucous as the night goes on with thirsty and hungry hordes lining the bar and petite dining room.

Over in the kitchen, familiar and approachable favorites rule the menu: *soupe à l'oignon*, wearing its traditional topper of broiled Gruyère on a moist crouton, oozes and bubbles over the sides of a ramekin. And an ample fillet of *saumon poché* napped in beurre blanc is the very essence of simplicity.

A lunch prix-fixe keeps the wallet light but belly full.

Lillie's Q

Barbecue

1856 W. North Ave. (at Wolcott Ave.)

Phone: 773-772-5500 Lunch & dinner daily
Web: www.lilliesq.com
Price: $$ Damen (Blue)

Bucktown's urban barbecue shack takes a scholarly approach to 'cue, as each table bears a caddy stocked with six regionally specific sauces for embellishing the slow-smoked meats to come. Cocktails served in Mason jars are a specialty made from "moonshine" offered at three proof levels, and servers in modern mechanic's shirts tend to the crowds clamoring for heaps of smoked meats rubbed in "Carolina dirt." Tri-tip is tender and pink-tinged after its time in the smoker with the joint's signature dry rub; while the succulent smoked hot link rests in a butter-griddled, top-sliced brioche bun served with Southern-style coleslaw.

And if at-home grilling is your thing, you'll be pleased to know that the mouthwatering sauces are available by mail order.

Mana Food Bar 

Vegetarian 

B4

1742 W. Division St. (bet. Paulina & Wood Sts.)

Phone: 773-342-1742 — Lunch Sat
Web: www.manafoodbar.com — Dinner nightly
Price: ⊕ — Division

Feeling like your body needs a jump-start? Mana, whose name translates to "the life force coursing through nature," is a good place to get your mojo back. Though welcoming to vegans, vegetarians, gluten-free diners, and anyone who's looking for a nutrient boost, it's not just health food: the small space also offers a full bar with sake cocktails, smoothies, and freshly squeezed juices.

Mana may be a tiny spot, but its diverse menu of vegetarian dishes is big on taste—and spice. Korean *bibimbap* mixes a roster of vegetables like pea pods, roasted carrots, and pickled daikon with a fresh sunny side-up egg; while horseradish and cracked black pepper sneak into macaroni and cheese.

House-made hot sauce with serranos and jalapeños adds extra pep to any dish.

Mexique

Mexican 

C5

1529 W. Chicago Ave. (bet. Armour St. & Ashland Ave.)

Phone: 312-850-0288 — Lunch & dinner Tue – Sun
Web: www.jbandala.mx/mexique
Price: $$ — Chicago (Blue)

Large groups fill most of the banquettes in this slender space, but a bar stretching half the length of the room makes it easy for smaller parties to stop in for a sip of sangria. A rear window offers a glimpse of Chef Carlos Gaytan at work in the kitchen, and congratulatory graffiti from visiting chefs provides a fun distraction on the way to the restroom.

While the chef's French-leaning dishes seem to have meandered too far from their Mexican soul, his cooking skills and hybrid approach still remain impressive. Take the delightful *pescamal* that sits in a pool of puréed black bean sauce humming with perfect heat; or *cordero*, which reveals lamb chops with a ruby-red center and salty feta. Vanilla ice cream and fresh berries finish a fine chocolate fondant.

Mindy's Hot Chocolate

Contemporary XX

B3

1747 N. Damen Ave. (bet. St. Paul Ave. & Willow St.)

Phone: 773-489-1747 — Lunch Wed – Sun
Web: www.hotchocolatechicago.com — Dinner Tue – Sun
Price: $$ — Damen (Blue)

Bucktown wouldn't be the same without this sweet spot run by pastry chef extraordinaire, Mindy Segal. Diners walk past decadent hot chocolate mix and cookies on display before hitting an industrial-chic space fitted with sleek dark wood, caramel-brown walls, and chocolate-toned leather banquettes. Get the point yet? Decadent chocolate is the name of the game here, though guests will be delighted to discover savory items beyond their expectations. Try the roasted tomato soup, garnished with bright green onion slivers; or the BLT with pesto aïoli, heirloom tomato, avocado, and thick, crispy maple-cayenne bacon.

An affogato—a scoop of coffee-cocoa nib ice cream paired with the chef's namesake hot chocolate—makes for the perfect finale.

Mirai

Japanese XX

B4

2020 W. Division St. (bet. Damen & Hoyne Aves.)

Phone: 773-862-8500 — Dinner nightly
Web: www.miraisushi.com
Price: $$ — Damen (Blue)

Mirai is a bit like Disney World. You know it's not real, but who cares? The Japanese food is westernized and by no means traditional, but unless you're dining out with Mr. Shinzo Abe, rest assured that nobody will cry foul.

Bold and appetizing flavors beg to take center stage. It's really all about the fish at this spot—just look around and you'll find most devotees feasting on sashimi, *unagi*, and maki. If raw fish doesn't float your boat, take a shot at one of the house specialties like *kani nigiri*, a baked king crab concoction. There is also a surfeit of hot dishes—think chicken *togarashi* with spicy, sweet, and tangy flavors. Affable and alert service combined with a relaxed atmosphere make this a hit among area residents.

Mott St.

Fusion

1401 N. Ashland Ave. (at Blackhawk St.)

Phone: 773-687-9977 — Lunch Sun
Web: www.mottstreetchicago.com — Dinner Tue – Sat
Price: $$ — Division

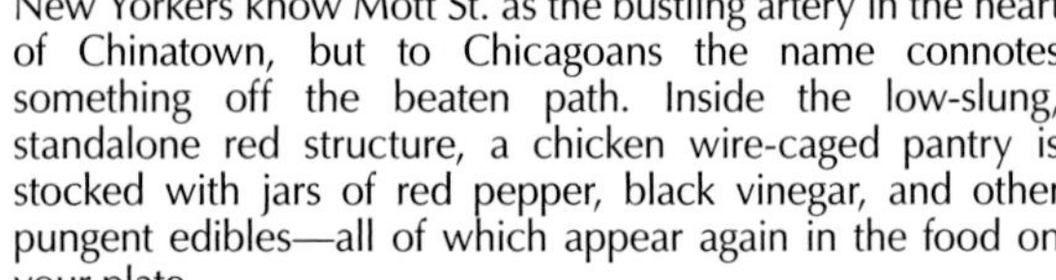

New Yorkers know Mott St. as the bustling artery in the heart of Chinatown, but to Chicagoans the name connotes something off the beaten path. Inside the low-slung, standalone red structure, a chicken wire-caged pantry is stocked with jars of red pepper, black vinegar, and other pungent edibles—all of which appear again in the food on your plate.

Offerings at this hip haven crisscross the globe, melding diverse ingredients for an utterly unique dining experience. Shredded kohlrabi substitutes green papaya for a Thai-inspired salad tossed with candied shrimp, poached chicken, and plenty of fresh herbs. Stuffed cabbage bears a Korean accent with tender chunks of slow-braised pork, tangy Napa cabbage kimchi, and crunchy sticky rice.

Nando Milano Trattoria

A4

2114 W. Division St. (bet. Hoyne Ave. & Leavitt St.)

Phone: 773-486-2636 — Dinner nightly
Web: www.nandomilano.com
Price: $$ — Division

A corner bar television constantly tuned to (European) football, vintage *aperitivo* posters, and a welcoming patio tailor-made for afternoon glasses of prosecco: charismatic host Dario Vullo has installed his own little slice of Milan in Wicker Park. The chic trattoria offers an intensely Italian menu and wine list to match the authentic accents of Vullo and family.

A trio of *arancini* are playfully prepared, with each rice ball sporting a unique shape—sphere, triangle, and cube—to denote a special filling like Bolognese ragù and smoked mozzarella; or mascarpone and spinach. House-made pastas like beet gnocchi in saffron sauce steal the show from equally flavorful and fresh focaccia sandwiches layered with creamy burrata and *Prosciutto di Parma*.

Oiistar

B3
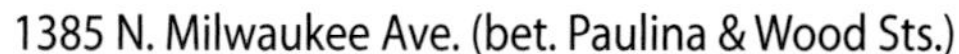

Asian

1385 N. Milwaukee Ave. (bet. Paulina & Wood Sts.)

Phone: 773-360-8791 — Lunch & Dinner Tue – Sun
Web: www.oiistar.com
Price: ⊜ — Damen (Blue)

It's easy to mistake Oiistar for yet another trendy ramen joint—but don't. Sure, it's got all the design hallmarks, from a minimalist wood-planked dining room and industrial open kitchen to a turned-up soundtrack, but the internationally influenced menu makes it much more than your average slurp shop.

In fact, "It's A Small World" could be the unofficial theme song for their lineup of steamed buns and comforting ramen bowls showcasing noodles, hand-pulled in-house, every day. The tempura cod bun is an enjoyable riff on a Baja fish taco complete with wasabi mayo and crunchy cabbage and fennel slaw; while the masala-spiced *tikkamen* ramen brings a belly-warming bowlful of toothsome noodles, deep-fried chicken thigh, braised bamboo shoots, and slow-cooked egg.

Owen & Engine

Gastropub

2700 N. Western Ave. (at Schubert Ave.)

Phone: 773-235-2930 — Lunch Sat – Sun
Web: www.owenengine.com — Dinner nightly
Price: $$

Owen & Engine's charm extends from its glossy black façade into its warm polished wood interior and all the way to the second-floor dining room that sees action into the wee hours. Brocade wallpaper, gas lights, and studded leather club chairs lend a Victorian feel. A frequently changing draft list always features a few selections pulled from a beer cask (or "engine"). British-inspired gastropub grub matches the impressive roster of brews and Pimm's cups. Bar nibbles like mustard-glazed soft pretzels with Welsh rarebit for dipping; or peanuts tossed in *sriracha*, Worcestershire, and brown sugar cater to the snacking sort. Hearty entrées like bangers and mash feature house-made Slagel Family Farm's pork sausage and potatoes smothered in onion gravy.

Piccolo Sogno

Italian XX

D5

464 N. Halsted St. (at Milwaukee Ave.)

Phone: 312-421-0077 | Lunch Mon – Fri
Web: www.piccolosognorestaurant.com | Dinner nightly
Price: $$ | Grand (Blue)

In-the-know locals craving mouthwatering Italian fare head to this swanky spot, usually packed with a dressy crowd. Inside, they are welcomed by a palette of rich, cool hues, crystal-beaded light fixtures that hang overhead, and an open kitchen boasting a wood-burning oven.

Piccolo Sogno's rustic yet refined menu offers traditional dishes with a twist. A version of the ubiquitous beet salad (both red and golden) is elevated here by shaved fennel, a drizzle of bright citrus oil, and a dollop of creamy, lush buffalo milk ricotta. If you need further encouragement, let us recommend the rabbit. Braised in a white wine sauce redolent of rosemary and lemon, the tender meat is served with wilted escarole and porridge-like semolina pudding.

Red Door

International 

B2

2118 N. Damen Ave. (at Charleston St.)

Phone: 773-697-7221 | Lunch Sat – Sun
Web: www.reddoorchicago.com | Dinner nightly
Price: $$

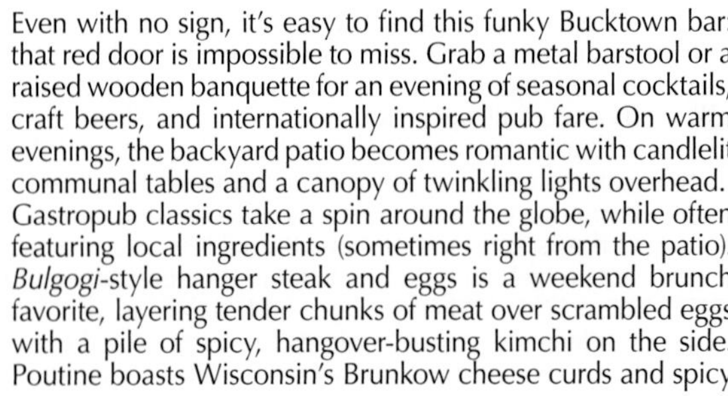

Even with no sign, it's easy to find this funky Bucktown bar: that red door is impossible to miss. Grab a metal barstool or a raised wooden banquette for an evening of seasonal cocktails, craft beers, and internationally inspired pub fare. On warm evenings, the backyard patio becomes romantic with candlelit communal tables and a canopy of twinkling lights overhead.

Gastropub classics take a spin around the globe, while often featuring local ingredients (sometimes right from the patio). *Bulgogi*-style hanger steak and eggs is a weekend brunch favorite, layering tender chunks of meat over scrambled eggs with a pile of spicy, hangover-busting kimchi on the side. Poutine boasts Wisconsin's Brunkow cheese curds and spicy curry gravy.

Ruxbin

American XX

851 N. Ashland Ave. (at Pearson St.)

Phone: 312-624-8509 — Dinner Thu – Mon
Web: www.ruxbinchicago.com
Price: $$ — Division

BYO

Refurbished and repurposed is the rationale behind Ruxbin's funky décor. In the tiny first-floor space, salvaged apple juice crates form wall panels and seat belts become chair backs. Up a few stairs, a stainless steel communal table offers a view into the semi-open kitchen.

From there, expect the kind of deeply creative cooking that demands respect—even with the occasional misstep. The tasting menu is presented as a list of items for diners to tick off their orders. Dishes include a composed salad of shaved root vegetables, apples, and spring onion with pumpernickel cubes in a Caesar-esque dressing. Their vegetarian take on carnitas feature jackfruit cooked until tender, served with a dollop of grits, smoky tomato sauce, and pickled vegetables.

Takito Kitchen

Mexican

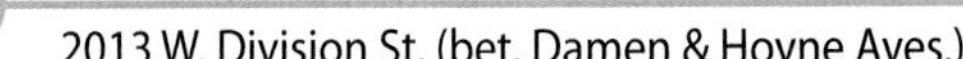

2013 W. Division St. (bet. Damen & Hoyne Aves.)

Phone: 773-687-9620 — Lunch Fri – Sun
Web: www.takitokitchen.com — Dinner Tue – Sun
Price: $$ — Division

Chicago's upscale taco circuit gets a new contender with Takito, where fresh ingredients make Latin-inspired food sing. Tequila takes pride of place in a chile-salted margarita, while skylights and mirrors make the narrow, mod-industrial space seem even brighter and larger. Sure, you can get a corn tortilla here, but sesame and hibiscus options let the kitchen get creative as evident in tacos filled with cornmeal-crusted redfish, beef *barbacoa*, or tamarind-chayote *pequin*. Shared plates like *sope de carne asada* blur culinary boundaries with the addition of Brunkow cheddar and green onion kimchi. It's an across-the-board mishmash of colorful flavors, but certainly a good way to go over the top.

Sister spot Bar Takito also boasts a notably concise menu.

Schwa ✿

Contemporary

B3

1466 N. Ashland Ave. (at Le Moyne St.)

Phone: 773-252-1466 Dinner Tue – Sat
Web: www.schwarestaurant.com
Price: $$$$ Division

BYO

There comes a point when pared-down style jumps from being easy-to-miss and becomes hard-to-forget. When a utilitarian and self-consciously bare-bones interior becomes attractively modern and industrial. When a lack of any FOH staff makes the service seem playfully all-hands-on-deck. The explicit rap music playing in the background reflects the deeply talented chefs' ethos, going well beyond laissez-faire to reach the point of "we don't give a damn." That said, you probably won't either—the food really is that good.

The extensive nightly tasting has no formal menu to speak of, but there are plenty of chatty servers ready to describe each dish, sometimes from over their shoulder by another table.

While the cuisine may seem more studied than sumptuous, it is a pleasure-filled adventure. Highlights include the signature *raviolo* filled with a gently cooked quail egg and fresh ricotta, swimming in brown butter with shaved black truffle. The excellent "fish fry" consists of a lightly battered and pearly white walleye fillet served with tender fava beans and two fried morsels of blackberry and cheese curds.

Cheesecake is also reinvented with layers of sharp Humboldt Fog, nasturtium purée, and nectarine.

Taus Authentic

International

B4

1846 W. Division St. (bet. Marion Ct. & Wolcott Ave.)

Phone: 312-561-4500 — Lunch Sun
Web: www.tausauthentic.com — Dinner Tue – Sun
Price: $$ — Division

You'll want to make an evening of it at this Wicker Park newcomer, where a stylish front lounge—complete with a working fireplace—makes for a cozy spot to enjoy a beer or cocktail. Then you may proceed to linger over a meal in the beautiful dining room, a modern vision of wood, powder blue velvet, and plate glass windows.

Chef Michael Taus has designed a menu made for grazing: think charcuterie, cheese, and starters including a sunchoke dosa. Made from lentils and basmati rice, this lacy crêpe is topped with bits of tender sunchokes in a spicy red curry sauce sweetened by golden raisins and candied pumpkin seeds. A tasting portion of pan-seared fluke, plated with sweet chili vinaigrette and a Korean-style pancake studded with dried shrimp, is equally delicious.

Taxim

Greek

B3

1558 N. Milwaukee Ave. (bet. Damen & North Aves.)

Phone: 773-252-1558 — Dinner nightly
Web: www.taximchicago.com
Price: $$ — Damen (Blue)

Though Taxim channels the spirit of Greece in its food, the casbah-esque décor takes inspiration from Turkey and other Mediterranean coastal neighbors. The large room glints with light from hanging Moorish lanterns and copper-topped tables. Share small plates on the sidewalk patio to take full advantage of Wicker Park people-watching.

Many of Taxim's dishes get a modern twist while remaining respectful to the islands' traditional cuisine. Wild Greek oregano and ouzo-preserved lemon offer a perfect balance to roasted Amish Miller Farms chicken; while *loukoumades* prove that no one can resist fried dough, especially when tossed in wildflower honey and topped with rosewater-infused pastry cream. The all-Greek wine list is an adventure for oenophiles.

tocco

Italian XX

1266 N. Milwaukee Ave. (bet. Ashland Ave. & Paulina St.)

Phone: 773-687-8895 — Dinner Tue – Sun
Web: www.toccochicago.com
Price: $$ — Division

Are we in Milan or Wicker Park? Tocco brings haute design and fashion to the table with such upscale textural touches as polished resin, faux ostrich skin, and bubblegum-pink accents in this sleek black-and-white space. Don your catwalk best before visiting: a fashion-centric display near a long communal table hints at the chichi theme present throughout.

The décor is cutting-edge, but the menu respects and returns to Italian standbys. *Gnocco fritto,* a dough pillow served with charcuterie, is irresistible to even the most willowy fashionistas; while cracker-crisp artisan pizzas from wood-burning ovens are equally pleasing. Traditional *involtini di pollo,* pounded thin and rolled around prosciutto, gets a hit of brightness from lemon and white wine sauce.

Trenchermen

Contemporary XX

2039 W. North Ave. (bet. Hoyne & Milwaukee Aves.)

Phone: 773-661-1540 — Lunch Sat – Sun
Web: www.trenchermen.com — Dinner nightly
Price: $$ — Damen (Blue)

In old-timey slang, a trencherman is a hearty eater and drinker, a definition that lets you know what you're in for at this glossy but comforting Wicker Park gastropub. Housed in a former Russian bathhouse, the black-and-white tiles and notched brick walls dividing the eclectic warren of rooms give a nod to the former tenant of this 1920s building.

Bar snacks and weekend brunch are taken just as seriously as full-on lunch and dinner here. Corned beef adds a manly touch to eggs Benedict, especially when drizzled with piquant *choron* sauce. Dense pretzel cinnamon rolls straddle the salty-sweet line. A menu favorite at any time of day, fried pickle tots are served with kicky beet-tinged red onion yogurt and thinly sliced chicken breast *bresaola*.

TWO

C5

1132 W. Grand Ave. (at May St.)

Phone: 312-624-8363 — Dinner Tue – Sun
Web: www.113two.com
Price: $$ — Chicago (Blue)

Two is an urban interpretation of a Midwest tavern that was set up by two owners, features second-hand furnishings, and has an address whose last digit is—you guessed it—the number two. Beyond the vintage Toledo scales, find a reclaimed wood-paneled space dressed with antique meat cleavers, quaint ceiling fans, and large barn doors.

This is a perfect lead into the farm-to-fork cuisine being whipped up in the open kitchen (the banquette across from it affords the best view). Start with classic Southern pimento cheese served in a miniature Mason jar alongside freshly grilled bread. Elegant small plates include pan-seared and spice-dusted halibut with fava beans and oyster mushrooms. On the sweet front, homemade puppy chow is chilled, crisp, and delicious.

Yuzu

B5

1751 W. Chicago Ave. (bet. Hermitage & Paulina Sts.)

Phone: 312-666-4100 — Lunch Mon – Sat, Dinner nightly
Web: www.yuzuchicago.com
Price: — Chicago (Blue)

Ancient and modern accents work in harmony at Yuzu, where hand-painted anime murals catch the eye above weathered plank wainscoting. A century-old wooden slab finds new life as a sushi counter, where diners sip sodas from Ball jars and groove to hip tunes.

Whole ginger- and garlic-glazed grilled squid is sliced into rings, then sprinkled with scallions and creamy jalapeño sauce. Succulent *robata*-grilled skewers, purchased by the piece, arrive with specialized accompaniments like marinated pork shoulder with sweet chili sauce or *kalbi*-glazed short rib. The *tobiko*-topped Black Sea roll is one of a roster of quirky but manageably sized maki, all of which arrive with an artistic flourish—think intricate, paisley-patterned sauces painted onto plates.

Chinatown & South

For years, the Red Line was the only true link between Chinatown and the South Loop. They may be neighbors geographically, but continue to remain distinct opposites in the culinary, architectural, and demographic spheres. Recent development on both sides of the line has brought the two worlds closer together, combining old and new flavors that make them irresistible to Chicago food lovers. The Great Chicago Fire spared many of the South Loop's buildings, making this architecture some of the oldest in the city. Residential palaces like the Glessner House and Clark House are now open for tours, but a quick walk along Prairie Avenue gives a self-guided view of marvelous mansions. Further north, those massive former lofts along Printers Row have been converted into condos, hotels, bookstores, and restaurants, as has the landmark Dearborn Station—the oldest train depot in Chicago.

SUN-UP TO SUNDOWN

The South Loop has the breakfast scene covered—quite literally—with dishes piled-high at casual neighborhood spots. Sop up an Irish Bennie adorned with corned beef hash or any number of egg favorites from frittata to French toast at **Yolk**, located on the southern end of Grant Park. The aptly named **Waffles** smothers its signature squares with both sweet and savory flavors. Varieties like cheddar cheese are topped with coffee-braised short ribs, while red velvet waffles come with strawberry compote and whipped cream cheese. As long as you're adding to your cholesterol count, stop at one of the many locations of **Ricobene's** for a breaded steak sandwich or big slab of juicy barbecue ribs.

If you're strolling through the Museum Campus for lunch, grab cash for a bite at **Kim & Carlo's Hot Dog Stand** between the Field Museum and Shedd Aquarium. Vegetarians applaud

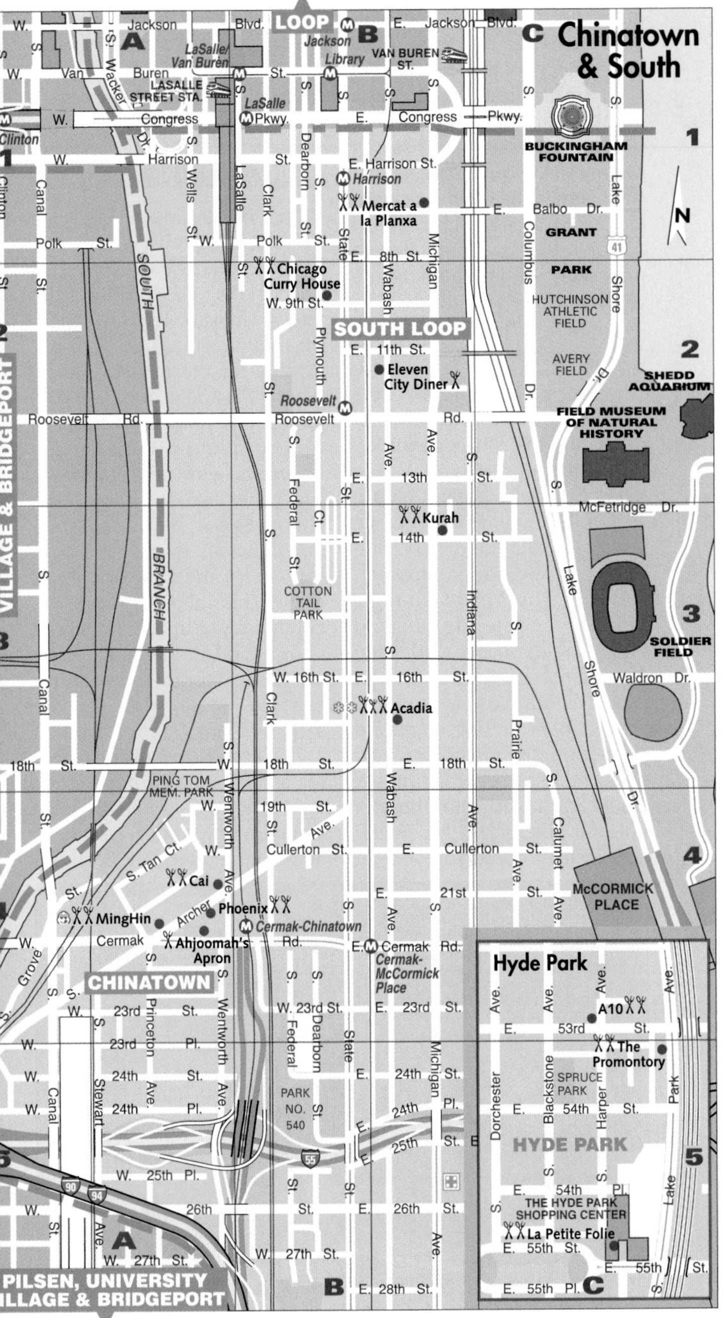
Chinatown & South
LOOP
SOUTH LOOP
CHINATOWN
Hyde Park
HYDE PARK
VILLAGE & BRIDGEPORT
PILSEN, UNIVERSITY
ILLAGE & BRIDGEPORT
A
B
C
1
2
3
4
5
N
Jackson Library
LaSalle/Van Buren
LASALLE STREET STA.
VAN BUREN ST.
LaSalle
Harrison
Roosevelt
Cermak-Chinatown
Cermak-McCormick Place
Clinton
BUCKINGHAM FOUNTAIN
GRANT PARK
HUTCHINSON ATHLETIC FIELD
AVERY FIELD
SHEDD AQUARIUM
FIELD MUSEUM OF NATURAL HISTORY
SOLDIER FIELD
McCORMICK PLACE
COTTON TAIL PARK
PING TOM MEM. PARK
PARK NO. 540
SPRUCE PARK
THE HYDE PARK SHOPPING CENTER
SOUTH BRANCH
Mercat a la Planxa
Chicago Curry House
Eleven City Diner
Kurah
Acadia
Cai
MingHin
Phoenix
Ahjoomah's Apron
A10
The Promontory
La Petite Folie
W. Jackson Blvd.
E. Jackson Blvd.
W. Van Buren St.
W. Congress Pkwy.
E. Congress Pkwy.
W. Harrison St.
E. Harrison St.
E. Balbo Dr.
Polk St.
E. 8th St.
W. 9th St.
E. 11th St.
Roosevelt Rd.
E. 13th St.
McFetridge Dr.
E. 14th St.
W. 16th St.
E. 16th St.
Waldron Dr.
18th St.
W. 18th St.
E. 18th St.
W. 19th St.
Cullerton St.
E. Cullerton St.
E. 21st St.
W. Cermak Rd.
E. Cermak Rd.
W. 23rd St.
E. 23rd St.
W. 23rd Pl.
W. 24th St.
E. 24th St.
W. 24th Pl.
E. 24th Pl.
E. 25th St.
W. 25th Pl.
W. 26th St.
E. 26th St.
W. 27th St.
E. 28th St.
S. Wacker Dr.
S. Canal St.
S. Wells St.
S. LaSalle St.
S. Clark St.
S. Dearborn St.
S. Plymouth Ct.
S. State St.
S. Wabash Ave.
S. Michigan Ave.
S. Columbus Dr.
S. Lake Shore Dr.
S. Federal St.
S. Indiana Ave.
S. Prairie Ave.
S. Calumet Ave.
S. Wentworth Ave.
S. Princeton Ave.
S. Stewart Ave.
S. Grove St.
S. Tan Ct.
W. Archer Ave.
E. 53rd St.
E. 54th St.
E. 54th Pl.
E. 55th St.
E. 55th Pl.
S. Dorchester Ave.
S. Blackstone Ave.
S. Harper Ave.
S. Lake Park Ave.
41
55
90
94

their special veggie dog with all the Chicago toppings, while everyone gets a great skyline view from Grant Park. For a glimpse of real Windy City politics in action, grab a seat at **Manny's**, the venerable coffee shop and deli; then sink your teeth into a giant pastrami on rye or a plate of crispy potato pancakes, while watching the city's wheelers and dealers do business.

When night falls, the South Loop really gets rocking. Buddy Guy himself often hits the stage at **Buddy Guy's Legends**, where live blues ring out nightly. Catch a set while digging into classic Southern soul food like fried okra, gumbo, or jambalaya. Similarly **The Velvet Lounge**, founded by late jazz legend Fred Anderson, moved from its original location in 2006, but still puts on a heckuva show. Other cutting edge and contemporary musicians also perform here several times a week. For a blast from the past but of a different sort, comedy and history come together at **Tommy Gun's Garage**. This dolled-up speakeasy hosts a riotous nightly dinner theater, allowing audiences to participate.

CHINATOWN

That ornate and arched gate at Wentworth Avenue and Cermak Road welcomes locals and visitors alike to one of the largest Chinatowns in America. This iconic structure is an apt symbol for the neighborhood, where the local population is still predominantly Chinese-American and history happily co-exists with contemporary life. The two-story outdoor **Chinatown Square** mall encompasses everything from restaurants and small boutiques to big banks, thereby giving the community a buzzing culinary and cultural introduction. Many of the restaurants here offer classic Chinese-American fare that is an amalgam of Sichuan and Cantonese cuisines, but for a homemade spread stock up on all things authentic from **Chinatown Market**. This large and "super" store is outfitted

with endless rows of Lee Kum Kee sauces, seafood, fresh produce, and more. At local standby **Go 4 Food**, a Sichuan beef lunch combo or wok-fried and hundred-spiced chicken continue to sate those pungent palates. Let the kids pick out a few intriguing Japanese sweets at **Aji Ichiban**, housed in the Chinatown Square mall, where bins filled with rainbows of foil-wrapped Japanese candy offer opportunities for tricks or treats. Unless you can read the characters on the wrappers, you're in for a surprise—though the store offers samples before charging by the pound. Home cooks as well as haute chefs know Chinatown isn't just a destination for dining out. It's also great for filling up on all the good eats necessary for a great home-cooked meal. In fact, the entire neighborhood is a specialty marketplace of sorts: find a mind-boggling array of fresh-pulled noodles at **Mayflower Food**; while Hong Kong-based tea shop, **Saint's Alp Teahouse**, serves quick snacks and a variety of tea-based drinks including the widely popular milk tea and taro milk tea—with or without tapioca pearls. Freshly baked fortune and almond cookies are a revelation at **Golden Dragon Fortune Cookies**, but those craving a wider range of sweets may pour over the cases at **Chiu Quon Bakery** filled with cakes and other cream- or custard-filled pastries. Meanwhile, additional inspiration can be found by perusing a cookbook (or ten) from the Chinese Cultural Bookstore. Finally, pay homage to the perennial city pastime by watching the White Sox do their thing on Guaranteed Rate Field, or the "Monsters of the Midway" take the gridiron inside Soldier Field's formidable walls.

Museums and learning centers showcase the Windy City's heritage from all angles. Apart from the stately collection of historic buildings in Grant Park's Museum Campus, this neighborhood is also home to Willie Dixon's Blues Heaven Foundation, whose mission is to preserve its musical legacy. With swooping green roof ornaments, the Harold Washington Library Center is impossible to miss, but an equally worthy site is the glass-ceilinged winter garden hidden inside. **Iron Street Farm**, a seven-acre urban field in Bridgeport, is part of Chicago's focus on eradicating food deserts within city limits. Here, local residents grow vegetables, raise chickens, and cultivate bees as part of the farm's educational programs. Respect!

Acadia ✿✿

Contemporary 

1639 S. Wabash Ave. (bet. 16th & 18th Sts.)

Phone: 312-360-9500 Dinner Wed – Sun
Web: www.acadiachicago.com
Price: $$$

Dining here is like being let in on a secret, uncovered along this rather unfortunate strip of no-man's land. The unexpected yet grand space employs nothing but neutral grays that extend from the concrete façade to the cushioned chairs and silvery beads dividing the center of this lofty room in half. Service is gracious and professional—the kind we should all expect but is hard to find.

Unusual and artful presentations may begin with canapés arriving in a box of moss or along a branch. Follow this with hamachi served as a brilliant study of flavor and balance, showcasing silky and beautifully marbled fish placed on a bed of coconut-infused rice pudding with dabs of black garlic, bits of finger lime, and lemongrass-infused chutney. Genius and luxury are at play in the sinfully rich Australian Wagyu beef, served red and fleshy with classic Bordelaise, roasted maitake to magnify the umami, chunks of sweet lobster, and lobster foam to lend an oceanic airiness to the plate.

Finish meals on a smooth and fudgy note with chocolate pudding cake accompanied by coconut gelée for striking visual contrast, a swipe of caramel, rum ice cream, candied black walnut, and toasty little slivers of coconut.

Ahjoomah's Apron

Korean

218 W. Cermak Rd. (bet. Archer & Wentworth Aves.)

Phone: 312-326-2800 Lunch & dinner daily
Web: www.ahjoomahchicago.com
Price: Cermak-Chinatown

Thanks to this modern, casual space, southside Chicagoans no longer need to head uptown for their fix of authentic Korean food. While there are no tabletop grills smoking up the dining room, the picnic-style tables fill quickly with generous portions of kitchen-grilled *bulgogi*, warming stews, and *banchan*.

A crimson kimchi *jjigae* broth, seamlessly balanced between sour and spicy, brims with soft chunks of tofu and pork. *Bibimbap* sizzles in a stone bowl, letting the requisite crispy crust form on the bottom while diners dig into a mountain of glistening sweet soy *kalbi*, crunchy vegetables, and fried egg. Want to feel virtuous about your meal? Wall posters tout the health benefits of traditional Korean ingredients like *doenjang*, an umami-rich soybean paste.

A10

1462 E. 53rd St. (at Harper Ave.)

Phone: 773-288-1010 Dinner nightly
Web: www.a10hydepark.com
Price: $$

A10 is a highway that winds through the Italian Riviera, but its detour through Hyde Park comes courtesy of prolific restaurateur, Matthias Merges. University of Chicago students and staff populate this split space, building a buzz over marble-topped rounds in the low-key bar area or dark wood tables in the convivial dining room.

Elegant presentations and ambitious creativity set this kitchen apart. Dishes deftly balance the rustic and sophisticated at a fantastic value, as in the pretty composition of charred and lightly blanched carrots over ricotta that is tinged pink from beet juice. Grilled salmon is beautifully cooked, flaky yet crisp-skinned, and served alongside creamy potato confit and large chunks of pickled cauliflower and carrots.

Cai

Chinese

A4

2100 S. Archer Ave. (at Wentworth Ave.)

Phone: 312-326-6888 Lunch & dinner daily
Web: www.caichicago.com
Price: $$ Cermak-Chinatown

Cai rolls out the red carpet for a lavish experience on the second floor of Chinatown Square, making it the local choice for celebratory seafood dinners or quick midday dim sum. The banquet hall-style room is grand and formal, complete with crystal chandeliers and professional service.

To say there's a lot to choose from is an understatement, as there are nearly 100 rolled, crimped, steamed, and fried dim sum options alone. Highlights include flaky puff pastry turnovers filled with sweet and savory barbecue pork; and large lotus leaves that envelop tender sticky rice mixed with chicken, liver, and crab. When the dim sum parade ends at 4:00P.M., the menu shifts to an equally vast selection of Cantonese dishes like crunchy stir-fried lotus root with ginger.

Chicago Curry House

Indian

B2

899 S. Plymouth Ct. (at 9th St.)

Phone: 312-362-9999 Lunch & dinner daily
Web: www.curryhouseonline.com
Price: $$ Harrison

Maybe you sniff the wafting aromas of ginger, garlic, and cumin first; maybe you hear the sitar tinkling its welcoming notes as you enter. Either way, you know immediately that Chicago Curry House is a commendable showcase of Indian and Nepalese cuisines.

The lunchtime buffet lets you eat your fill for under $12, with crispy *papadum* and baskets of naan; while dinner features an à la carte of faves including Nepalese *khasi ko maasu* with bone-in goat bobbing in a velvety cardamom- and black pepper-sauce. *Tandoori* chicken is a smoky, moist delight; and butter chicken, creamy and rich in a tomato- and *garam masala*-spiced gravy, is done just right. The staff has helpful suggestions for dealing with the area's draconian parking restrictions; call ahead for tips.

Eleven City Diner

Deli

B2

1112 S. Wabash Ave. (bet. 11th St. & Roosevelt Rd.)

Phone: 312-212-1112 Lunch & dinner daily
Web: www.elevencitydiner.com
Price: ⊕⊕ Roosevelt

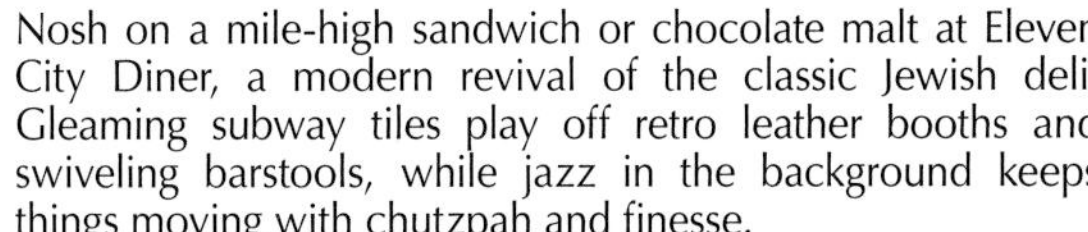

Nosh on a mile-high sandwich or chocolate malt at Eleven City Diner, a modern revival of the classic Jewish deli. Gleaming subway tiles play off retro leather booths and swiveling barstools, while jazz in the background keeps things moving with chutzpah and finesse.

Diner standards include patty melts, sandwiches piled with corned beef or pastrami, knishes, and latkes. Bubbie's chicken soup comes brimming with a fluffy matzo ball the size of a baseball; while Junior's cheesecake from Brooklyn or a triple-decker wedge of red velvet cake sates all the sweet-loving guests. A full-service deli counter offers salamis and smoked fish to-go. For a true blast from the past, stop by the candy stand near the entry, stocked with Bazooka Joe and other favorites.

Kurah

Middle Eastern

B3

1355 S. Michigan Ave. (at 14th St.)

Phone: 312-624-8611 Lunch & dinner daily
Web: www.kurahchicago.com
Price: $$ Roosevelt

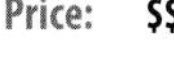

The phrase "small plates" doesn't always translate to "great value," but Kurah offers an exception to the rule with its affordable selection of shareable, Middle Eastern-influenced dishes. Featuring Arabic-inspired wallpaper and upholstered seats, the setting is as warm and cozy as the open grill blazing away in the kitchen.

Build a meal from hot and cold tapas options like *muthowma*, a blend of silky potatoes and whipped garlic that's perfect for scooping onto warm pita bread. Larger meat platters like a single juicy lamb and beef *kifta kabob*, served with roasted vegetables and golden saffron rice, make a hearty meal for one. For dessert, dark chocolate oozes invitingly between layers of phyllo and crushed walnuts in a tasty twist on the classic baklava.

La Petite Folie

French XX

C5

1504 E. 55th St. (at Harper Ave.)

Phone: 773-493-1394 — Lunch Tue – Fri
Web: www.lapetitefolie.com — Dinner Tue – Sun
Price: $$

Though its tree-lined courtyard off 55th Street may not be as picturesque as the Tuileries, La Petite Folie remains a transporting Gallic hideaway in Hyde Park. The graceful lace-curtained dining room and curvaceous wood bar draws scholarly types from nearby University of Chicago, with prices that cater to student budgets.

A retinue of French classics like whole trout Grenobloise are refreshed by seasonal market ingredients at the hands of Chef/co-owner Mary Mastricola. Slices of smoked duck drizzled with black currant vinaigrette get an earthy touch from apple-walnut compote in an elegant lunch salad. Even the wine list chosen by Mastricola's husband Michael is an all-French affair, with numerous by-the-glass choices from Bordeaux to Chablis.

Mercat a la Planxa

Spanish XX

B1

638 S. Michigan Ave. (at Balbo Ave.)

Phone: 312-765-0524 — Lunch & dinner daily
Web: www.mercatchicago.com
Price: $$ — Harrison

Within a cavernous space in the Renaissance Blackstone hotel, Mercat a la Planxa recreates the hustle and bustle of a Spanish marketplace with an extensive menu of Catalan tapas. The dining room's tightly packed tables are perfect for grazing, and soaring ceilings along with cathedral windows overlooking Grant Park, impress locals and out-of-towners alike.

Plump, crunchy *gambas al ajillo* are bathed in buttery garlic sauce with a hint of lemon, and servers add to the excitement by drizzling jus over skewers of bacon-wrapped lamb loin medallions at the table. This is the kind of place where nary a splash of sauce is left behind, so use those slices of brioche—with a swipe of sweet onion purée for good measure—to sop up every last delicious drop.

MingHin

Chinese XX

A4

2168 S. Archer Ave. (at Princeton Ave.)

Phone: 312-808-1999 — Lunch & dinner daily
Web: www.minghincuisine.com
Price: ©© — Cermak-Chinatown

Conveniently situated on the ground level of Chinatown Square, MingHin is a stylish standby that draws a diverse crowd to the neighborhood. Spacious dining rooms separated by wooden lattice panels offer seating for a number of occasions, from casual booths and large banquet-style rounds to specially outfitted tables for hot pots.

Dim sum is a popular choice even on weekdays, with diners making selections from photographic menus rather than waiting for a passing cart. Among the numerous options, juicy *har gao*, stuffed with plump seasoned shrimp, always hit the spot. Pan-fried turnip cakes are simultaneously crispy and creamy, studded with bits of pork and mushroom. Fluffy and subtly sweet Malay steamed egg cake is a rare find for dessert.

Phoenix

Chinese XX

A4

2131 S. Archer Ave. (bet. Princeton & Wentworth Aves.)

Phone: 312-328-0848 — Lunch & dinner daily
Web: www.chinatownphoenix.com
Price: ©© — Cermak-Chinatown

Dim sum lovers get the best of both worlds at Phoenix, a comfortable room that boasts a grand view of the Chicago skyline. Here, stacks of bamboo baskets are wheeled to tables on signature silver trolleys for a classic dim sum experience—yet each diner's selection is cooked to order for truly fresh and steaming hot bites. The proof is in the soft and poppable shrimp-and-chive dumplings and the fluffy white buns stuffed with chunks of barbecue pork.

Those looking for larger portions will appreciate the meandering menu, which also boasts Hong Kong-style stir-fry and clay pot dishes alongside Americanized Chinese classics. Fillets of steamed sea bass swim in soy oil on a large oval platter, sprinkled with a touch of slivered scallion to brighten the delicately flaky fish.

The Promontory

American XX

C5

5311 S. Lake Park Ave. West (bet. 53rd & 54th Sts.)

Phone: 312-801-2100 Lunch & dinner daily
Web: www.promontorychicago.com
Price: $$

Equal parts restaurant, watering hole, and music venue, The Promontory brings a much-needed gathering place to the Hyde Park community. Under lofty ceilings trimmed with black iron beams and sleek wood accents, urbanites sip hand-crafted cocktails around a central bar.

A white-hot fire blazes away in the open kitchen, providing the "hearth to table" food trumpeted on the menu. Smoky roasted feta arrives in a pool of balsamic vinegar and oil with a generous assortment of briny olives, while shatteringly crisp black trumpet mushrooms and pickled shallot add piquant crunch to Nantucket bay scallops. At dessert, sweet brûléed marshmallow and a scoop of graham cracker ice cream sit atop a moist chocolate soufflé for a reverse take on s'mores.

The sun is out – let's eat alfresco! Look for 🏖.

Gold Coast

GLITZ & GLAMOUR

The moniker says it all: the Gold Coast is one of the Windy City's most posh neighborhoods, flaunting everything from swanky high-rises along Lake Shore Drive to dazzling boutiques dotting Michigan Avenue. Stroll down the Magnificent Mile only to discover that money can indeed buy it all. Then, head over to Oak Street for yet another spree and watch millionaires mingle over Manolos while heiresses rummage for handbags.

APPLAUDING THE ARTS

Through all this glamor, Gold Coast architecture is not just notable but stunning. And, mansions crafted in regal Queen Anne, Georgian Revival, or Richardsonian Romanesque styles are unequivocally breathtaking. However, this neighborhood is not all about the glitz; it is also deeply committed to the arts, housing both the Museum of Contemporary Art as well as the world-leading Newberry Library. Culture vultures are sure to uncover something edgy and unique at A Red Orchid Theater, after which the exotic Indian lunchtime buffet at **Gaylord** seems not only opportune, but perhaps obligatory? This prized subterranean location, with its spelled-out menu items and well-stocked bar, is sought by both aficionados as well as anyone hungering for free appetizers during happy hour. Nearby, **Le Cordon Bleu College of Culinary Arts** continues to train students (read: hot chefs in the making) on the classics, as well as the next food fad in Chicago kitchens.

RAUCOUS NIGHTS

It's a well-known fact that the Gold Coast also knows how to party. Visit any nightclub, pub, or restaurant along Rush and Division to get a sense of how the cool kids hold it down—until well after dawn. By then, find breakfast on the burner at the **Original Pancake House**. This may seem like a lowbrow treat for such a high-brow neighborhood, but really can there be anything more rewarding than fluffy pancakes, towering waffles, and sizzling skillets after a late-night? Another perfect place to start your day is at Italian deli **L'Appetito**, which also serves up hearty breakfasts, baked goods, and Italian-style sammies. But, rest assured as there is also some darn good junk food to be had in this white-gloved capital of prosperity. American comfort classics like sliders, burgers, and mac and cheese find their way into the menu at **LuxBar**, a dynamic lounge and bar with some of the

best people-watching in town. Need some sweet? Make your way to one of **Teuscher's** outposts for decadent dark chocolate or even **Corner Bakery Cafe** for a fleet of bakery fresh treats—the golden-brown cinnamon crème cake topped with crumbles of cinnamon streusel and powdered sugar has been drawing residents for over two decades and is dubbed a signature for good reason.

A QUICK FIX

With so many awards under its belt and boasting the best ingredients in town, **Gold Coast Dogs** is packed to the gills (er, buns), perpetually. Inside, everyone is either a regular or on the verge of becoming one—thanks in large part to their deliciously charred dogs, usually topped with gooey cheddar. Or, simply humor your hot dog hankering by joining the constant queue outside **Downtown Dogs**. Surely these robust eats should be sealed by a cup that revives? **TeaGschwendner** is just the spot where locals have been known to lose themselves in a world of exotic selections. And, if you don't feel like steeping your own "Sencha Claus" blend, then snag a seat at **Argo Tea** where clouds of whipped cream and flavorful iced drinks are all part of the carte—it's just like Starbucks without the coffee! Serious cooks and gourmands make a beeline for **The Spice House**, where a spectrum of high quality and often esoteric spices, seasonings, and rubs (ground and blended in-house) make for an integral part of a dinner party at home.

HEAVEN ON EARTH

In keeping with its quintessentially elegant and old-world repute, the Gold Coast allows you to don Grandma's pearls for afternoon tea at **The Drake's Palm Court**. Daintily sip, not slurp, your tea while listening to the gentle strumming of a harp and sampling a tasty selection of sandwiches, pastries, and scones. If it's good enough for the Queen, it will certainly do. Also housed in The Drake, warm and luxurious **Cape Cod Room** is famous for seafood and old-world cocktails, presented in oversized brandy snifters. And, over on Delaware Place, fine wines and cocktails aren't the only thing heating up the scene at **Drumbar**—a rooftop spot at the Raffaello Hotel that lets the fashionable crowd frolic alfresco at night (and during the day on Sunday).

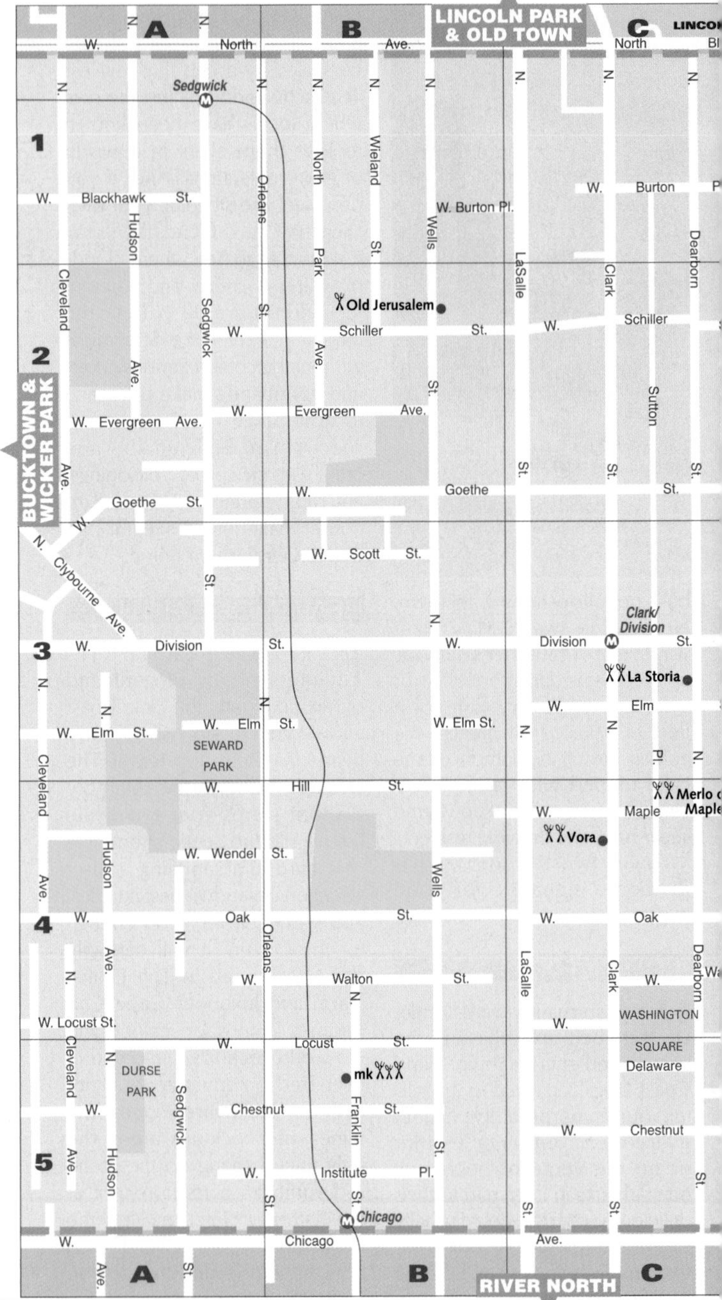

LINCOLN PARK & OLD TOWN
BUCKTOWN & WICKER PARK
RIVER NORTH
Sedgwick
Clark/ Division
Chicago
Old Jerusalem
La Storia
Merlo
Vora
mk
SEWARD PARK
DURSE PARK
WASHINGTON SQUARE
W. North Ave.
W. Blackhawk St.
W. Burton Pl.
W. Burton
W. Schiller St.
W. Evergreen Ave.
W. Goethe St.
W. Scott St.
N. Clybourne Ave.
W. Division St.
W. Elm St.
W. Hill St.
W. Maple
W. Wendel St.
W. Oak St.
W. Walton St.
W. Locust St.
W. Delaware
W. Chestnut St.
W. Institute Pl.
W. Chicago Ave.
N. Cleveland Ave.
N. Hudson Ave.
N. Sedgwick St.
N. Orleans St.
N. North Park Ave.
N. Wieland St.
N. Wells St.
N. LaSalle St.
N. Clark St.
N. Sutton Pl.
N. Dearborn St.
N. Franklin St.

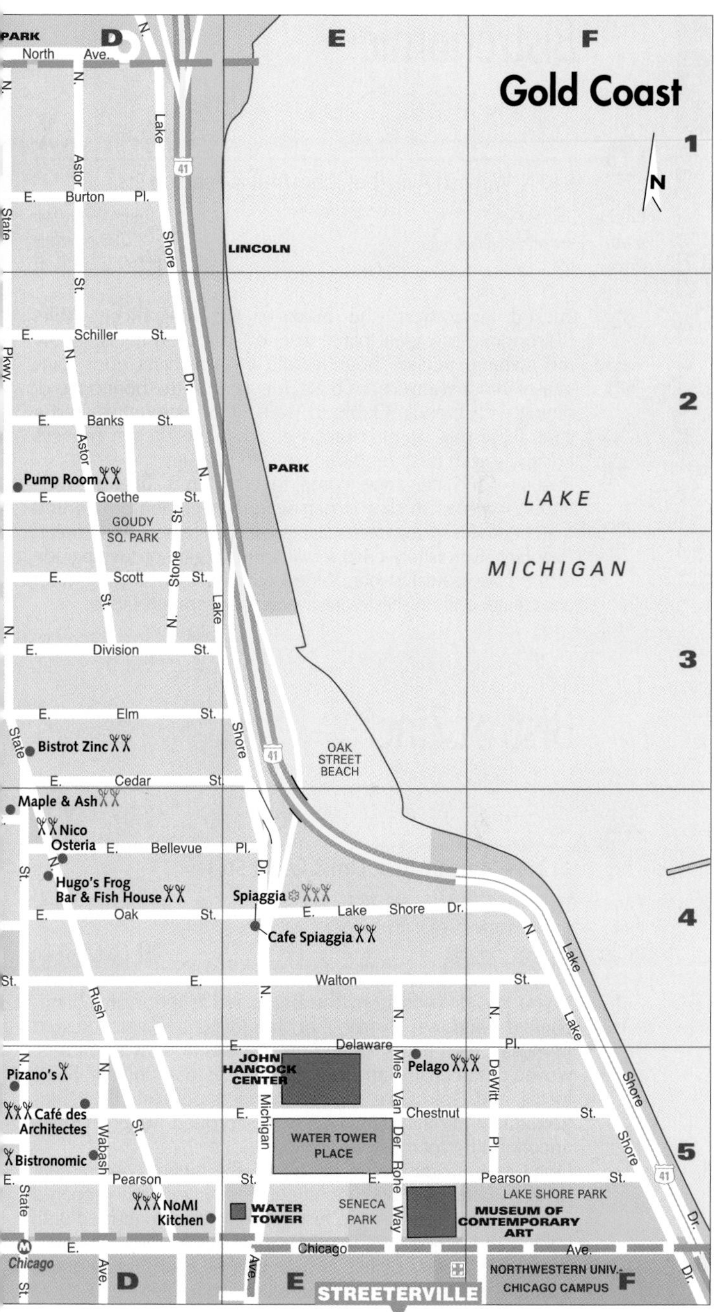
Gold Coast
N
D
E
F
1
2
3
4
5
PARK
North Ave.
LINCOLN
PARK
LAKE
MICHIGAN
E. Burton Pl.
E. Schiller St.
E. Banks St.
E. Goethe St.
GOUDY SQ. PARK
E. Scott St.
E. Division St.
E. Elm St.
E. Cedar St.
E. Bellevue Pl.
E. Oak St.
E. Lake Shore Dr.
E. Walton St.
E. Delaware Pl.
E. Chestnut St.
E. Pearson St.
E. Chicago Ave.
N. Astor St.
N. Lake Shore Dr.
N. State Pkwy.
N. Stone St.
N. State St.
Rush St.
N. Wabash Ave.
N. Michigan Ave.
N. Mies Van Der Rohe Way
N. DeWitt Pl.
41
OAK STREET BEACH
Pump Room
Bistrot Zinc
Maple & Ash
Nico Osteria
Hugo's Frog Bar & Fish House
Spiaggia
Cafe Spiaggia
Pelago
Pizano's
Café des Architectes
Bistronomic
NoMI Kitchen
JOHN HANCOCK CENTER
WATER TOWER PLACE
WATER TOWER
SENECA PARK
LAKE SHORE PARK
MUSEUM OF CONTEMPORARY ART
NORTHWESTERN UNIV.-CHICAGO CAMPUS
Chicago
STREETERVILLE

Bistronomic

French XX

D5 840 N. Wabash Ave. (bet. Chestnut & Pearson Sts.)

Phone: 312-944-8400 Lunch Wed – Sun
Web: www.bistronomic.net Dinner nightly
Price: $$ Chicago (Red)

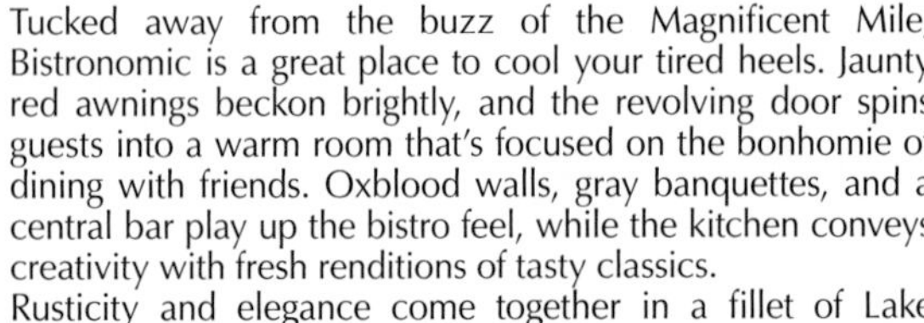

Tucked away from the buzz of the Magnificent Mile, Bistronomic is a great place to cool your tired heels. Jaunty red awnings beckon brightly, and the revolving door spins guests into a warm room that's focused on the bonhomie of dining with friends. Oxblood walls, gray banquettes, and a central bar play up the bistro feel, while the kitchen conveys creativity with fresh renditions of tasty classics.

Rusticity and elegance come together in a fillet of Lake Superior whitefish that is pan-seared to golden-brown and matched with spring ratatouille, preserved lemon, and puréed eggplant. Exquisitely crisp *feuilletine* is a glamorous upgrade to the classic Kit Kat bar, folded with hazelnuts, bittersweet chocolate, and finished with a sweet-tart orange sauce.

Bistrot Zinc

French XX

D3 1131 N. State St. (bet. Elm & Cedar Sts.)

Phone: 312-337-1131 Lunch & dinner daily
Web: www.bistrotzinc.com
Price: $$ Clark/Division

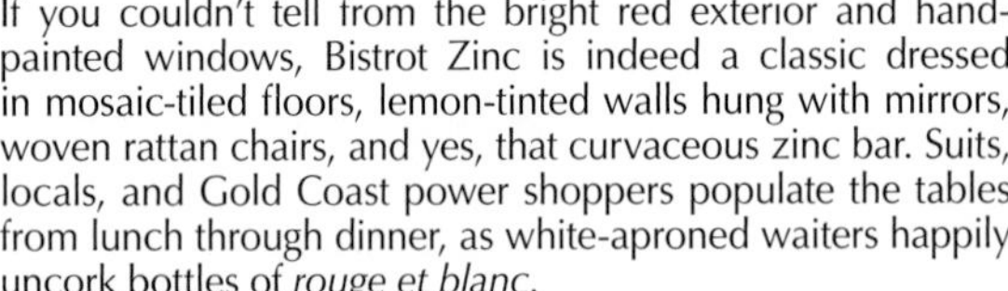

If you couldn't tell from the bright red exterior and hand-painted windows, Bistrot Zinc is indeed a classic dressed in mosaic-tiled floors, lemon-tinted walls hung with mirrors, woven rattan chairs, and yes, that curvaceous zinc bar. Suits, locals, and Gold Coast power shoppers populate the tables from lunch through dinner, as white-aproned waiters happily uncork bottles of *rouge et blanc*.

Don't look for modern surprises on the menu; contentment here is attained through uncomplicated but expertly prepared French dishes from frites to frisée. Whole trout, pan-fried until golden and napped with butter sauce, hits all the right notes; while daily standards like croque monsieur or French onion soup are enhanced by more ambitious monthly specials.

Café des Architectes

Contemporary XXX

D5

20 E. Chestnut St. (at Wabash Ave.)

Phone: 312-324-4063 Lunch & dinner daily
Web: www.cafedesarchitectes.com
Price: $$$ Chicago (Red)

European sophistication lends extra polish to this shimmering spot in the Sofitel Hotel, where "Bonjour" is passed around freely by the mostly French staff. The dining room is just as chic, with crimson banquettes, black-and-white portraits of the city's architectural marvels, and windows with striking steel accents.

The seasonally shifting small plates are simple and creative, like a single Wianno oyster dabbed with fennel cream and crowned with spoonfuls of both sturgeon and faux citrus caviar. Follow this up with such precisely executed items as a potato-leek *velouté* flavored with crawfish tails and scallion crème fraîche. Those hankering for a charcuterie-focused meal may look to the "Chestnut Provisions prix fixe," which at $39, is quite a steal.

Cafe Spiaggia

Italian XX

E4

980 N. Michigan Ave. (at Oak St.)

Phone: 312-280-2750 Lunch & dinner daily
Web: www.spiaggiarestaurant.com/cafe
Price: $$ Chicago (Red)

The revamped look at this café is fresh, modern, and stunning and yet it retains its rustic soul. The clean and sophisticated combination of white marble tables with black cushioned chairs complement the oversized windows' lake views. Gold accents add a sense of luxury and aesthetic appeal to the space, not unlike its über-elegant sibling Spiaggia down the hall.

Like the singular décor, the menu also presents something unique. It is offered as a series of vegetable-focused small plates as well as a handful of larger entrées for two, like the deeply satisfying hunk of pork shoulder, honey-roasted slowly and carefully until it nearly falls off the bone. Standout pasta includes *gemelli* coated in a tomato sauce studded with cubed *guanciale*, *coppa*, and brined artichokes.

Hugo's Frog Bar & Fish House

American XX

D4

1024 N. Rush St. (bet. Bellevue Pl. & Oak St.)

Phone: 312-640-0999 — Lunch Sat – Sun
Web: www.hugosfrogbar.com — Dinner nightly
Price: $$ — Clark/Division

Housed in a sprawling setting adjacent to big brother Gibson's, Hugo's always seems packed. The vast dining room sets white linen-topped tables amid dark polished wood and pale walls decorated with a mounted swordfish, fish prints, and model ships. Hugo's bar draws its own crowds with abundant counter seating.

The menu focuses on a selection of fish preparations as well as steaks and chops. These are supplemented by stone crab claws, oysters, crab cakes, chowders, and sautéed frog's legs. Speaking of which, the restaurant takes its name from the nickname of owner Hugo Ralli's grandfather, General Bruce Hay of Her Majesty's Imperial Forces.

Bring a football team to share a slice of the Muddy Bottom Pie, a decadent (and enormous) ice cream cake.

La Storia

Italian XX

C3

1154 N. Dearborn St. (bet. Division & Elm Sts.)

Phone: 312-915-5950 — Lunch Sat – Sun
Web: www.lastoriachicago.com — Dinner nightly
Price: $$$ — Clark/Division

Tucked into a gorgeous townhouse along Chicago's Gold Coast, this Italian charmer woos with pretty patios, sexy dark panel walls, and conversation-worthy murals by Edward Sorel. The result is a casual, clubby feel; and the first floor, with its low wood beam ceilings, offers great views of Dearborn Street.

Chef Justin Ferguson, who oversees the rest of the Ideology's portfolio of restaurants (including Biggs, Blue Door Farm Stand and Chicago Q), takes the reins here, pushing out a finely executed Italian menu. Try the notable *pollo Milanese*. While it may seems like a predictable standard, La Storia's version is laid over excellent liver mousse and strewn with crispy fried capers as well as peppery watercress to give it a solid leg up on the competition.

Maple & Ash

Steakhouse XX

D4

8 W. Maple St. (bet. Dearborn & State Sts.)

Phone: 312-944-8888 — Dinner nightly
Web: www.mapleandash.com
Price: $$$$ — Clark/Division

Every meal here is like a party, especially if you arrive with an above-average appetite. The space feels as dynamic as the neighborhood, with a serious lounge downstairs and enormous dining room and open kitchen upstairs.

The menu offers different formats, but the one that seems to be earning attention and topping tables is the "I Don't Give A (*ahem*)" prix fixe, for a premium price. In keeping with the steakhouse theme, portions are as gargantuan as the dining rooms themselves. A wedge salad is a veritable meal of crisped bacon and marinated cherry tomatoes piled over slabs of iceberg, draped with blue cheese dressing. The Siberian caviar is as good as its copious accompaniments, ranging from potato chips to cornichons. Steaks are thick, juicy and just right.

Merlo on Maple

Italian XX

C4

16 W. Maple St. (bet. Dearborn & State Sts.)

Phone: 312-335-8200 — Dinner nightly
Web: www.merlochicago.com
Price: $$$ — Clark/Division

Inside a graciously decorated Victorian townhouse, Chef/owner Luisa Silvia Marani proudly showcases the bounty of her native Bologna with an Emiliana-inflected accent and delicious Northern Italian fare. Her frequently changing roster of luscious dishes serve as edible billboards for the foods of the region—think *mortadella di Bologna* and *tartufi neri del'Umbria*.

Rabbit ragù clings to delicate parsley-flecked bow tie pasta tossed with *Parmigiano Reggiano* and copious butter. Wine-braised bone-in lamb shank, served in its own rich sauce, needs little else to shine. Signature *budino di mascarpone, cioccolato e caffé* is the standard-bearer for proper tiramisù, accompanied by tart sugar-coated red currants to offset the creamy sweetness.

mk

American 

B5

868 N. Franklin St. (bet. Chestnut & Locust Sts.)

Phone: 312-482-9179 Dinner nightly
Web: www. mkchicago.com
Price: $$$ Chicago (Brown)

After nearly two decades in business, larger than life "mk" still welcomes all to Chef/owner Michael Kornick's eponymous flagship. Rich brown tones warm up the former paint factory's lofty interior, which features a skylit space that's beloved citywide for big nights and romantic evenings.

There's a seasonal dish here to sate every appetite, whether diners are seated at linen-draped tables or perched on sleek stools in the lounge area. Bar bites offer upscale indulgences like bison sliders tucked into bone marrow-buttered focaccia, while a dual preparation of tartares—yellowfin tuna with Moroccan olives complementing Scottish salmon with charred red onion—could be a meal on its own. For dessert, citrusy "Where troubles melt like lemon drops" is every bit as charming as its name.

Nico Osteria

Italian XX

D4

1015 N. Rush St. (at Oak St.)

Phone: 312-994-7100 Lunch & dinner daily
Web: www.nicoosteria.com
Price: $$$ Chicago (Brown)

Buzz-worthy and a hit since day one, Chef Paul Kahan's area darling happens to be one of the most likeable restaurants around. Think of it as more trendsetting than trendy. The dining room enhances the Mediterranean ambience with subway-tile floors and plenty of natural light. The accommodating staff ensures that no one leaves disappointed. The menu focuses on Italian-leaning seafood dishes, so it is an ideal stop for inspired crudo like fluke with ice-wine vinegar, fennel, and breadcrumbs.

Take a counter seat before the open kitchen to see just how the Kindai tuna with black trumpet mushrooms and kumquat comes together. The regional menu may go on to highlight dishes with boldy flavored seafood, like chili-cured swordfish with thin, house-made *grissini*.

NoMI Kitchen

D5

800 N. Michigan Ave. (entrance on Chicago Ave.)

Phone: 312-239-4030 — Lunch & dinner daily
Web: www.nomirestaurant.com
Price: $$$ — Chicago (Red)

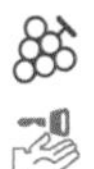
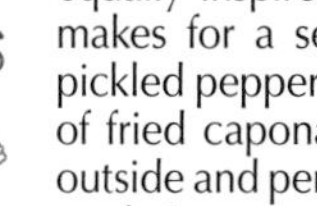
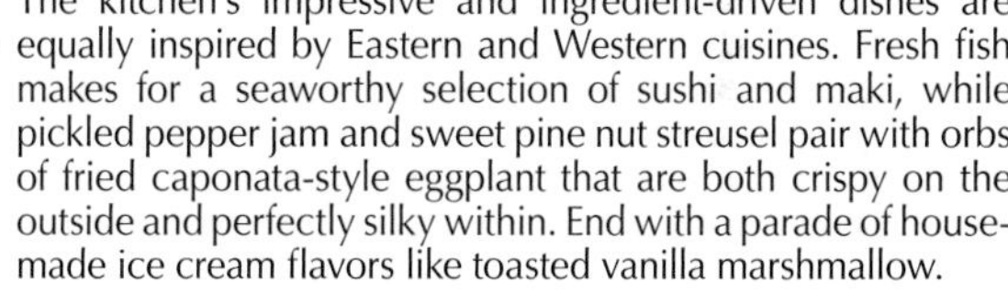

A hushed aerie awaits on the seventh floor of the Park Hyatt at NoMI Kitchen. Let the dapper staff whisk you through the hotel lobby and elevator to a glassed-in dining room with Water Tower views. A semi-open kitchen doesn't detract from the lush but restrained décor, and a breezy terrace offers an alfresco option with a different menu.

The kitchen's impressive and ingredient-driven dishes are equally inspired by Eastern and Western cuisines. Fresh fish makes for a seaworthy selection of sushi and maki, while pickled pepper jam and sweet pine nut streusel pair with orbs of fried caponata-style eggplant that are both crispy on the outside and perfectly silky within. End with a parade of house-made ice cream flavors like toasted vanilla marshmallow.

Old Jerusalem

Middle Eastern 

B2

1411 N. Wells St. (bet. North Ave. & Schiller St.)

Phone: 312-944-0459 — Lunch & dinner daily
Web: N/A
Price: — Sedgwick

Set on a charming stretch of the Windy City, this family-run favorite has been eagerly accommodating its happy customers for years. The menu features a large section of tasty vegetarian options, but the true focus is on Lebanese classics like tabbouleh with cracked wheat, scallions, and tomatoes, seasoned with lemon, olive oil, and plenty of green parsley. Hummus arrives rich with tahini, perhaps accompanying the likes of grilled chicken kebabs and traditional flatbreads. Finish with flaky, sweet and syrupy baklava.

While the décor may not impress, the space manages to feel clean, cozy and comfortable for everyone. Very reasonable prices, hospitable service, and generous portions make this *the* neighborhood go-to—whether dining in or taking out.

Pelago

E5

201 E. Delaware Pl. (at Mies van der Rohe Way)

Phone: 312-280-0700 Lunch & dinner daily
Web: www.pelagorestaurant.com
Price: $$$ Chicago (Red)

This jewel box of a spot is fittingly set adjacent to the Raffaello Hotel. Oozing with elegance, it boasts a crisp style via large windows, tasteful artwork, and comfortable leather seats. An azure-blue color theme ensures the mood is serene. If the décor doesn't evoke the Med, then the Italian-leaning dishes will do the trick. *Taralli ricotta alla salsiccia* features ampersand-shaped pockets filled with ricotta and bathed in a white wine sauce enriched by *Parmigiano Reggiano* for a carbo-licious feast. *Guazzetto di cernia e capesante*, or grouper and scallops in a subtle tomato broth, is matched with escarole for all that's wholesome in this world.

Some may swap dessert for cheese, but don't forgo the *frollino*—a cookie ring filled with mango-mascarpone sabayon.

Pizano's

D5

864 N. State St. (bet. Chestnut St. & Delaware Pl.)

Phone: 312-751-1766 Lunch & dinner daily
Web: www.pizanoschicago.com
Price: ⊜ Chicago (Red)

While Chicago may be hailed as home of the deep-dish pizza, the relatively thin crusted pies at Pizano's earn their own devotees by leaving a bit more room for piling on delicious toppings. This cozy local spot recalls Italian-American style without feeling like a chain-restaurant cliché; even the waitstaff's genuine warmth is palpable. Of course, the crowds come for the crust, which is flaky, buttery, thin (by local standards), and perfectly crisp. Their pizzas are some of the best in town, which should be no surprise as pizza has long been the family calling: owner Rudy Malnati's father founded Pizzeria Uno.

The "thinner" offspring at Pizano's sates its growing fan base from multiple locations, and even ships to those far from the Second City.

Pump Room

American XX

D2

1301 N. State Pkwy. (at Goethe St.)

Phone: 312-229-6740
Web: www.pumproom.com
Price: $$

Lunch Sat – Sun
Dinner nightly
Clark/Division

The location is just part of the charm, so if you find yourself waiting, there are plenty of public spaces and cafés within this architecturally interesting neighborhood, just a stroll away from the shopping district or lake. Inside, the sunken dining room is surrounded by an elevated line of dining tables.

Everything here seems well-orchestrated, beginning with the roasted carrot and avocado salad, tossed with crunchy pumpkin seeds, sour cream, and citrus vinaigrette. Homemade ravioli are simply excellent, filled with ricotta and bathed in butter along with ramps, fava beans, and asparagus. Signature desserts are pure pleasure. Be sure to try the salted caramel ice cream sundae with candied peanuts, salty popcorn, whipped cream, and chocolate sauce.

Vora

Asian XX

C4

1028 N. Clark St. (bet. Maple & Oak Sts.)

Phone: 312-929-2035
Web: www.vorachicago.com
Price: $$

Lunch & dinner daily
Clark/Division

Whether you're in the mood for Chinese, Japanese, Thai, Vietnamese, or Korean, Vora is sure to please with its menu of pan-Asian cooking. The food is quick, inexpensive, and a hit among younger diners. And while the kitchen here seems driven to be more crowd-pleasing than authentic, everyone leaves happy (especially after a fishbowl-sized lychee Bellini or two).

Mix and match stir-fries may throw tradition to the wind rather than in the wok, but combinations like sliced beef with udon in a white wine sauce are well-prepared and tasty—don't hesitate to up the spice level. *Moo shoo* pork should probably go by another name here, but this dish with shredded vegetables and flour wraps is very good indeed. Taiwanese options include oyster omelets and dim sum-like treats.

Spiaggia ✿

Italian XXX

E4

980 N. Michigan Ave. (at Oak St.)

Phone: 312-280-2750 Dinner nightly
Web: www.spiaggiarestaurant.com
Price: **$$$$** Chicago (Red)

There are many reasons why Spiaggia remains one of Chicago's most beloved Italian restaurants. There are high-end bells and whistles aplenty, but to hear the staff recite the effort and intricacies of, say, the *culurgiones* is to compel you to order them. These curious "ravioli" of sorts deliver pure pleasure, filled with lamb, fava beans, and shallots, then baked and served over a pool of fava sauce with crisp radishes. Even the bread here is a noteworthy artisanal assortment, including a crusty little *pain boule* begging to be smeared with butter. A steak is then treated with particular care—in this case the perfectly marbled ribeye, which is dry-aged for 45 days before being cooked to a medium rare and topped with shaved *bottarga* and "brown cow" parmesan, alongside ramps, oyster mushrooms, and an intriguing espresso-Hollandaise sauce.

Come dessert, the tiramisu has all the flavors and notes of the classic, but is deconstructed with contemporary style.

All in all, to dine at Spiaggia is to celebrate a Chicago grande-dame. The dining room is designed with marble columns and terraces to make the most of its dramatic views—an idyllic spot to appreciate the Magnificent Mile by night.

KEMPER
LINNEA

Humboldt Park & Logan Square

A charming pair of lively North Side neighborhoods, Humboldt Park and Logan Square have for long been revered as Chicagoland's heart and soul. They may reside a few steps off the beaten path, but locals here still live to eat and can be found perusing the wares of global grocers, secret bodegas, and those fine falafel shops. **Smalls** is one such tasty smoke hut that churns out familiar barbecue dishes alongside Asian comfort food. Here, hickory-smoked brisket on Texas toast with Thai-style "tiger cry" sauce has earned an army of devotees for good reason. Koreatown is a prized thoroughfare spanning miles along Lawrence Avenue and preparing faithful meals that commence with *banchan,* followed by *galbi, bulgogi,* or *bibimbap.* **Joong Boo Market** is a gem in Avondale flaunting specialties from rice cakes and ground red pepper flakes to dried vegetables and seaweed snacks. Stroll further along these tree-lined streets dotted with quaint buildings and trendy shops, until you land upon **Bang Bang Pie Shop**. Here, handmade, buttery biscuits are likely to keep you inside—indefinitely. But, make sure to step out and into **Global Garden**, a community venture (or "refugee training farm") where immigrants grow produce for sale at local farmer's markets or CSAs. Other like-minded operations include **Campbell Co-op** or **Drake Garden** whose harvest of vegetables and plants unite the neighborhood's diverse groups while ensuring gorgeous greenery amid the city. Humboldt Park is also home to a vibrant Puerto Rican community—just look for Paseo Boricua, the flag-shaped steel gateway demarcating the district along Division Street. These storefronts are as much a celebration of the diaspora as the homeland, with

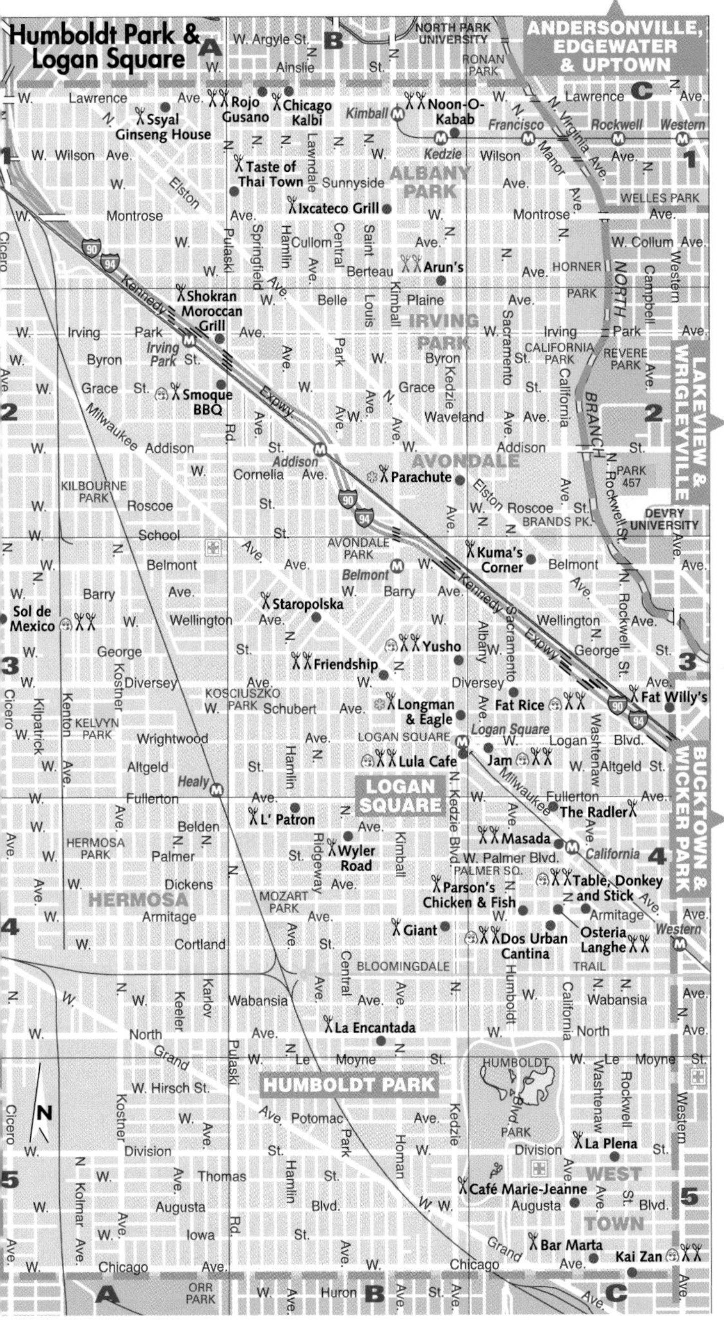
Humboldt Park & Logan Square
ANDERSONVILLE, EDGEWATER & UPTOWN
LAKEVIEW & WRIGLEYVILLE
BUCKTOWN & WICKER PARK
NORTH PARK UNIVERSITY
RONAN PARK
ALBANY PARK
IRVING PARK
AVONDALE
LOGAN SQUARE
HERMOSA
HUMBOLDT PARK
WEST TOWN
KILBOURNE PARK
KELVYN PARK
HERMOSA PARK
KOSCIUSZKO PARK
AVONDALE PARK
MOZART PARK
PALMER SQ.
HORNER PARK
CALIFORNIA PARK
REVERE PARK
WELLES PARK
PARK 457
BRANDS PK.
DEVRY UNIVERSITY
ORR PARK
BLOOMINGDALE TRAIL
NORTH BRANCH
Rojo Gusano
Chicago Kalbi
Noon-O-Kabab
Ssyal Ginseng House
Taste of Thai Town
Ixcateco Grill
Arun's
Shokran Moroccan Grill
Smoque BBQ
Parachute
Kuma's Corner
Staropolska
Sol de Mexico
Yusho
Friendship
Fat Rice
Fat Willy's
Longman & Eagle
Lula Cafe
Jam
The Radler
L' Patron
Masada
Wyler Road
Table, Donkey and Stick
Parson's Chicken & Fish
Giant
Dos Urban Cantina
Osteria Langhe
La Encantada
La Plena
Café Marie-Jeanne
Bar Marta
Kai Zan
Kimball
Kedzie
Francisco
Rockwell
Western
Irving Park
Addison
Belmont
Logan Square
Healy
California
Kennedy Expwy.
Elston Ave.
Milwaukee Ave.
Grand Ave.
Lawrence Ave.
Wilson Ave.
Montrose Ave.
Irving Park Ave.
Addison St.
Belmont Ave.
Diversey Ave.
Fullerton Ave.
Armitage Ave.
North Ave.
Division St.
Chicago Ave.
Cicero Ave.
Pulaski Rd.
Kedzie Blvd.
Western Ave.
Logan Blvd.
W. Palmer Blvd.
Humboldt Blvd.

an impressive array of traditional foods, rare ingredients, and authentic *pernil*. In fact, the annual **Puerto Rican Festival** features four days of festivity, fun, and great food. You can also get your fill of Caribbean cuisine in these parts, but for serious Latin food, dash over to **Café Colao**, a Puerto Rican coffee shop selling pastries and sandwiches. Get here before the crowds for a cheese-and-guava *pastelillo* or Cuban sandwich with *cafe con leche*, of course.

Bill Dugan's **The Fishguy Market** has been serving Michelin-starred restauwrants for decades, while also renting space to **Wellfleet**, a popular luncheonette named after the Cape Cod fishing town. Here fish fans are always in good hands thanks to the kitchen's creative renditions of fresh crustaceans. If steaming hot dogs are a custom in Chicago, then **Jimmy's Red Hots** is the standard bearer of this neighborhood. Meanwhile, the great value found at **Dante's Pizzeria** may only be exceeded by its larger-than-life, exceedingly tasty pies. Speaking of which, the aptly named "inferno" comes with pepperoni, sausage, bacon and fresh garlic—just in case those blazing hot peppers aren't enough. Alternatively, take a real gamble and go for the slice of the day. Then, look to **Grandma J's Local Kitchen** for a breakfast spread rife with deliciously unique sides—think French toast sticks or kale chips. Pastries take the cake at **Shokolad** and the staff at this Ukrainian haunt know how to keep your eyes on the prize: a stacked-to-the-top glass bakery case showcases its wares to great effect. Their signature cheesecake lollipops may not hail from the Old Country, but rest assured that they are very tasty.

LOGAN SQUARE

An eclectic mix of cuisines combined with historic buildings and charming boulevards attracts everybody from hipsters and working-class locals, as well as artists and students to this lovely quarter. Within the culinary community, a blend of home chefs, star cooks, and staunch foodies can be found plunging into the products at **Kurowski's Sausage Shop**, a respected butcher specializing in handmade cuts of Polish meats. Novices take note: pair a flavorful sausage with toasted rye before picking up pickles to-go from the old-school and always-reliable **Dill Pickle Food Co-op**. Carrying on this cultural explosion, Logan Square is also home to **Johnny's Grill**, a neighborhood diner that has been revived by a formally trained pastry chef. But the greasy spoon spirit lives on in dishes like the fried fish sandwich, flat top double cheeseburger, and bottomless fresh brewed Intelligentsia coffee. Also of epicurean note is **Logan Square Farmers Market** selling everything ingestible from raw honey to organic zucchini; while the uniquely sourced and beautifully packaged brews at **Gaslight Coffee Roasters** are a caffeine junkie's real-life fantasy.

Just as kids delight in a day spent at **Margie's Candies** for homemade chocolates, adults eagerly await a night out at **Scofflaw** for gin-infused libations and secret menu combinations. Of course, the tiki craze is thriving at local cocktail legend Paul McGee's **Lost Late Tiki Bar**, slinging rum based delights. On the opposite end, students prepare for an impromptu dinner with *nonna* by buying up all things authentic from **Half Italian Grocer**. Food wonks however shop till they drop at **Independence Park Farmers Market** for a divine dinner back home. Less locally traditional but just as tantalizing is **Jimmy's Pizza Café**, justly mobbed for its mean rendition of a New York-style slice. Albany Park is another melting pot of global foods and gastronomic retreats minus the sky-high price. Plan your own Middle Eastern feast with a spectrum of cheeses, spreads, and flatbreads from **Al-Khyam Bakery & Grocery**, tailed by perfect baklava from **Nazareth Sweets**. But, if meat is what you're craving, then join the crowds of carnivores at **Charcoal Delights**, a time-tested burger joint.

Arun's

B1 Thai XX

4156 N. Kedzie Ave. (at Berteau Ave.)

Phone: 773-539-1909 Dinner Thu – Sat
Web: www.arunsthai.com
Price: $$$$ Kedzie (Brown)

Dining at Arun's feels like attending a dinner party hosted by a well-traveled friend. Covered wall-to-wall in rich carpeting and filled with artwork and figurines, the dining room feels homey and intimate. Adding to the ambience, the kitchen offers a choice of ten- or 12-course chef's tastings nightly in lieu of à la carte.

The dishes on each tasting menu shift according to the chef's whims, and some are more successful than others. Courses range from the familiar and comforting to the innovative: crisp, shatteringly light batter coats two thin strips of pork belly; a hearty chunk of beef tenderloin melts into rich spice-infused *massaman* curry; and a squirt of lemon balances the fragrant coconut broth and crushed chili peppers of *mee kati* noodles.

Bar Marta

American 

C5

2700 W. Chicago Ave. (at Washtenaw Ave.)

Phone: 773-697-4489 Dinner Tue – Sat
Web: www.barmarta.com
Price: $$

Hidden in plain sight is this cozy, clandestine, and downright delicious speakeasy-cum-restaurant—and it is destined to become a neighborhood favorite. Upon arrival, make your way inside to find a stylish crowd enjoying cocktails at the marble bar, soaking in the sultry tunes, and basking in the candlelight. Service is deceptively good—relaxed but on the ball. And the prices are reasonable, considering the quality of food. Dig into a warm bowl of succulent, tender-braised octopus interspersed with coins of fingerling potatoes; or toothsome, hand-cut pasta tossed in creamy *cacio e pepe*.

A generous wedge of silky chocolate ganache featuring a dark cookie crumb is topped with a cloud of freshly whipped cream, which serves as a clean foil to the richness beneath.

Café Marie-Jeanne

American 

1001 N. California Ave. (at Augusta Blvd.)

Phone: 773-904-7660 Lunch & dinner Wed – Mon
Web: www.cafe-marie-jeanne.com
Price: $$

Straddling a rapidly gentrifying intersection of this neighborhood dotted with trendy restaurants, pubs, and the like, Café Marie-Jeanne is laid-back and welcoming—just the way you hope your favorite neighborhood café is going to be. The airy interior owns an almost European sensibility, but the cooking is straight out of an American playbook: think PB&J sandwiches, griddle cakes, and veggie pot pies.

From breakfast to dinner, the menu is eclectic and flexible, allowing customers to mix and match mains and sides. A quarter smoked chicken is brined to juicy perfection and coated in an irresistibly sweet glaze. Tender sides like roasted and charred squash arrive fragrant with toasted hazelnuts, pepitas, crispy sage and a melted brown sugar glaze.

Chicago Kalbi

3752 W. Lawrence Ave. (bet. Hamlin & Lawndale Aves.)

Phone: 773-604-8183 Dinner Wed – Mon
Web: www.chicago-kalbi.com
Price: $$

Take me out to the ballgame—or the barbecue joint where a ballplayer would feel right at home. At this quirky spot, autographed baseballs line the shelves, while photographs and posters of ballplayers paper the walls. The cluttered décor never deters locals from frequenting this modest yet welcoming home to Korean barbecue.

Start with a less than traditional but tasty starter of *banban* tofu, topped with cucumbers, shredded daikon pickles, and a nest of nori beneath fermented soybean paste. Gas grills at each table give off an intoxicatingly savory perfume as patrons take their time searing their choice of well-marbled marinated beef, including the always-popular *bulgogi* or *kalbi*, then cool their palates with an array of *banchan*.

Dos Urban Cantina

Mexican XX

C4

2829 W. Armitage Ave. (at Mozart St.)

Phone: 773-661-6452 Dinner nightly
Web: www.dosurbancantina.com
Price: $$

After several years at Topolobampo, the husband-wife duo behind this gem have taken their knowledge and skills to craft this consistently delicious and inventive cuisine. And, the chefs' deep understanding of Mexican ingredients has allowed them to create elegant and well-priced compositions. Chunks of slowly braised pork carnitas are hearty, tender, and brought to an entirely new level with squash that pops with bright flavor—all balanced with a bracing tomatillo broth. For dessert, indulge in excellent Mexican sugar pie topped with whipped cream and pecan toffee that is out of this world.

The space is comfortable and roomy so that the steady stream of thirty-somethings never make it feel crowded. Curved booths and romantic lighting lend a soft feel.

Fat Rice

Macanese XX

C3

2957 W. Diversey Ave. (at Sacramento Ave.)

Phone: 773-661-9170 Lunch Wed – Sun
Web: www.eatfatrice.com Dinner Tue – Sat
Price: $$ Logan Square

Not familiar with the food of Macau? Not to worry—Fat Rice turns the uninitiated into believers nightly. In fact, the restaurant's thriving success led to an expansion that includes a cocktail lounge and bakery next door. Bar seating around the open kitchen gives a bird's-eye view of the mélange of ingredients used in each dish, though servers are happy to walk any guest through the intoxicating mashup of Portuguese-meets-Asian cuisine.

Sharing is recommended for the namesake *arroz gordo*, a paella-esque blend of meat, shellfish, and pickles. Pillowy bread pairs well with crisp chili prawns stuffed with a flavorful blend of fermented black beans and garlic; while chrysanthemum gelée served with jackfruit and peanuts is a sweet 'n salty thrill.

Fat Willy's

C3

2416 W. Schubert St. (at Artesian Ave.)

Phone: 773-782-1800 Lunch & dinner daily
Web: www.fatwillys.com
Price: $$

With piles of hickory and applewood stacked at the entrance and the sweet-spicy aroma of smoke filling the air, Fat Willy's telegraphs an authentic barbecue experience from the outset. Vintage hand mixers decorate one wall, but this isn't a precious farmhouse bakery—the meat is front and center, as indicated by the rolls of paper towels and sheets of Kraft paper laid out over gingham tablecloths.

Signature baby back ribs are pink and glistening with fat after a slow smoke, and a duo of house-made barbecue sauces lets diners kick things up as desired. Minced fresh garlic adorns the pulled pork sandwich, with a few shakes of seasoned vinegar for extra oomph. After those savory indulgences, a slice of cool, creamy peanut butter mousse cake is just the ticket.

Friendship

B3

2830 N. Milwaukee Ave. (bet. Dawson & Kimball Aves.)

Phone: 773-227-0970 Lunch & dinner daily
Web: www.friendshiprestaurant.com
Price: $$ Logan Square

Innovative Chinese cuisine and sophisticated cocktails make this hip Logan Square venue worth seeking out. Inside the dimly lit space, wood-lined walls, sleek banquettes, linen-draped tables, and polished copper accents play off a palette of rich neutrals to lend a modern, upscale vibe.

Friendship's spirited menu offers both traditional cuisine and enticing departures. Fruit juices and liquors enhance items like Barbarian beef with a chili-cabernet sauce. Then, Champagne lemon chicken, XO brandy beef *chow fun*, and sizzling Xi'an pork with a red chili-and-black bean sauce all boast salty, sweet, and spicy notes. For a sweet finish, opt for one of the more western-leaning desserts or simply settle for the ultimate *coup d'etat*—a chocolate fortune cookie.

Giant

B4

3209 W. Armitage Ave. (bet. Kedzie & Sawyer Aves.)

Phone: 773-252-0997 Dinner Tue – Sat
Web: www.giantrestaurant.com
Price: $$

Jason Vincent returns to the Chicago dining scene with this fabulous new restaurant.

The menu is a listing of cozily familiar dishes (think onion rings, crab salad, and baby back ribs), albeit drummed up with unique accents reflecting the chef's distinctive style. The petite space is simple and lovely, with a modern-rustic décor and a genuinely nice neighborhood vibe. A chef's counter in the back offers an up-close-and-personal kitchen experience. Kick things off with the excellent Jonah crab salad, served with soft, pillowy waffle-cut potato fritters and freshly made cocktail sauce. Then move on to the "Pici with chew," thick strands of *pici* noodles cooked to a conservative al dente, and tossed with smoky bacon, chopped jalapeños, and breadcrumbs.

Ixcateco Grill

Mexican

B1

3402 W. Montrose Ave. (bet. Bernard St. & Kimball Ave.)

Phone: 773-539-5887 Dinner Tue – Sun
Web: www.ixcatecogrill.com
Price: $$ Kedzie (Brown)

$ BYO

Servers stand erect as soldiers at Ixcateco Grill, their pressed white shirts tucked into immaculate black pants. It's a sight you wish you'd see more often—the unmistakable feeling that the staff cares deeply about your experience at this delicious Mexican hot spot. The colorful space, painted in bright shades of orange, green, and fuchsia, only adds to the bonhomie.

Chef Anselmo Ramírez, a veteran of Frontera Grill and Topolobampo, knows his way around Southern Mexican food. Try the irresistible *picaditas*, a pair of tender little masa canoes filled with savory chicken carnitas, pickled cactus, avocado cream, and *queso fresco*; or the wonderfully complex and authentic *pollo en mole negro*, sporting that perfect, complex blend of sweet and spicy *mole*.

Jam

American 

3057 W. Logan Blvd. (at Albany Ave.)

Phone: 773-292-6011 — Lunch Thu – Tue
Web: www.jamrestaurant.com
Price: Logan Square

Hiding in plain sight, Jam remains the sweetheart of brunch-o-philes who won't settle for some greasy spoon. White walls and stone tables punctuated by lime-green placemats give a gallery-like feel to the space; while a friendly welcome and open kitchen keep things homey.

Creative and refined versions of brunch faves from Chef Jeffrey Mauro set this kitchen apart. For instance, French toast features brioche slices soaked in vanilla and malt-spiked custard, cooked sous vide, and then caramelized in a sizzling pan. Garnished with lime leaf-whipped cream and pineapple compote, this staple is sure to cure any hangover. Then braised beef and tomato *crema* are rolled into buckwheat crêpes and crowned by a sunny-side up egg for an elegant take on the breakfast burrito.

Kai Zan

Japanese

2557 ½ W. Chicago Ave. (at Rockwell St.)

Phone: 773-278-5776 — Dinner Tue – Sat
Web: www.eatatkaizan.com
Price: $$

Despite doubling its space a few years ago, Kai Zan is still the kind of place that needs a reservation well in advance. Located on an otherwise solitary stretch of Humboldt Park, the space is particularly charming and makes you feel like you are stepping into a cozy neighborhood *izakaya* tucked away in a remote Japanese fishing hamlet. Savvy diners book a seat at the marble sushi counter to watch chefs and twin brothers Melvin and Carlo Vizconde perform their magic up close.

The brothers turn out sophisticated, creative dishes that are decked with myriad sauces, flavors and textures. Non-traditional sushi, nigiri, *yakitori*, as well as classic bar bites like *takoyaki* and *karaage* are all crafted with precise details and impeccable ingredients.

Kuma's Corner

C3

2900 W. Belmont Ave. (at Francisco Ave.)

Phone: 773-604-8769 — Lunch & dinner daily
Web: www.kumascorner.com
Price: ⊜

Even vegans know the cult following of Kuma's Corner, though there's absolutely nothing for them on the menu at this heavy metal burger joint on an unassuming Avondale corner. It's not for the faint of heart: between the crowds, the crunching blasts of sound, and the NC-17 artwork. Steady yourself with a beer or Bourbon while waiting for a table and a juicy patty.

The lines wouldn't be stretching out the door if the kitchen weren't cranking out kick-ass burgers. The menu features more than a dozen options of 10-oz. monsters served on pretzel rolls with myriad toppings like roasted garlic mayonnaise, house-made hot sauce, and pepper jack cheese. Almost as famous, mac and cheese with add-ins offers a comparably artery-clogging change of pace.

La Encantada

Mexican

B4

3437 W. North Ave. (bet. Homan & St. Louis Aves.)

Phone: 773-489-5026 — Dinner Tue – Sun
Web: www.laencantadarestaurant.com
Price: ⊜

Encantada is Spanish for enchanting, and this family-run spot more than lives up to its name. Royal-blue, golden-yellow, and exposed brick walls are hung with gallery-style artwork (most of which is for sale), and contemporary Latin tunes waft through the air. Culinary inspiration begins in the family's hometown, Zacatecas, but pulls from around Mexico with delectable results.

Enchiladas rojas, a Zacatecan specialty, are as authentic as one could wish. Two small, salted beef-filled tortillas are draped with earthy salsa *rojas* for muted chili heat, while avocado and *crema fresca* bring depth to a rustic chicken tortilla soup. The chewy, caramelized crust on pan-fried plantains is textbook perfect, served with a dollop of cinnamon-laced cream.

La Plena

Puerto Rican

C5

2617 W. Division St. (bet. Rockwell St. & Washtenaw Ave.)

Phone: 773-276-5795 — Lunch & dinner Thu – Mon
Web: N/A
Price: ☺

BYO

Owners Epi and Soraya Velez have created a warm and welcoming haven for anyone hoping to enjoy a little piece of Puerto Rico in Chicago. Their home-style cooking would make any Boricua proud, offering standards from *mofongo* to *lechon* and even the holiday favorite of *coquito*—with much less of the heaviness often associated with the traditional cuisine.

As the story goes, the *jibarito* was created by Chicago's Puerto Rican community, and La Plena's rendition—featuring thin steak strips, garlicky mayonnaise, and melted cheese between fried flattened plantains—is an exceptional example. For dessert, dig into a slice of dense, eggy flan while you take in the dining room's custom murals that showcase Puerto Rico's beaches and countryside.

L' Patron

B4

3749 W. Fullerton Ave. (bet. Hamlin & Ridgeway Aves.)

Phone: 773-799-8066 — Lunch & dinner Wed – Mon
Web: N/A
Price: ☺

BYO

This local, no-frills and much-loved taqueria may have moved locations, but in its new digs, things remain largely the same. Signature lime-green and bright orange hues continue to decorate the interior space, which also features counter service, blaring *bachata* to keep you moving as you munch, and those wonderfully soft and flavorful homemade tortillas, tortas, tacos, and burritos.

Ultra-fresh dishes are assembled to order, like the taco *al pastor*, filled with sumptuous chunks of achiote-marinated pork and topped with chopped onion and cilantro. Then a version with carne asada may be offered, packed with grilled, well-seasoned beef; while crisp tortilla chips, still warm from the fryer, are addictive companions for scooping up chunky, garlicky guacamole.

Longman & Eagle ✿

Gastropub

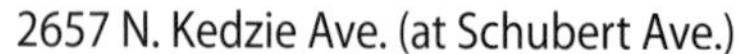

B3

2657 N. Kedzie Ave. (at Schubert Ave.)

Phone: 773-276-7110 Lunch & dinner daily
Web: www.longmanandeagle.com
Price: $$ Logan Square

Situated on a trendy corner and marked by a single ampersand over the door, this is the ultimate merging of the Old World and New Order. It's where remnants of a glorious past live in harmony with chefs who prefer bandanas and beards to toques. The cuisine is as haute as ever despite the saloon-like feel.

From early to late, Millennials never seem to tire of this local hangout. Its numerous dining nooks include the happening bar that pours exceptional cocktails, boisterous front dining room, and exposed brick alcove for both space and privacy.

Although the lunch menu offered here is particularly limited, the kitchen does boast a "go bold or go home" sort of creative flair—even though it may at times get lost in endless dots and drizzles of garnish. And while the à la carte items sound complex, superb taste is at the center of each dish. Don't miss the signature "duck in a jar" that is turned out into a bowl to better appreciate the succulent array of hearty duck pastrami, duck confit and rice beans balanced with intriguing notes of sweet acidity from fresh raspberries and cubes of vinegar jelly. Distinct desserts may include a chocolate-pecan praline, Bourbon caramel, and espresso terrine garnished with shards of burnt honey and smooth malt ice cream.

Lula Cafe

American XX

2537 N. Kedzie Ave. (off Logan Blvd.)

Phone: 773-489-9554 — Lunch & dinner Wed – Mon
Web: www.lulacafe.com
Price: $$ — Logan Square

Despite a gleamingly renovated kitchen, neighborhood darling Lula Cafe remains the same beloved hangout it's always been. No matter what's on the constantly evolving menu, the fresh, seasonal, and always original fare keeps the casual spot slammed with the creative denizens of Logan Square from morning to night.

The mouthwatering fixings in Lula's Royale breakfast sandwich change with the seasons and might include thin slices of meaty, tender short rib, a sunny-side up farm egg, smoky cumin aïoli, and bitter orange jam served alongside a salad of vinegary carrot, daikon, and cilantro. Sweet teeth are satisfied by a tall wedge of double-layered carrot cake complete with crème anglaise and a luxurious spoonful of strawberry preserves on the side.

Masada

2206 N. California Ave. (bet. Lyndale & Palmer Sts.)

Phone: 773-697-8397 — Lunch Sat – Sun
Web: www.masadachicago.com — Dinner Tue – Sun
Price: — California (Blue)

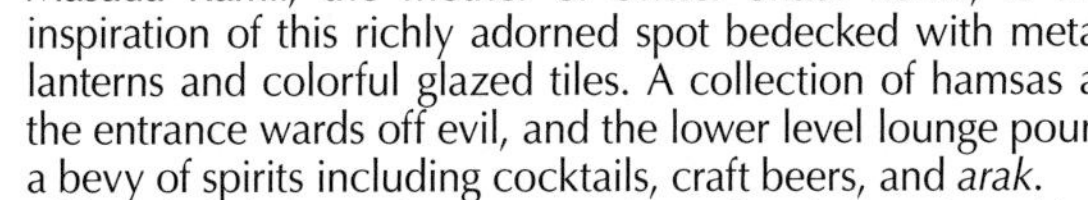

Masada Ramli, the mother of owner Shadi Ramli, is the inspiration of this richly adorned spot bedecked with metal lanterns and colorful glazed tiles. A collection of hamsas at the entrance wards off evil, and the lower level lounge pours a bevy of spirits including cocktails, craft beers, and *arak*.

Although kebabs and wraps can be ordered, there's nothing commonplace about Masada's home-style cooking. Instead, imagine the likes of lamb's kidney and heart sautéed with onions and oyster mushrooms; or *fetit betinjan*, crunchy pita cubes and roasted eggplant dressed with tahini, pomegranate molasses, and lemon. A number of vegan options abound and attract, including *koshari*, a hearty mélange of rice, lentils, and gluten-free pasta, accompanied by spicy tomato sauce and tart pickles.

Noon-O-Kabab

B1 Persian XX

4661 N. Kedzie Ave. (at Leland Ave.)

Phone: 773-279-9309 Lunch & dinner daily
Web: www.noonokabab.com
Price: ¢¢ Kedzie (Brown)

A bustling lunch crowd appreciates the welcoming hospitability at this family-run Persian favorite in the heart of the North Side. Intricate tilework and patterned wall hangings offset the closely spaced linen-topped tables and add touches of elegance to the homey space.

A basket of warm pita bread and a bowl of salty Bulgarian feta, parsley, and raw onions sate the appetites of those perusing the kababs on the menu. Succulent, hand-formed lamb *koubideh* and beef tenderloin skewers are juicy and charred with a hint of spice, and vegetarian offerings like *tadiq* with *ghormeh sabzi* play up the textural contrast of crispy pan-browned saffron rice against flavorful stewed spinach. Sample a glass of "awesome" house Earl Grey tea steeped with cardamom and ginger.

Osteria Langhe

C4 Italian XX

2824 W. Armitage Ave. (bet. California Ave. & Mozart St.)

Phone: 773-661-1582 Dinner nightly
Web: www.osterialanghe.com
Price: $$ California (Blue)

Osteria Langhe offers Logan Square a genuine taste of Italy—Piedmonte, to be exact. Partners Aldo Zaninotto and Chef Cameron Grant have created a sophisticated yet welcoming contemporary space, with warm, glowing bulbs that protrude from the walls, bare wood tables and metal chairs lining the floor. Additionally, a communal table at the restaurant's entrance, is visible through its garage-like glass façade.

The regionally focused food and wine list celebrates the Italian way of eating ("slow food") with legendary Piedmontese pasta like the *tajarin*, a plate of deliciously eggy noodles twirled around savory ragù, diced carrots and bright green parsley. Dinner specials offer great value, most notably the Trifecta Tuesday $38 prix-fixe.

Parachute ✿

Fusion

3500 N. Elston Ave. (at Troy St.)

Phone: 773-654-1460 Dinner Tue – Sat
Web: www.parachuterestaurant.com
Price: $$

Husband-and-wife chef team Johnny Clark and Beverly Kim have put their little corner of Avondale on Chicago's culinary map with this hip and homey bistro. Young foodies fill the space every night, whether seated at tables lining the wooden banquette or perched on colorful stools dotting a double-sided slab of counter, half of which faces the open kitchen.

Clark and Kim's exemplary cuisine results from a deep understanding of the Korean pantry as well as a brilliant application of au courant technique to seasonal product. Baked potato *bing* bread, the restaurant's signature flaky flatbread carb-bomb, is stuffed with melted scallions and bacon bits, topped with nutty sesame, and served with sour cream butter. Then, cauliflower is deep-fried, set over cool, herbaceous raita, and studded with shards of spicy *tandoori* chicken skin; while *dukbokki*, Korean rice cakes, are pan-crisped and combined with bits of succulent goat meat sausage and refreshingly bitter wilted rapini.

Desserts are a stellar finish—think silky panna cotta served with a soy sauce-caramel drizzle and topped with popped corn, or a novel take on the fruit crisp with buckwheat, Bing cherries, ginger-spiced broth, and scoop of *sakura* ice cream.

Parson's Chicken & Fish

American

2952 W. Armitage Ave. (at Humboldt Blvd.)

Phone: 773-384-3333 — Lunch & dinner daily
Web: www.parsonschickenandfish.com
Price: $$ — California (Blue)

For the young professionals and new families of gentrifying Logan Square, Parson's Chicken & Fish is a lively but low-key hangout that hits all the bases. It's equally appropriate for a midday snack with the kids or a late-night munchies run, and the stay-and-play vibe extends to on-site activities like a winter ice skating rink or summer ping pong tables.

As per the name, poultry and seafood offerings are house specialties, with signature golden-fried chicken (and equally popular Negroni slushies) on many tables. An aïoli-smeared brioche bun holds a piping-hot fillet of beer-battered fish topped with crisp slaw and house hot sauce. Dessert isn't made in house, but no matter; neighboring Bang Bang Pie Shop provides daily slices of sweetness.

The Radler

German

C4

2375 N. Milwaukee Ave. (bet. California & Fullerton Aves.)

Phone: 773-276-0270 — Lunch Sat – Sun
Web: www.dasradler.com — Dinner Tue – Sun
Price: $$ — California (Blue)

With around 20 suds on tap and more than 95 bottles to sample, The Radler is everything you want in a beer hall. The restaurant may be young, but the space retains an old soul thanks to communal benches that hearken back to the days of Bavarian *biergartens*. The enormous "Bohemian Export" beer mural that commands guests' attention is original to the building—a happy discovery during demolition. A stack of small plates on each table sends the message that everything on the menu is meant for sharing.

Food here may be crafted with drinking in mind, but that does not undermine its delicious creativity. Try the deep-golden pork loin schnitzel with bacon-braised lentils, dried Mission figs, and smoky cream sauce, balanced with a light green salad and charred lemon.

Rojo Gusano

Mexican 

3830 W. Lawrence Ave. (at Avers Ave.)

Phone: 773-539-4398
Web: www.rojogusano.com
Price: $$

Lunch Sat – Sun
Dinner nightly

You wouldn't expect to find this breezy urban beach oasis in Albany Park, but here it is: Rojo Gusano brings its cheery, laid-back cantina vibe to the Northwest side via bare wooden tables, bright paintings and a surfboard on the walls. But it's the delicious little menu, which arrives humbly on a folded piece of paper, which really sets the tone.

Fresh tortillas, high quality ingredients, and solid cooking technique result in an array of enticing and affordable tacos, from classic pork *pibil* to Korean barbecue and green curry shrimp. There are also guacamoles, salsas, and a few small bites like chicken *pibil tamale* or the portobello empanada, to choose from. Whatever you order, be sure to end with Dudley's chocolate tamal.

Shokran Moroccan Grill

Moroccan 

A2

4027 W. Irving Park Rd. (bet. Keystone Ave. & Pulaski Rd.)

Phone: 773-427-9130
Web: www.shokranchicago.com
Price: ⊜

Dinner Wed – Mon
Irving Park (Blue)

BYO

Embrace Moroccan hospitality to the fullest and bone up on your Arabic at Shokran, where the country's culinary culture is displayed in a romantic setting. Nooks and crannies throughout the dining rooms offer intimacy; take a seat among the cozy cushioned banquettes and prepare to say "shokran" (thank you) repeatedly as courses come your way.

Traditional dishes offer the most authentic experience, like sweet and savory *bastilla*, a flaky pastry starter that's large enough to serve two, stuffed with spiced chicken and dusted with cinnamon. Famously rustic, the lamb Marrakesh tagine features a meaty bone-in shank adorned with bitter slivers of preserved lemon and surrounded by sweet peas, whole black olives, and tender quartered artichoke hearts.

Smoque BBQ

Barbecue

A2

3800 N. Pulaski Rd. (at Grace St.)

Phone: 773-545-7427 Lunch & dinner Tue – Sun
Web: www.smoquebbq.com
Price: Irving Park (Blue)

Smoque opens for lunch at 11:00 A.M., but a crowd of devotees can be found lining up for a barbecue fix long before then. Once inside, peruse the chalkboard menu, then order cafeteria-style before staking your claim among the communal seating while waiting (and salivating).

The half-and-half sandwich, piled with pulled pork and brisket, is the best of both worlds, with chunky shreds of tender pork and spice-rubbed slices of pink-rimmed beef spooned with vinegary barbecue sauce. The usual side dish suspects like zingy, crisp coleslaw and deeply smoky baked beans are anything but standard here, complementing the 'cue as they should. For a sweet finish, look no further than pecan bread pudding drizzled with salted caramel-Bourbon sauce.

Sol de Mexico

Mexican

A3

3018 N. Cicero Ave. (bet. Wellington Ave. & Nelson St.)

Phone: 773-282-4119 Lunch & dinner Wed – Mon
Web: www.soldemexicochicago.com
Price: $$

Far more authentic than the average chips-and-salsa joint, Sol de Mexico brightens the scene and palate with a lively atmosphere (cue the mariachi music!) and delectable house specialties. Walls painted in tropical pinks, blues, and oranges are a cheerful canvas for Dia de los Muertos artifacts.

To sample the kitchen's skill, start with *sopes surtidos "xilonen"*—four molded masa cups with a variety of fillings like caramelized plantains doused in sour cream or tender black beans topped with crumbly house-made chorizo. Then, move on to the *pollo en mole manchamanteles*, which translates to "tablecloth stainer." Rich and slightly bitter with a comforting nuttiness, the aptly named mahogany sauce begs to be sopped up with freshly made tortillas.

Ssyal Ginseng House

Korean

A1

4201 W. Lawrence Ave. (at Keeler Ave.)

Phone: 773-427-5296 Lunch & dinner Mon – Sat
Web: www.ssyal.com
Price: 

With Ssyal Ginseng House's invigorating *samgyetang* at their doorstep, it's a wonder anyone in Albany Park ever gets sick. Since 1993, the sunny spot has served this restorative dish, featuring an entire Cornish game hen stuffed with glutinous rice, jujubes, and whole garlic cloves in an earthenware bowl of delicately flavored ginseng broth.

Equal care and skill goes into the rest of the Korean specialties on offer, all of which are presented with kind, attentive service. *Oden ttuck-bok-gi* is piled high in a chewy mix of thin fish cake strips, glutinous rice cakes, and shredded carrots and cabbage tossed in sweet and spicy *gochujang*. For an immunity boost in your own kitchen, take home some of Ssyal's house-dried ginseng or ginger candies.

Staropolska

Polish

B3

3030 N. Milwaukee Ave. (bet. Lawndale & Ridgeway Aves.)

Phone: 773-342-0779 Lunch & dinner daily
Web: www.staropolskarestaurant.com
Price:

Fans of traditional Polish cooking know to proceed to this Logan Square mainstay. If a stroll past nearby Kurowski's Sausage Shop doesn't put you in the mood for some meaty, belly-busting cuisine, then one step inside this Old World-style sanctum certainly will.

Polish pilsners and lagers are poured at the bar and pair perfectly with the stuffed and slow-cooked plates sent out by the kitchen. Pierogies are a staple, and are offered here with a variety of sweet and savory embellishments. Stuffed cabbage is available with a meatless mushroom filling, and house specialties include the *placek po wegiersku*: a light and tender griddled potato pancake folded over chunks of pork and bell pepper slices, braised in a tomato and sweet paprika sauce.

Table, Donkey and Stick

Austrian

2728 W. Armitage Ave. (bet. California Ave. & North Point St.)

Phone: 773-486-8525 — Dinner nightly
Web: www.tabledonkeystick.com
Price: $$ —  Western (Blue)

When American comfort food just won't suffice, look to Table, Donkey and Stick for a helping of cozy Alpine fare. The rustic inn-inspired setting reflects its reputation as a gathering place where friends meet at the inviting bar or settle in at communal tables for whimsical, creative compositions.

Though the food is European-influenced, ingredients from local farms make their way into many dishes. Caraway seeds spice up duck meatballs nestled among springy egg noodles with dehydrated sauerkraut and shaved salted egg yolk, and honeycomb tripe wins new fans when fried to a crisp and topped with house-made giardiniera. For a sweet take on the traditional baked good, try the pretzel-shaped puff pastry sprinkled with candied mustard seeds.

Taste of Thai Town

Thai

B1

4461 N. Pulaski Rd. (at Sunnyside Ave.)

Phone: 773-299-7888 — Lunch & dinner daily
Web: N/A
Price: ⊜

BYO

Well-regarded Thai restaurateur Arun Sampanthavivat expands his influence with this second sibling, a casual and welcoming gathering place housed in a former police station. The menu showcases a taste of each of Thailand's diverse regions, though many diners will be familiar with the offerings on hand. The mouthwatering aromas of each dish are matched in many cases by eye-watering spice.

Pad see ew retain their chewy bite when tossed with crisp veggies like *gai lan* and green beans, and is served with a caddy of sugar, pickled jalapeños, and chili sauce to customize your preferred level of heat and sweet. A cup of pepper pork curry, the chef's specialty, bobs with tender pork belly in a balanced and sumptuous turmeric-tinged sauce.

Wyler Road

American

3581 W. Belden Ave. (at N. Central Park Ave.)

Phone: 773-661-0675 Lunch & dinner daily
Web: www.wylerroad.com
Price: ⊜

Opened as a day-into-late-night eatery near Logan Square, Wyler Road takes the American love for a good sandwich to new heights. Think 20+ varieties of creative sandwiches straddling all walks of appetite: from veal-heart Phillys to fried clam belly rolls; vegetarian sandwiches; and familiar favorites like Reubens. Each of them is deliciously "cheffed up" with unique toppings and detailed execution.

Fitted with a stylish, rustic interior, Wyler Road is part diner and part watering hole, with wood planks as well as a long bar punctuated with teal metal stools. The casual, young and laid-back service staff is a good fit for the easygoing crowd, which streams in late into the evening for post-drink munchies and one last round of cocktails.

Yusho

Japanese 

2853 N. Kedzie Ave. (bet. Diversey Pkwy. & George St.)

Phone: 773-904-8558 Lunch Sun
Web: www.yusho-chicago.com Dinner Mon – Sat
Price: $$ Logan Square

Matthias Merges, a Trotter vet, applies his impressive technical skills to bar food at this fun ode to an *izakaya*—Chicago style. Just off the beaten path from its Logan Square brethren, Yusho draws a crowd into its expansive room featuring a rustic-chic mix of weathered wood, plaid-upholstered booths, and Danish midcentury-style chairs. Diners show up in droves for a mashup of Japanese treats, finished with big flavor.

Start with steamed buns or crispy chicken bits before lingering over the "Logan Poser Ramen" showcasing thick, al dente strands in spicy *tonkotsu* broth. A poached hen egg and crispy pig's tail croquette take it over the top. Vegetarians may delight in pickled gobo root salad mingled with Asian pear, black plum slices and silky tofu-*tobanjan* dressing.

Lakeview & Wrigleyville

Lakeview is the blanket term for the area north of Lincoln Park, including Roscoe Village and Wrigleyville (named after its iconic ball field). Keeping that in mind, enjoy a boisterous game with maximum conveniences at a Wrigley Field rooftop like **Murphy's Bleachers**, where hot dogs and hamburgers are washed down with pints of beer. When the beloved Cubs finish their season each October, don't despair, as these American summertime classics continue to shape the neighborhood's cuisine. Thanks to a large Eastern European population, a sumptuous supply of sausages and wursts can be found in a number of casual eateries or markets, including **Paulina**—a local institution where expected items like corned beef and lamb are offered beside more novel delights like ground venison and loin chops. This is also a hot spot among local Swedish families, who come for time-tested plates of pickled Christmas ham or even cardamom-infused sausages. Other residents may opt to sojourn to **Ann Sather**, a sweet brunch spot branded for its baseball glove-sized cinnamon buns.

CLASSIC CHICAGO

Diners are all the craze in this area, starting with **Glenn's** whose menu reads like a seafaring expedition with over 16 varieties of fish on offer. And between its kitchen's savory egg specialties, 30 types of cereal, and a blackboard menu that makes Egyptian tombs look brief, this is a veritable big city sort of spot and flaunts something for everyone. Similarly, the Windy City's passion for the humble hot dog is something to write home about, and Lakeview offers plenty of proof. Case in point—the dogs and burgers at **Murphy's Red Hots**, which may be simple in presentation are in fact amazing in taste. But, keep in mind that this location has outdoor picnic tables and no inside seating.

BAKING IN BAVARIA

Even Chicagoans can't survive on hot dogs alone. Thankfully, Lakeview has an antidote for practically every craving imaginable. Should you have a hankering for Bavarian baked goods, for instance, **Dinkel's Bakery** is right around the corner. Originally opened by a master baker from Bavaria in 1922, this family-run business (in its current locale since 1932) is renowned for faithful renditions of strudels, *butterkuchen*, and stollen. Their big breakfast sandwich, Dinkel's Burglaur, may be less traditional but is just as tasty—not unlike those decadent donuts. Items here can be purchased fresh, but are also available frozen for shipping to lucky out-of-town fans.

FASCINATING FOOD FINDS

For a different type of high, stop by south-of-the-border sensation, **5411 Empanadas**. This food truck-turned-storefront sells Argentinian empanadas with such inventive fillings as malbec beef or chorizo with *patatas bravas*. It also showcases impressive Latin sweets like *alfajores* to go with good, strong coffee. Connoisseurs of quality-baked goods will want to pop into **Bittersweet Pastry Shop**, where Chef/owner Judy Contino has been whipping up luscious desserts for almost two decades. It's a one-stop shop for everything from breads, pastries, and cupcakes, to exquisitely sculpted wedding confections. Those seeking a classic American experience should proceed to **The Roost Carolina Kitchen** for a 24-hour buttermilk-brined, hotter-than-hot take on the popular Southern fried hot chicken sandwich. Another laudation, even if it comes in buttery and sugary packages to these neighborhoods, is **City Caramels**—home to some lip-smacking treats. Settle in before making your way through Bucktown (by way of coffee-inspired caramels with chocolate-covered espresso beans); Lincoln Square (toasted hazelnuts anybody?), and Pilsen (Mexican drinking chocolate with ancho chili) along with their respective caramel and candy cuts. If savory bites are more your style, trek to **Pastoral**, commonly hailed as one of the country's top destinations for cheese. Their classic and farmstead varietals, fresh breads and olives, as well as intermittently scheduled tastings are a local treasure. An offbeat yet quirky vibe is part and parcel of Lakeview's fabric; and testament to this fact can be found at **The Flower Flat**, boasting a comforting breakfast or brunch repast in an actual flower shop. Meanwhile, **Uncommon Ground** is as much a restaurant serving three square meals a day as it is a coffee shop revered for its live music talent and performances. During the months between June and September, stop by at any time to admire their certified organic sidewalk garden before tasting its bounty on your plate, inside. And a few more blocks north, aspiring young chefs with big dreams proudly present a wholesome grab-n-go restaurant called **Real Kitchen**. Here on the menu, home-style items like baked Amish chicken are paired with a unique and crusty pork belly sandwich to reflect each chef's take on a favored classic.

ROSCOE VILLAGE

Everyone loves a rollicking street fair, and this nabe's **Shock Top Oyster Fest** featuring an incredible music and beer selection as well as worthy guests of honor (maybe a certain mollusk believed to have aphrodisiac qualities) doesn't disappoint. In fact, nostalgic New Yorkers and transplants should take note: Roscoe Village is also home to **Apart Pizza**, Chicago's very own homage to the thin-crust pie. (Just remember, you're in deep-dish land, so you might want to refrain from admitting just how much you enjoyed it!) And finally, because no feast is complete without sweet, bide some time at **Black Dog** whose creamy gelato concoctions count renowned local chefs among their fans.

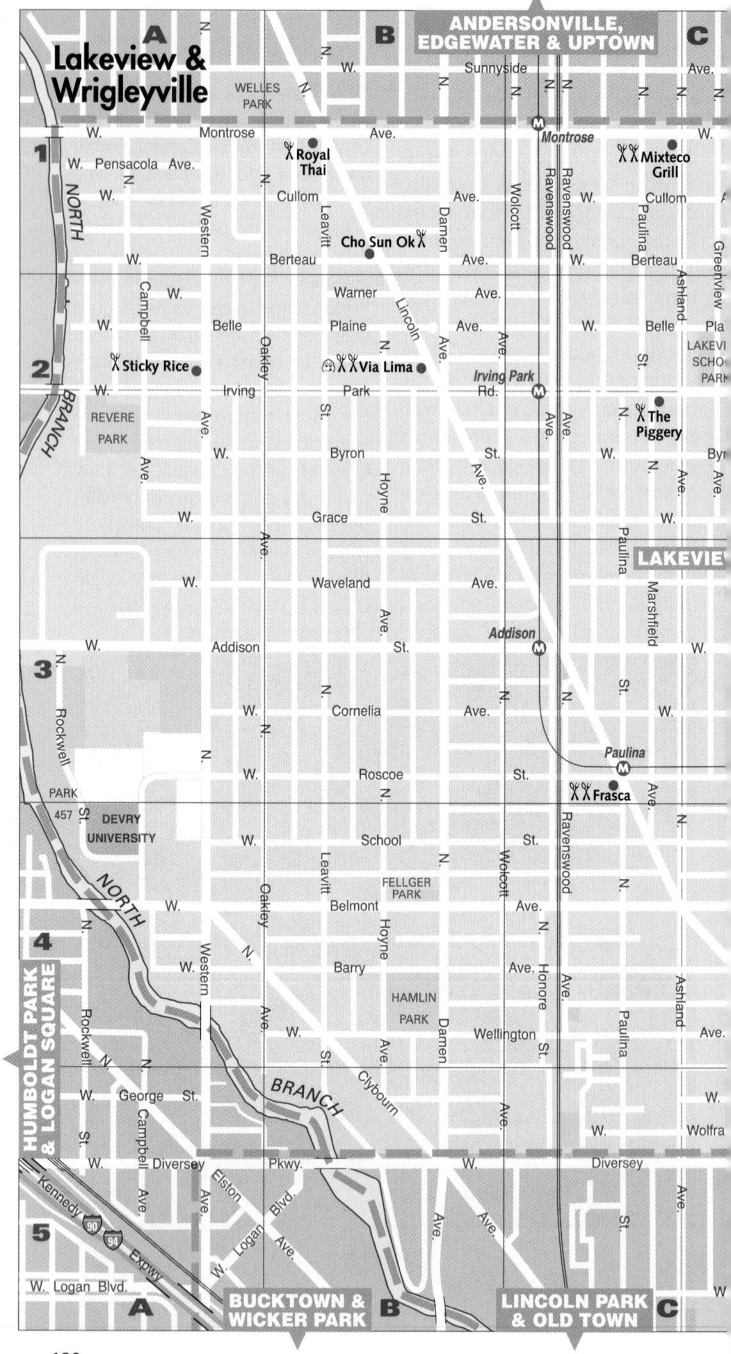
Lakeview & Wrigleyville
ANDERSONVILLE, EDGEWATER & UPTOWN
HUMBOLDT PARK & LOGAN SQUARE
BUCKTOWN & WICKER PARK
LINCOLN PARK & OLD TOWN
LAKEVIEW
Royal Thai
Mixteco Grill
Cho Sun Ok
Sticky Rice
Via Lima
The Piggery
Frasca
Montrose
Irving Park
Addison
Paulina
WELLES PARK
REVERE PARK
DEVRY UNIVERSITY
FELLGER PARK
HAMLIN PARK
NORTH BRANCH
W. Montrose Ave.
W. Pensacola Ave.
W. Cullom Ave.
W. Berteau Ave.
W. Warner Ave.
W. Belle Plaine Ave.
W. Irving Park Rd.
W. Byron St.
W. Grace St.
W. Waveland Ave.
W. Addison St.
W. Cornelia Ave.
W. Roscoe St.
W. School St.
W. Belmont Ave.
W. Barry Ave.
W. Wellington Ave.
W. George St.
W. Diversey Pkwy.
W. Logan Blvd.
N. Lincoln Ave.
N. Clybourn Ave.
N. Elston Ave.
Kennedy Expwy
N. Western Ave.
N. Campbell Ave.
N. Rockwell St.
N. Oakley Ave.
N. Leavitt St.
N. Hoyne Ave.
N. Damen Ave.
N. Wolcott Ave.
N. Ravenswood Ave.
N. Honore St.
N. Paulina St.
N. Marshfield Ave.
N. Ashland Ave.
N. Greenview Ave.
Sunnyside Ave.
PARK 457
90
94
A
B
C
1
2
3
4
5

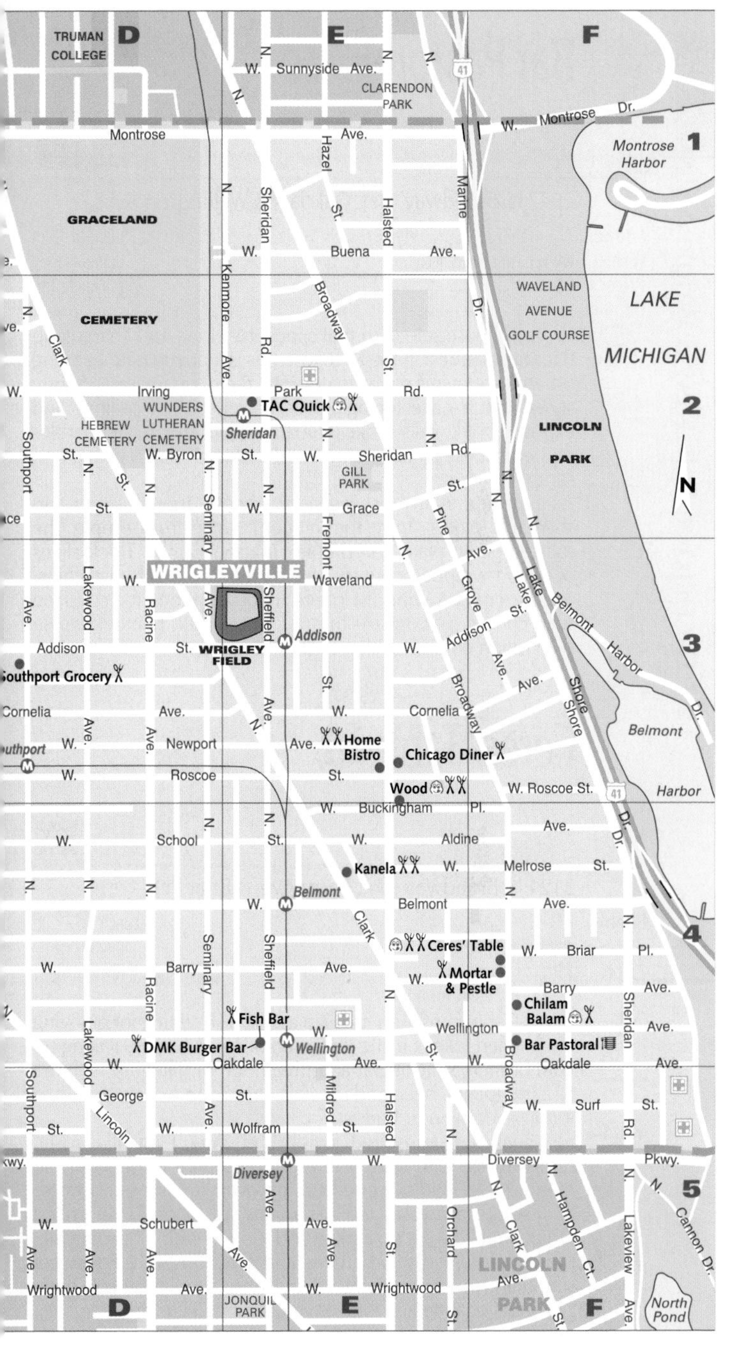
D
E
F
TRUMAN COLLEGE
GRACELAND CEMETERY
HEBREW CEMETERY
WUNDERS LUTHERAN CEMETERY
CLARENDON PARK
GILL PARK
WAVELAND AVENUE GOLF COURSE
LINCOLN PARK
LAKE MICHIGAN
Montrose Harbor
Belmont Harbor
WRIGLEYVILLE
WRIGLEY FIELD
JONQUIL PARK
North Pond
TAC Quick
Southport Grocery
Home Bistro
Chicago Diner
Wood
Kanela
Ceres' Table
Mortar & Pestle
Chilam Balam
Bar Pastoral
Fish Bar
DMK Burger Bar
Sheridan
Addison
Belmont
Wellington
Diversey
Southport
1
2
3
4
5
N

Bar Pastoral

International

F4

2947 N. Broadway (bet. Oakdale & Wellington Aves.)

Phone: 773-472-4781 — Lunch Sat –Sun
Web: www.pastoralartisan.com — Dinner nightly
Price: $$ — Wellington

With a cheese selection that spans the globe and charcuterie flaunting the best in the Midwest, this is a prized haunt among urbanites craving some wine with their savory eats. Subtly styled like a cave for aging, its barrel-vaulted ceilings and exposed brick walls evoke intimacy. A half-moon bar, marble-topped cheese counter, and wood tables let guests gather and sample.

As expected, many dishes feature cheese, though larger and shareable plates "from the kitchen" range from simple (the roasted garlic plate) to complex (rack of lamb). Thick slices of bacon-wrapped country pâté are studded with pistachios. And, a concise wine list offers unique options for coupling with cheese, of course—the raw cow's milk Kentucky Rose with onion chutney is thoroughly delicious.

Ceres' Table

Italian XX

F4

3124 N. Broadway (bet. Barry Ave. & Briar Pl.)

Phone: 773-922-4020 — Lunch Sat – Sun
Web: www.cerestable.com — Dinner nightly
Price: $$ — Belmont (Brown/Red)

Ceres' Table continues its reign as a stylish setting for enjoying the kitchen team's rustic Italian cooking. Whether waking up with brunch, snacking at aperitivo hour, or filling up with the $22 trio (pizza, beer, and dessert), there's an excuse to stop in for any occasion or budget.

Seasonal Italian-inspired cuisine offering elegantly rustic dishes made with solid skill are represented throughout the menu. Here, find a wood-burning oven turning out a range of first-rate pizzas as well as mains like a perfectly grilled whole branzino set on a plate and topped with a heaping pile of lightly dressed salad greens and shaved radish. For sweet simplicity, try the Tuscan *torta della nonna* with buttery baby pine nuts coating a wedge of vanilla-tinged custard pie.

Chicago Diner

Vegetarian

E3

3411 N. Halsted St. (at Roscoe St.)

Phone: 773-935-6696 — Lunch & dinner daily
Web: www.veggiediner.com
Price: ☺ — Addison (Red)

"Meat free since '83" is the slogan at Chicago Diner, where servers have been slinging creative, healthy fare to grateful vegetarians and vegans for decades. The ambience evokes a neighborhood diner with fire engine-red tables, black vinyl chairs, and raised booths. And the food? It looks and tastes the part. Crispy seitan buffalo wings cool down the spice factor with vegan ranch dressing; while *flautas* filled with mashed potato, faux cheese, and jalapeños are served with flavorful fixings so that the meat is never missed. With a popular brunch menu, gluten-free choices and a stronghold on the vegan scene, you can expect a line. So, get here early or hope for good Karma—and a seat.

A second location in Logan Square continues to garner an impressive following.

Chilam Balam

Mexican 

F4

3023 N. Broadway (bet. Barry & Wellington Aves.)

Phone: 773-296-6901 — Dinner Tue – Sat
Web: www.chilambalamchicago.com
Price: $$ — Wellington

$ BYO

Chilam Balam's cozy subterranean space feels like an undiscovered hideaway, but the secret of this lively Mexican hot spot is out. Though waits can be long, the accommodating staff goes the extra mile to mix up margaritas with BYO tequila or walk guests through the rotating roster of shared plates.

Familiar favorites and seasonal specials make for a festive mix of adventurous, yet universally pleasing dishes. Flat corn tortillas form a sandwich-style enchilada, stuffed with fork-tender beef brisket and topped with crunchy strands of sweet potato slaw. Salty chorizo and green papaya *tlacoyos* show that opposites attract, and peanut butter empanadas—primed for dipping in Oaxacan chocolate sauce and dulce de leche—take a childhood favorite to new heights.

Cho Sun Ok

Korean

B1

4200 N. Lincoln Ave. (at Berteau Ave.)

Phone: 773-549-5555 — Lunch & dinner daily
Web: www.chosunokrestaurant.com
Price: ⊕⊕ — Irving Park (Brown)

BYO

As tempted as you might be to judge this book by its brisk, unsmiling cover, don't. Instead, enter the cozy, wood-paneled den and raise that first delicious forkful to your mouth.

Take a cue from the regulars and start with *galbi*, a crave-worthy signature that glistens from a sweet and garlicky soy marinade and warrants good old-fashioned finger-licking. *Haemul pajeon* stuffed with squid and scallions is a crisp, golden-fried delight; and *kimchi jjigae* is a rich, bubbling, and nourishing broth packed with soft tofu and tender pork. Summer calls for a taste of the *bibim naengmyeon*—a chilled broth floating with buckwheat noodles, fresh veggies, Asian pear, and crimson-red *gochujang* all tossed together for a delicious reprieve from the city's sweltering heat.

DMK Burger Bar

American 

E4

2954 N. Sheffield Ave. (at Wellington Ave.)

Phone: 773-360-8686 — Lunch & dinner daily
Web: www.dmkburgerbar.com
Price: ⊕⊕ — Wellington

Outside, towering neon "DMK" letters shine like a beacon for burger fanatics; inside, craft beers gush from taps and attentive, accommodating servers sling mile-high piles of fries. With blaring music and church pew-lined banquettes, it's a cool and modern hang for families and friends of all ages.

Sate salt cravings with a batch of batter-fried okra pods and tangy pickle spears dipped in creamy herbed ranch. Then order by number to get the creative grass-fed burger of your choice. The #3 takes on a Reuben with pastrami, sauerkraut, and Gruyère; while #9 is the platonic ideal of a patty melt, with smoked Swiss cheese, caramelized onions, and chewy bacon between caraway-studded slices of rye bread. Save room for #15—the always-interesting daily special.

Fish Bar

Seafood

2956 N. Sheffield Ave. (at Wellington Ave.)

Phone: 773-687-8177 — Lunch & dinner daily
Web: www.fishbarchicago.com
Price: $$ — Wellington

Chicago may not be known for local seafood, but Fish Bar makes sure to handpick the best from both the Atlantic and Pacific coasts to fill its chilled coffers. A blackboard above the semi-open kitchen lists the fresh daily fish and oyster offerings, ready to be shucked, steamed, fried, and grilled for guests lining up at the wood bar that snakes around the room.

The casual menu pays homage to classic coastal fish shacks, yet throws in a few gussied-up items like tartare and octopus *à la plancha*. Bowls of gumbo stick to the classic recipe with zippy andouille sausage, okra, and chunks of blue crab. The Satchmo po'boy is a mouthful, combining fried rock shrimp and crawfish tails along with slaw and sweet pickles in a traditional, buttery split-top roll.

Frasca

Italian

3358 N. Paulina St. (at Roscoe St.)

Phone: 773-248-5222 — Lunch Sat – Sun
Web: www.frascapizzeria.com — Dinner nightly
Price: $$ — Paulina

The warmth of the wood-burning brick oven and the list of well-priced wines is enough to entice Lakeview's young professionals into the friendly confines of Frasca. Amidst a décor inspired by the restaurant's name ("branch" in Italian), lively groups and intimate dates sample wine flights and split appetizers like charred Brussels sprouts and cauliflower florets tossed with bacon and briny capers.

Chewy pizza crusts blistered from the heat of the oven are laden with market-fresh toppings. The *salsiccia* adds shaved pickled fennel and delicate, wispy fronds to handfuls of crumbled fennel seed sausage and pools of melted Havarti. Grab extra forks for the moist tiramisu with a generous inch-thick layer of cocoa-dusted mascarpone mousse.

Home Bistro

American XX

E3

3404 N. Halsted St. (at Roscoe St.)

Phone: 773-661-0299 — Lunch Sun
Web: www.homebistrochicago.com — Dinner Tue – Sun
Price: $$ — Belmont (Brown/Red)

BYO

Home dishes up loads of charm with a healthy dash of humor in the heart of Boystown. Flickering tea lights on the closely packed bistro-style tables faintly illuminate cozy orange walls painted with food-related quotes. Chef Victor Morenz's eclectic menu picks up influences from around the globe, but each dish is consistently gratifying.

Southern meets south of the border in crisp fried oyster tacos with pickled pepper remoulade. Candied kumquats and olive tapenade contrast pleasantly with buttery seared duck breast, and a dense cube of warm, fudgy chocolate cake placed over a swipe of coconut peanut butter is a decadent finale. Plan for an early evening if you're looking forward to a quiet meal; at peak hours, those orange walls really reverberate.

Kanela

American XX

E4

3231 N. Clark St. (bet. Belmont Ave. & School St.)

Phone: 773-248-1622 — Lunch daily
Web: www.kanelabreakfastclub.com
Price: ⊜ — Belmont (Brown/Red)

If there's one thing Chicago does really well, it's brunch. And, this breakfast club is just the place to have it—with a Bloody Mary or four. A comfortable setting makes Kanela feel more like a home away from home for many residents. The cozy dining room packs in hungry diners on weekends, but the flung-open windows and efficient kitchen keep everyone happy. Since the name is Greek for "cinnamon," their eponymous signature pastry is appropriately loaded with spiced sugar, vanilla frosting, and blueberries. A flight of French toast sweetens the deal for indecisive types, but savory palates have a host of options too—the Lorraine scramble with Gruyère and peppered bacon?

Cocktails, fresh-squeezed juices, smoothies and Julius Meinl coffee cover all the beverage bases.

Mixteco Grill

Mexican 

C1

1601 W. Montrose Ave. (at Ashland Ave.)

Phone: 773-868-1601 — Lunch Sat – Sun
Web: www.mixtecogrill.com — Dinner nightly
Price: $$ — Montrose (Brown)

BYO

Floor-to-ceiling windows that wrap around the corner of Montrose and Ashland are flanked by cheerful orange curtains that imitate Mixteco's fiery and flavorful Mexican fare. A large open kitchen splits the casual dining space, giving the front room's patrons a firsthand look at the mesquite-fired grill and from-scratch preparations.

Non-traditional menu items might miss the mark here and there, but familiar dishes don't disappoint—and neither do the reasonable prices that pull in crowds of regulars. Shredded chicken enchiladas (wrapped with house-made tortillas) balance earthy, complex *mole negro* with a burst of brightness from radish matchsticks, cilantro, and raw onion. Thick and creamy refried black beans ensure that no one leaves hungry.

Mortar & Pestle

International 

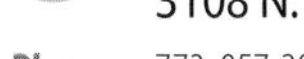

F4

3108 N. Broadway (at Barry Ave.)

Phone: 773-857-2087 — Lunch Wed – Mon
Web: www.mortarandpestlechicago.com
Price: — Wellington

BYO

This charming neighborhood brunch spot arrives courtesy of Chefs Stephen Ross and Stephen Paul, who worked together at Table 52. The farmhouse-designed space is rustic, welcoming, and full of personal touches, like reclaimed wood tables and vintage stained glass windows. And the service is genuinely friendly—coffee is poured the minute you sit down, and the chefs often appear to greet guests in person.

The kitchen's slogan is "globally inspired cuisine, rooted in tradition" and their globe-trotting ingredients—merguez sausage, cheese curds, romesco sauce—wind their way into a delicious array of brunchy items. Standards like eggs Benedict and French toast get sweet elevation from unexpected, upscale elements like King crab or even foie gras torchon.

The Piggery

American 

C2

1625 W. Irving Park Rd. (at Marshfield Ave.)

Phone: 773-281-7447 — Lunch & dinner daily
Web: www.thepiggerychicago.com
Price: $$ — Irving Park (Brown)

The bacon is back—as well as the ham, the shoulder, and the rest of the pig too. This Lakeview sports bar and shrine to all things porcine pays homage to its whimsical ways by way of kitschy pig paraphernalia that shares shelf and wall space with flat-screens tuned to Cubs and Sox games, naturally.

The menu may be hell for vegans, but it's a pork lover's paradise: cuts from every part of the animal find their way into nearly each dish, from hearty ham-stuffed burgers to the signature bacon-wrapped jalapeño poppers. Gently charred slabs of ribs basted with the Piggery's own heady barbecue sauce are teeth-sinkingly tender. Even salads may give you the meat sweats, with pulled pork or buffalo chicken—and bacon, of course—offered as toppings.

Royal Thai

Thai

B1

2209 W. Montrose Ave. (bet. Bell Ave. & Leavitt St.)

Phone: 773-509-0007 — Lunch & dinner Wed – Mon
Web: www.royalthaichicago.com
Price: — Western (Brown)

BYO

This wonderful family-owned and operated restaurant, situated opposite Lincoln Square, has been at it for over two decades. Royal Thai's secret to longevity? Tasty, downright solid cooking at unbeatable prices. The dining space itself is simple enough—clean, no frills, with bare wood tables, pale beige walls, and a few colorful lanterns hanging in the windows.

The regulars here love the Panang curry and crispy pad Thai (among others), but nearly everything on this sublime menu is pristine, perfectly balanced in flavor and straight-up delicious—and heat preference is asked upon each order. Try the *phla pla krob*, thin fillets of deep-fried white fish tossed in a lime sauce with lots of herby cilantro, lemongrass, mint and red pepper.

Southport Grocery

American

3552 N. Southport Ave. (bet. Addison St. & Cornelia Ave.)

Phone: 773-665-0100 Lunch daily
Web: www.southportgrocery.com
Price: ⊜ Southport

Equal parts specialty grocery and upscale diner, this Southport Corridor hot spot draws quite a crowd. Local products and in-house goodies are stocked in the front of the narrow space, while the rear offers comfortable banquettes for a casual sit-down meal.

Breakfast is served as long as the sun shines, with options like a freshly baked and buttered English muffin stuffed with ginger-sage sausage, a vibrant orange sunny side-up egg, and sweet pepper jelly. A side of red bliss potatoes sweetens the deal, but if you're really looking for something sugary, the grilled coffee cake is a double-layered cinnamon and cream cheese delight. Craving more of your meal? You're in luck: certain menu items, denoted with an asterisk, are available for purchase up front.

Sticky Rice

Thai

4018 N. Western Ave. (at Cuyler Ave.)

Phone: 773-588-0133 Lunch & dinner daily
Web: www.stickyricethai.com
Price: ⊜ Irving Park (Blue)

BYO

There's no dearth of Thai joints in this neighborhood, but Sticky Rice stands out—not only for its focus on Northern Thai specialties, but also for the quality and abundance of dishes made to order. Sunny and citrus-hued, it's the kind of place where those who dare to step outside their satay-and-pad Thai comfort zone will be greatly rewarded.

Luckily, the extensive menu makes it easy to do just that. Tender egg noodles absorb the fragrant coconut curry in a bowl of *kow soy* that's redolent of citrusy coriander and served with pickled greens and cilantro. Duck *larb* is zippy and full of spice, with an unforgettable tart-and-sweet dressing. Hint: use the spot's namesake sticky rice to temper the heat while soaking up every last drop.

TAC Quick

Thai

E2

1011 W. Irving Park Road (bet. Seminary & Sheffield Aves.)

Phone: 773-327-5253 — Lunch & dinner daily
Web: www.tacquick.com
Price: — Sheridan

The focus at this Wrigleyville institution is on speedy, authentic Thai food—and that's exactly what you'll get. The restaurant may have recently moved around the corner from its original location, but long-time loyalists can count on a similar setting that is still within earshot of the rumbling El.
Two laminated menus—one with standard fare, and another "secret" listing with more traditional dishes—ensure there's something for everyone. It's hard to resist double-dipping a stack of glistening, charred *moo ping* pork skewers in sour, spicy, and sweet sauce, or finishing every flaky morsel of *pad ped pla duk* (fried catfish with creamy green curry). Spice crazed? You're in luck—TAC Quick's heat level is perhaps the most authentic around.

Via Lima

Peruvian 

B2

4024 N. Lincoln Ave. (bet. Cuyler Ave. & W. Irving Park Rd.)

Phone: 773-348-4900 — Lunch Sun
Web: www.vialimachicago.com — Dinner Tue – Sun
Price: $$ — Irving Park (Brown)

Via Lima infuses a chic, contemporary personality into the typical rustic atmosphere of a Peruvian restaurant. Here, Lakeview residents pack themselves into comfortable booths upholstered in colorful fabrics, sharing dishes from a refined menu of familiar classics or tucking into larger entrées at bare wood tables.
A bracingly sour *leche de tigre* broth infused with fiery South American *rocoto* chili adds zing to market-fresh fish ceviche, while starchy corn kernels and a scoop of creamy sweet potatoes tame the heat. *Choclo* soufflé blends a fluffy, mildly sweet corn cake with meltingly tender duck confit to balance sweet and savory; while Lucuma mousse subtly showcases the vibrant marigold-hued Peruvian fruit, topped with a spoonful of fresh vanilla whipped cream.

Wood 

Contemporary 

E3

3335 N. Halstead St. (at Buckingham Pl.)

Phone: 773-935-9663 — Lunch Sun
Web: www.woodchicago.com — Dinner nightly
Price: $$ — Belmont (Brown/Red)

You might think everyone comes to Wood for the great music and cheeky cocktail list (Strictly Platonic, anyone?), or even the audaciously dubbed "Morning Wood" brunch on weekends. But really, it's Chef Ashlee Aubin's menu that keeps this sleek dining space packed every night. Generous portions and that irresistibly lively atmosphere (a little bit sophisticated, a little bit disco) only seal the deal.

Aubin has crafted a rotating, seasonal menu that's concise but packs a hefty punch. Imagine wood-oven flatbreads, topped with fennel sausage and wilted greens, melt-in-your-mouth steak tartare, or tangles of *spaghetti con vongole*. Dinner on the other hand might involve a juicy bone-in pork chop, hearty cheeseburger, tender roasted chicken, or seared scallops.

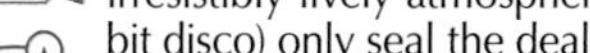

Your opinions are important to us. Please write to us directly at: michelin.guides@us.michelin.com

Lincoln Park & Old Town

The congregation of history, commerce, and nature is what makes Lincoln Park and Old Town one of Chicago's most iconic districts. Scenically situated on Lake Michigan's shore, the eponymous park offers winter-weary locals an excuse to get out. And if that isn't enticing enough, the park also keeps its patrons happy with a spectacular array of cafés, restaurants ranging from quick bites to the city's most exclusive reservations, and takeout spots offering picnic-perfect products. Populated by college grads, young families, and wealthy upstarts, as well as home to more than a handful of historic districts, museums, shopping, music venues, and the famous (not to mention, free) zoo, Lincoln Park flourishes as a much sought-after destination year-round.

DELICIOUS DINING

Wallet-happy locals and well-heeled gourmands make reservations to come here and dine at some of the most exclusive restaurants in town. But beyond just glorious white-glove restaurants, there's more delicious eating to be done in this area. During the weekend, these streets are jumping thanks to a combination of plays, musicals, bars, and scores of high-rises housing affluent and brash yuppies. On Wednesdays and Saturdays during the **Green City Market**, the south end of the park is transformed into hipster chef-foodie central. With the aim to increase availability of top produce and to improve the link between farmers and local producers with restaurants and food organizations, this market works to educate the

Windy City's masses about high-quality food sourcing. (In winter it is held across the street inside the Peggy Notebaert Nature Museum).

Lincoln Park's outpost of **Floriole Café & Bakery** brought about much jubilation, and along with it, a regular fan following. In fact, the aromas wafting from freshly baked breads, pastries, and cookies never fail to tempt onlookers. For the recreational chef, **Read it & Eat** is a kitchen workshop that doubles as a fully stocked bookstore housing a fantastic selection of cookbooks. Check out their calendar of food-centric events—from informative hands-on classes to drool-worthy book launches. Like many foods (Juicy Fruit, Cracker Jack, and Shredded Wheat, for example), it is said that the Chicago-style dog may have originated at the Chicago World's Fair and Columbian Exhibition in 1893. Others credit the Great Depression for its birth. Regardless of its origin, one thing is for certain— chef-driven **Franks 'n' Dawgs** is this city's most desirable hot dog destination. By cooking with only fresh, locally sourced ingredients, these hand-crafted creations are sure to hit the spot. Similarly, **The Wieners Circle** is as known and loved for its delicious dogs and fries, late hours (as late as 5:00 A.M.), and intentionally rude service. Red meat fiends may choose to carry on the party at **Butcher & the Burger** as they do their part to stay at the helm of the burger game, or linger at **Gepperth's Meat Market**, which was established in 1906 when the neighborhood was comprised of mostly Hungarian and German settlers. Old-world butchery is the dictum here with knowledge that has been passed down for generations. If prime cuts and all the trimmings come to mind, you know you've arrived at the right place. Meanwhile the ocean's bounty can be relished in all its glory at **Half Shell**. Here, the cash-only policy has done nothing to deter crowds from consuming platters of crab legs and briny oysters. Wash down these salty delights with a cool sip from a choice selection at **Goose Island Brewery**—makers of the city's favorite local beers. Keep up this alcohol-fueled fun at **Barrelhouse Flat**, which is always hip and happening thanks to a litany of hand-crafted punches. Then wind up in time—for brunch perhaps?—at **The Drinkingbird**. From a sweet and stirring sake punch to spicy house-made sausages, their carte du jour is nothing less than satisfying.

Lincoln Park is also one of the most dog-friendly areas around, but then what else would you expect from a neighborhood named after a huge expanse of grass? Big bellies and bold palates with Fido in tow are forever filling up on artisanal goods at **Blue Door Farm Stand**. This particularly edgy grocery-cum-café also doubles as a watering hole and breakfast hot spot for lunching ladies who can be found picking at kale salads or indulging in grilled cheese sammies. If that doesn't bring a smile, the deep-fried oreos at **Racine Plumbing** or decadent popcorn from **Berco's** boutique will certainly do the trick. To keep that sugar rush going, **Cocoa + Co.** is a chocoholic's dream. This candy shop and café stocks a heavenly collection of chocolate treats and pastries from around the world, as well as comforting cups of hot cocoa and coffee. Feeling those sugar blues? Burn off the calories with a good laugh at The Second City, the country's foremost comedy club.

The Old Town quarter has a few quaint cobblestoned streets that are home to the Second City comedy scene (now with a Zanies, too, for even more laughs). Also nestled here is June's annual must-see (and must-shop) Old Town Art Fair; the Wells Street Art Fair; as well as places to rest with beers and a groovy jukebox—maybe the **Old Town Ale House**? However, Wells Street is the neighborhood's main drag, and is really where browsing should begin.Any epicurean shopping trip should also include **The Spice House** for its exotic spice blends, many named after local landmarks; or **Old Town Oil** for hostess gifts like infused oils and aged vinegars. Prefer a sweeter vice? **The Fudge Pot** tempts with windows of toffee, fudge, and other chocolate-y decadence. Lastly, you may not be a smoker, but the Up Down Cigar is worth a peek for its real cigar store Indian carving.

STEPPENWOLF

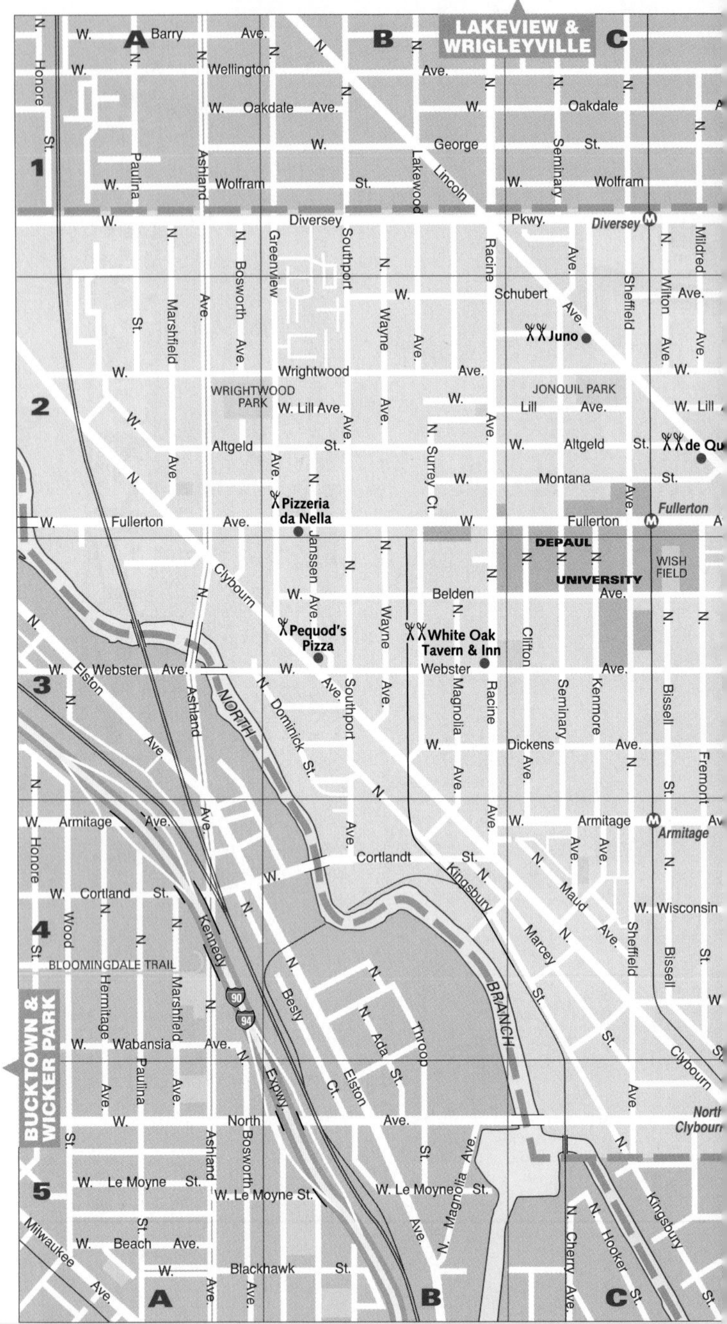
LAKEVIEW & WRIGLEYVILLE
BUCKTOWN & WICKER PARK
A
B
C
1
2
3
4
5
W. Barry Ave.
W. Wellington Ave.
W. Oakdale Ave.
Oakdale
W. George St.
W. Wolfram St.
Wolfram
W. Diversey Pkwy.
Diversey
W. Schubert Ave.
W. Wrightwood Ave.
WRIGHTWOOD PARK
W. Lill Ave.
Lill Ave.
JONQUIL PARK
W. Altgeld St.
W. Montana St.
W. Fullerton Ave.
Fullerton
DEPAUL UNIVERSITY
WISH FIELD
W. Belden Ave.
W. Webster Ave.
W. Dickens Ave.
W. Armitage Ave.
Armitage
W. Cortlandt St.
W. Cortland St.
W. Wisconsin
W. Wabansia Ave.
W. North Ave.
W. Le Moyne St.
W. Beach Ave.
W. Blackhawk St.
N. Honore St.
N. Paulina
N. Ashland Ave.
N. Lakewood
N. Lincoln
N. Seminary
N. Racine Ave.
N. Marshfield Ave.
N. Bosworth Ave.
N. Greenview Ave.
N. Southport Ave.
N. Wayne Ave.
N. Sheffield Ave.
N. Wilton Ave.
N. Mildred Ave.
N. Surrey Ct.
N. Janssen Ave.
N. Clybourn Ave.
N. Elston Ave.
N. Dominick St.
N. Magnolia Ave.
N. Clifton Ave.
N. Kenmore Ave.
N. Bissell St.
N. Fremont St.
N. Kingsbury St.
N. Maud Ave.
N. Marcey St.
N. Wood St.
N. Hermitage Ave.
BLOOMINGDALE TRAIL
N. Kennedy Expwy.
90
94
N. Besly Ct.
N. Ada St.
N. Throop St.
N. Elston Ave.
N. Cherry Ave.
N. Hooker St.
N. Milwaukee Ave.
NORTH BRANCH
North Clybourn
Juno
de Qu
Pizzeria da Nella
Pequod's Pizza
White Oak Tavern & Inn

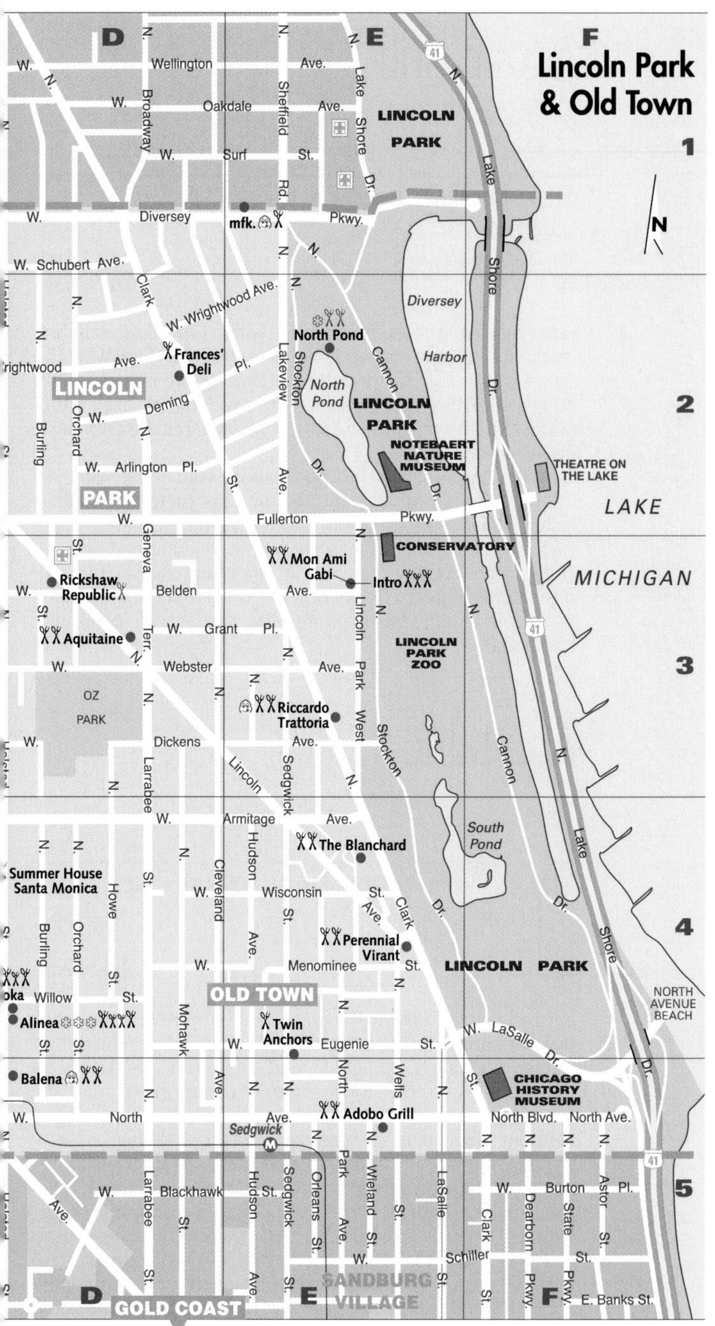

Lincoln Park & Old Town
LINCOLN PARK
North Pond
Frances' Deli
mfk.
Mon Ami Gabi
Intro
Rickshaw Republic
Aquitaine
Riccardo Trattoria
The Blanchard
Summer House Santa Monica
Perennial Virant
Alinea
Balena
Twin Anchors
Adobo Grill
NOTEBAERT NATURE MUSEUM
CONSERVATORY
LINCOLN PARK ZOO
THEATRE ON THE LAKE
CHICAGO HISTORY MUSEUM
NORTH AVENUE BEACH
LAKE MICHIGAN
OLD TOWN
GOLD COAST
SANDBURG VILLAGE
OZ PARK
Diversey Harbor
South Pond
Sedgwick

Adobo Grill

Mexican

E5

215 W. North Ave. (bet. Wells & Wieland Sts.)

Phone: 312-266-7999 — Lunch Sun
Web: www.adobogrill.com — Dinner nightly
Price: $$

Sedgwick

A fire may have caused their move within Old Town, but their margaritas are still shaken tableside and better than ever. The space is tastefully decorated with dark wood, rich red walls hung with Mexican paintings, and a welcoming back patio. Many remember Adobo for its tasty drinks, but the cooking is just as adept.

Guacamole is mashed to-order before your eyes, with just the right amount of jalapeños to suit your preference. Other dishes show a bit of fusion, like the *ceviche de atun* made with sashimi-grade tuna tossed with cucumbers, serrano chilies, and creamy avocado in ginger-soy sauce. Tacos *al pastor* offer tender chunks of roasted pork and caramelized pineapple topping fresh corn tortillas. Desserts are pleasantly traditional.

Aquitaine

American

D3

2221 N. Lincoln Ave. (bet. Belden & Webster Aves.)

Phone: 773-698-8456 — Dinner nightly
Web: www.aquitainerestaurant.com
Price: $$ — Fullerton

When Lincoln Park locals want French-inspired cuisine, they head to Aquitaine for a taste of Chef/owner Holly Willoughby's refined cooking. Dim lighting and subtle brocade details on the walls keep the long, narrow dining room casually romantic, with enough simple sophistication to swing a Saturday night date or weekday post-work dinner. A well-priced wine list only adds to the elegant appeal.

Large chunks of succulent lobster are a luxe touch in a ramekin of tender potato gnocchi bathed in creamy sauce. Eggplant, olive, and tomato relish gives double-cut lamb chops a Provençal spin, heightened by a drizzle of basil pesto. Textbook-perfect crème brûlée needs only a tap of the spoon to send its delicate sugar crust splintering into the silken custard.

Alinea ✿✿✿

Contemporary XXXX

D4

1723 N. Halsted St. (bet. North Ave. & Willow St.)

Phone: 312-867-0110 Dinner Wed – Sun
Web: www.alinearestaurant.com
Price: $$$$ North/Clybourn

Billed as a reinvention but what in reality was more a renovation, the "new" Alinea is no longer a freewheeling circus of culinary showmanship. The entire space is now more subdued, with fewer stunts and minimal pomp. It offers maturity, substance, soul, and a level of infectious confidence unknown in its previous incarnation. This restaurant is more about you (the guest) than them (Chef Grant Achatz and his deeply talented team). Service, too, has never been more attentive and engaged, thanks to a staff who bring both humor and personality to the meal.

The menu style has been completely revamped, so even the most frequent visitor will have some surprises in store. There are three seating options, each with its own menu. The Salon is the most modest with eleven courses, while the Gallery offers a few more dishes with copious bells and whistles. The third and most opulent is the Kitchen Table, where outright bacchanalia ensues for a price tag that will probably leave Nick Kokonas the only one smiling. (Actual prices vary according to the date and time of your pre-paid reservation.)

Highlights are always whimsical, sometimes experimental, and may include scented vapors, smoke, and balloons.

Balena

Italian 

D5

1633 N. Halstead St. (bet. North Ave. & Willow St.)

Phone: 312-867-3888 Dinner nightly
Web: www.balenachicago.com
Price: $$ North/Clybourn

Balena effortlessly blends rusticity and contemporary design in its prime Lincoln Park location. Lofty ceilings and industrial accents are a simple but statement-worthy juxtaposition against wooden floors and tables—and an appealingly inviting backdrop for a menu of inventive but solid takes on Italian cuisine. Knowledgeable, on-point service makes the meal even more divine.

Start with a choice from the large vermouth selection and a round of burrata with pickled mustard seeds and fresh mint, ready to be piled on *lardo*-brushed toast. Or sink your teeth into wood-fired pizza with a parade of toppings like pistachio pesto and crisp mortadella. For dessert, brandy-soaked cherries add boozy warmth to caramel *budino* with salty-sweet praline crumble.

The Blanchard

French XX

E4

1935 N. Lincoln Park West (at Lincoln Ave.)

Phone: 872-829-3971 Dinner Tue – Sun
Web: www.theblanchardchicago.com
Price: $$$

In a minimalist but elegant space that complements its picturesque Lincoln Park environs, The Blanchard serves up sophistication with a side of well-executed French bistro food. Petite portions still satiate thanks to the richness of classic dishes like rillettes, duck à l'orange, and foie gras preparations.

Escargots à la Bourguignonne start the meal on a luxurious note, with six plump morsels sitting on a knob of mushroom duxelles and bathed in garlic butter, parsley, and breadcrumbs. Lightly caramelized capers and a brown butter sauce garnish two thin fillets of Dover sole meunière, alongside a streak of green pea tendril-pommes purée. Lush passion fruit curd and a sprinkle of lavender buds enhance a moist and chewy coconut financier.

Boka ✿

Contemporary XxX

1729 N. Halsted St. (bet. North Ave. & Willow St.)

Phone: 312-337-6070 — Dinner nightly
Web: www.bokachicago.com
Price: $$$ — North/Clybourn

Housed in an affluent part of town, find a small walkway that leads into this elaborate, handsome, and very sultry dining room. There are three different seating areas and each exudes class with a bit of romance, whimsy, and occasional quirk (note the escutcheon-covered doorway and capricious paintings). Against dark pebbled walls, find oversized horseshoe booths, long banquettes, and mirrored light bulbs casting funky shadows. The semi-outdoor solarium has a living wall of moss and ferns. Servers are friendly and genuine without a hint of pretense.

This is the kind of place where one can sink in and not care to leave.

Chef Lee Wolen's menu may be modern, but it is widely appealing with a Mediterranean edge. Begin with translucent slivers of fresh sea bass that get a pleasant bite from almond crumble and perfect flavor from a subtle dab of citrusy *yuzu kosho*. Then, deliciously tender and evenly pink Colorado lamb is served with a harmonious hodgepodge of creamy yogurt, charred lettuce, and nearly sweet baby potatoes. For dessert, an airy and whipped mound of praline-flavored mousse is set beside milk ice cream, which serves as a cooling counterpoint to the nutty flavors throughout and makes for a fine ending.

de Quay

Fusion 

2470 N. Lincoln Ave. (bet. Altgeld & Montana Sts.)

Phone: 872-206-8820 | Lunch Sun
Web: www.dequay-chicago.com | Dinner Tue – Sun
Price: $$ | Fullerton

Given its history as a former colony, the Dutch have developed a great deal of appreciation for Indonesian culinary traditions. And, Chef/owner David de Quay pulls from his family heritage to bring the two together at his eponymous restaurant. Delft pottery houses and sleek teak wall accents are visual mementos of this union.

On the menu, sweet-and-sour *babi panggang* departs from its traditional pairing with roast pork to heighten succulent grilled shrimp and fragrant lemongrass *lumpia*. Crisp-edged dumplings enclose a creamy potato-and-Gouda filling that is studded with bacon and English peas. Chewy house-made *stroopwafels* sandwich warm spiced caramel with vanilla bean-flecked ice cream for an unforgettable *finis*.

Frances' Deli

D2

2552 N. Clark St. (bet. Deming Pl. & Wrightwood Ave.)

Phone: 773-248-4580 | Lunch daily
Web: www.francesdeli.com
Price: ⊜

Frances' Deli is the type of quaint, lived-in diner everyone dreams of having just around the corner from home. Lucky Lincoln Park residents get that wish fulfilled at this authentic pre-war haunt packed with American antiques and memorabilia—where weekend waits are the norm as half the neighborhood vies for a place at one of the closely spaced tables.

As with any good diner, breakfast all day certainly hits the spot. The deli roasts its own meats and does Jewish-American staples right, from flavorful, crisp-tender potato pancakes to oversized pastrami and brisket sandwiches with all the fixings (slaw, fries, and potato salad). As long as you're going for the full nostalgia trip, slurp down a made-to-order milkshake or malt.

Intro

Contemporary

E3

2300 N. Lincoln Park West (at Belden Ave.)

Phone: 773-868-0002 Dinner Wed – Sun
Web: www.introchicago.com
Price: $$$

This jewel-box of a dining room tucked away in the Belden-Stratford has evolved from a sort of restaurant incubator hosting a series of chefs and their limited-run concepts, into a sure-footed operation consistently headed by Chef Stephen Gillanders. Blonde wood, a chic mix of furniture styles, and espresso-stained tables are an appropriate backdrop for the sophisticated clientele Intro receives.

This talented kitchen sends out prettily plated fare like white shrimp transformed into ceviche with habanero-spiked lemon juice and toasted pepitas, or Faroe Island salmon brushed with miso and encrusted with wild mushrooms. Specials, perhaps inspired by a trip to Korea, prove that this kitchen remains creatively untethered.

Juno

C2

2638 N. Lincoln Ave. (bet. Seminary & Sheffield Aves.)

Phone: 773-935-2000 Dinner Tue – Sun
Web: www.junosushichicago.com
Price: $$$ Diversey

Raw fish with a side of creativity differentiates Juno from the rest of this city's sushi brethren. Inside, a rather plain and dimly lit bar up front gives way to the more contemporary, bright and airy dining room, which is a huge hit among locals looking to get all dressed for a night out. The menu offers cool bites like the Juno queen, a special nigiri of salmon topped with scallop and potato crunch; and hot treats like honey-glazed quail.

Chef B.K. Park's omakase must be ordered 24 hours in advance. Try cleverly spun morsels like gently torched prawn with pineapple salsa, pickled garlic oil-drizzled New Zealand King salmon, soy-marinated sea eel dabbed with ground sesame seeds, and spicy octopus *temaki*—it's a feast well worth the extra effort.

mfk.

E1

432 W. Diversey Pkwy. (bet. Pine Grove Ave. & Sheridan Rd.)

Phone: 773-857-2540 — Lunch Wed – Sun
Web: www.mfkrestaurant.com — Dinner nightly
Price: $$ — Diversey

"First we eat, then we do everything else," said M.F.K. Fisher, the food writer who serves as both the inspiration and namesake for this young neighborhood darling. Thanks to large windows, whitewashed brick walls, and gleaming silver-and-white tilework, the subterranean space manages to evoke a breezy seaside oasis. And with a seafood-centric menu featuring modern interpretations of Iberian-inspired plates, the food follows suit.

The ocean's bounty is showcased in simple but flavorful dishes like crispy fried prawn heads served with a nutty *salbitxada* sauce for dipping; and bowls of cataplana stew with fresh clams, crunchy shrimp, and grilled cobia collar. A crumbly slice of Basque cake and an expertly pulled *cortado* ends the meal on a high note.

Mon Ami Gabi

French 

E3

2300 N. Lincoln Park West (at Belden Ave.)

Phone: 773-348-8886 — Lunch Sun
Web: www.monamigabi.com — Dinner nightly
Price: $$

A real French bistro can give an American steakhouse a run for its money in the meat department any day, and the 11 different steak preparations on Mon Ami Gabi's menu (all served with crispy golden frites) are justly impressive. Beyond the butcher case, a selection of satisfying Francophile classics keeps the sophisticated Chicago contingent returning to this cozy, stylish standby.

Tradition reigns in the kitchen, where the emphasis is on flavorful and unpretentious dishes like seafood *pot-au-feu* bobbing with scallops and pepper-crusted cod fillet in a tasty fennel broth. Pickled cornichons and warm toast points make a meal out of house-made country pâté. And for an indulgent finish, split a plate of warm caramel-drizzled pineapple crêpes.

North Pond ✿

Contemporary XX

E2

2610 N. Cannon Dr.

Phone: 773-477-5845 — Lunch Sun
Web: www.northpondrestaurant.com — Dinner Wed – Sun
Price: $$$

This charming Arts and Crafts building may have started as a warming shelter for park ice skaters back in 1912, but today it is a celebratory and cozy setting that makes you want to light a fire and pop open some champagne. Exposed brick, that roaring fireplace, and large windows overlooking the park and lake make the rooms feel warm and pleasant.

A commitment to agriculture is clear in everything: seed packets arrive with the check and each bottle of wine has a one-dollar surcharge that is donated to charities like the Lincoln Park Conservancy or Chicago Rarities Orchard Project.

Chef Bruce Sherman has a particular style that almost seems to fly in the face of those minimalist competitors who use menus to list single ingredients. Here, dishes are described comprehensively as a flurry of ingredients that may not seem to fit together, but they always do with great success. Try neatly trimmed Arctic char that is slow-roasted for silken texture, then served with embellishments like house-made sauerkraut, mustard seeds, candied walnuts, and Dauphine potatoes. A duo of strip steak and spoon-tender Porter-braised short rib arrives with pan-crisped black pepper spaetzle, Brussels sprouts, and beet-apple purée.

Pequod's Pizza

Pizza X

B3

2207 N. Clybourn Ave. (at Webster Ave.)

Phone: 773-327-1512 — Lunch & dinner daily
Web: www.pequodspizza.com
Price: — Armitage

Ditch your diet, grab your fellow Blackhawks fans, and head to this Lincoln Park stalwart for some of the best pies in town. Christened for Captain Ahab's sailing ship, Pequod's menu promises smooth sailing for sports bar noshers, featuring a lineup of shareable bar snacks such as wings and mozzarella sticks, hearty sandwiches like tender Italian beef, and both thin-crust and deep-dish pan pizzas.

Grab that cutlery before digging into the buttery crust of each deep-dish pie, ringed with blackened cheese at the edges. Toppings like pepperoni, fresh garlic, and crunchy sautéed onions are generously layered between tart tomato sauce and handfuls of cheese for an oozy jumble in every bite. A towering wedge of fudge cake awaits those with room for dessert.

Perennial Virant

American XX

E4

1800 N. Lincoln Ave. (at Clark St.)

Phone: 312-981-7070 — Lunch Sat – Sun
Web: www.perennialchicago.com — Dinner nightly
Price: $$

Housed along tony Lincoln Avenue and packed with patrons to match, this Paul Virant operation is a "perennial" hit. Take the time to truly appreciate the philosophy followed at his haute farm-to-table spot, where local, sustainable cuisine combines with a minimalist décor featuring lush earth tones and chandeliers crafted from repurposed jars.

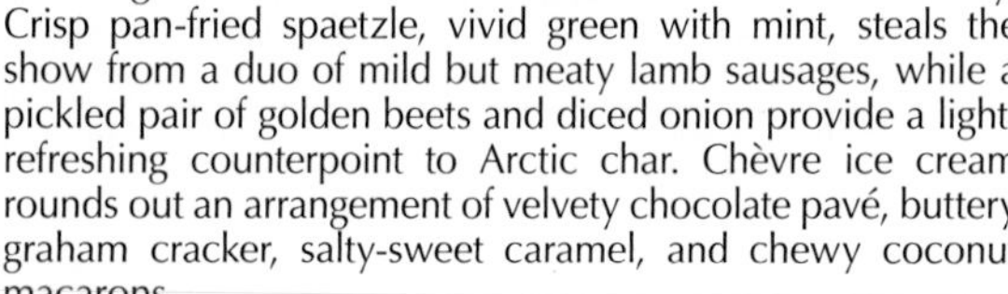

Each ingredient-driven dish honors farmers and seasonality. Crisp pan-fried spaetzle, vivid green with mint, steals the show from a duo of mild but meaty lamb sausages, while a pickled pair of golden beets and diced onion provide a light, refreshing counterpoint to Arctic char. Chèvre ice cream rounds out an arrangement of velvety chocolate pavé, buttery graham cracker, salty-sweet caramel, and chewy coconut macarons.

Pizzeria da Nella

1443 W. Fullerton Ave. (bet. Greenview & Janssen Aves.)

Phone: 773-281-6600 — Lunch & dinner daily
Web: www.pizzeriadanella.com
Price: $$ — Fullerton

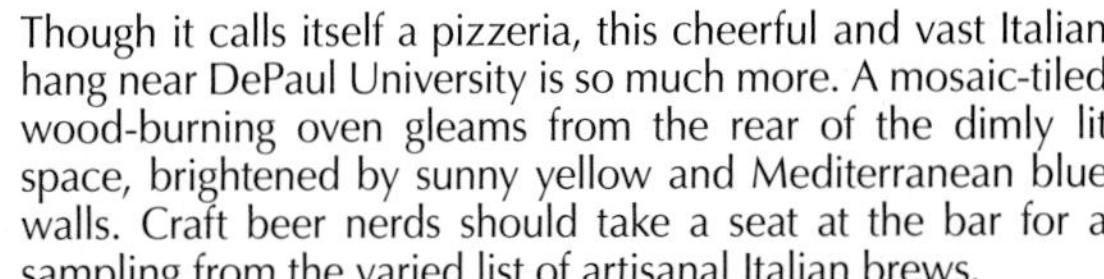

Though it calls itself a pizzeria, this cheerful and vast Italian hang near DePaul University is so much more. A mosaic-tiled wood-burning oven gleams from the rear of the dimly lit space, brightened by sunny yellow and Mediterranean blue walls. Craft beer nerds should take a seat at the bar for a sampling from the varied list of artisanal Italian brews.

Authentic Neapolitan pizzas share menu space with modern stuffed "bomba" pies like the Ciotta Ciotta, which mounds a deli case's worth of *salumi* and cheeses between two pizza dough rounds. Pasta selections are equally sprawling, and include fresh combinations like pappardelle with plump mussels, black truffles, and pecorino. Limoncello-soaked strawberries over homemade sponge cake keep the finale light.

Riccardo Trattoria

E3

2119 N. Clark St. (bet. Dickens & Webster Aves.)

Phone: 773-549-0038 — Dinner nightly
Web: www.riccardotrattoria.com
Price: $$

The timeless wood-and-cream décor doesn't resemble an Italian *nonna's* kitchen, but no matter—the soulful personality of Chef/owner Riccardo Michi and his cache of family recipes make his eponymous restaurant a second home to nearly half the neighborhood. It's a spot that's suited for flirty date nights, boisterous dinners, and every occasion in between.

As befits the word "trattoria," rustic Italian preparations take precedence, but the simplicity satisfies. Chunks of pork sausage add heft to a heaping bowl of hand-rolled cavatelli bathed in a light tomato cream sauce, and curls of grilled calamari need only a squirt of lemon, splash of olive oil, and sprinkle of parsley to sing. For dessert, a thin, buttery tart shell cradles tender wine-poached pears.

Rickshaw Republic

D3

2312 N. Lincoln Ave. (bet. Belden Ave. & Childrens Plz.)

Phone: 773-697-4750 — Lunch Fri – Sun
Web: www.rickshawrepublic.com — Dinner Tue – Sun
Price: ⚭ — Fullerton

BYO

The captivating flavors of Southeast Asian street food are matched by the creative design at this friendly, family-run Lincoln Avenue space. Color and pattern collide as parasols, puppets, and bird cages vie for attention with abstract Indonesian wood carvings. Once the food arrives, though, the spotlight shifts to the aromatic plates.

Start with crisp *martabak* crêpes that hold a savory combination of beef, onions, and egg. Then move on to lemongrass-braised chicken thighs in a turmeric-tinged coconut curry with sweet and spicy tamarind *sambal* and pickled cabbage. Surprise your palate with *es cendol*, a mix of coconut milk and green *pandan* jelly in palm sugar syrup. Finally, take one of Mama Setiawan's homemade *sambals* home to bring color to your cooking.

Summer House Santa Monica

American

D4

1954 N. Halsted St. (bet. Armitage Ave. & Willow St.)

Phone: 773-634-4100 — Lunch & dinner daily
Web: www.summerhousesm.com
Price: $$ — Armitage

Sunny days and southern California come to Lincoln Park in the form of this bright and breezy restaurant that resembles a beach house, albeit an enormous one with lots of house guests. It's the perfect choice for a summer's day—and not a bad one in the colder months either, if you're having a quick bite before the theater or want to shake off those winter blues for a while. There's even a countdown showing the number of days till summer.

The menu proves a good fit for the surroundings by keeping things easy. There are sandwiches, tacos, and salads, but it's the meat and fish from the wood-fired oven that stand out. For dessert, choose a big cookie from the counter by the entrance. There's also a pizza restaurant and bar attached.

Twin Anchors

Barbecue

E4

1655 N. Sedgwick St. (at Eugenie St.)

Phone: 312-266-1616
Web: www.twinanchorsribs.com
Price: $$

Lunch Sat – Sun
Dinner nightly
Sedgwick

Within the brick walls that have housed Twin Anchors since 1932, generations have made their way across the checkerboard linoleum floor to throw a quarter in the jukebox and get saucy with a slab of their legendary ribs in one of the curved booths. Though the bar is wall-to-wall on weekends, most weekdays are low-key, with families and groups ready for a casual night out.

Fall-off-the-bone baby back ribs are the real deal, made with a sweet and spicy rub, served with their own "zesty" sauce or the newer Prohibition version, with brown sugar and a wallop of ghost-pepper heat. Classic sides like onion rings, baked beans, or hearty chili round out the meal.

If there's a wait at this no-reservations spot, try the beer of the month while cooling your heels.

White Oak Tavern & Inn

American

B3

1200 W. Webster Ave. (at Racine Ave.)

Phone: 773-248-0200
Web: www.whiteoakchicago.com
Price: $$

Lunch Tue – Sun
Dinner Tue – Sat
Armitage

Having evolved into a more relaxed spot for lunch or dinner with very approachable cooking, the appealingly rustic White Oak Tavern & Inn flaunts a detailed study in creative flavor combinations and technical finesse. Service may be hit or miss here, but with the Midwestern farm at its forefront, every ingredient on this multi-category menu is of irreprehensible quality. The menu features such hearty all-American staples as chicken wings, pork meatballs and pimento cheese. And their in-house bread program is an unexpected treat. Find evidence of this in the much-loved cheeseburger, with its buttered and charred potato bun sandwiching a juicy beef patty and all the necessary trappings.

A freshly baked chocolate chip cookie is a suitable finale.

Loop

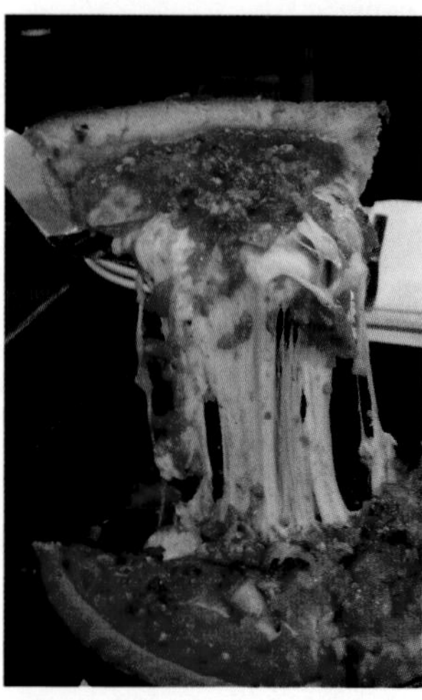

The relentless pace and race of Chicago's main business district is named after the "El" tracks that make a "loop" around the area. Their cacophony may be an intrinsic part of the soundtrack of the Windy City, but that isn't to say that this neighborhood doesn't have a culinary resonance as well. In fact, it is one that is perpetually evolving with the region. It wasn't that long ago that the Loop turned into no-man's land once the business crowd headed home for the night.

However thanks to a revitalized Theater District, new residential high-rises, sleek hotels, and student dorms, the tumbleweeds have been replaced with a renewed dining scene, wine boutiques, and gourmet grocery stores that stay open well past dusk. In fact, as a testament to the times, local foodies and visitors can contact the Chicago Cultural Center's "culinary concierges" with any food tourism-related queries.

SENSATIONAL SPREADS

Start your voyage here by exploring **Block 37**, one of the city's original 58 blocks. It took decades of hard work and several political dynasties, but the block now houses a five-story atrium with shopping, restaurants, and entrances to public transportation. Next up: **Tesori**, an Italian trattoria that has a buzzing space serving hand-crafted pastas to a corporate crowd. Top off these savory bites with a bit of sweet at the Chicago outpost of NYC hot spot, **Magnolia Bakery**.As per tradition, folks get in line here for treasures such as banana pudding and melt-in-your-mouth cupcakes. For those watching their waistline, probiotic **Starfruit Cafe**—with delicious frozen yogurts—is like heaven on earth. And, catering to the clusters of office types in the Loop, are several fast food options on the Pedway level (a system of tunnels that links crucial downtown buildings underground, which is a godsend during those brutal Chicago winters.) For a quick grab-and-go lunch, **Hannah's Bretzel** is top-notch. Lauded as "über sandwich makers," their version of the namesake, crafted from freshly baked German bread, features ultra-tasty fillings (imagine a grass-fed sirloin sammie spread with nutty Gruyère, vine tomatoes, and horseradish aïoli). While summer brings a mélange of musical acts to Millennium Park, Grant Park, and the Petrillo Music Shell that are just begging for a picnic, winter evenings are best spent at **The Walnut Room**. Besides fantastic people-watching, a family-friendly vibe, and stunning Christmas décor, this Marshall Fields favorite also warms the soul with comfort food like Mrs. Hering's Chicken Pot Pie—the recipe for which dates back to 1890. Foodies can also be found feasting at **Park Grill**, a full-service restaurant flanked by an ice rink in the winter. Of course, no trip to Chicago, much less the Loop, would be complete without munching on Italian specialties from **Vivere**—which is a beloved local institution that seamlessly blends formality with spirited charm in a handsome, wood-toned space.

TOURING & CAROUSING

Calling all sweet tooths: with flavors like maple-bacon and pistachio-Meyer lemon, you will be hard-pressed to stop at just one donut variety at the delicious **Do-Rite**. But, if dessert doesn't do it for you, eat your way through the city by way of **Tastebud Tours'** Loop route, whose stops include hot dogs, pizza, as well as **The Berghoff**—one of the city's oldest restaurants known for its enormous steins of beer. Word on the street is that none of the "slices" in Chicago are considered legit without a deep-dish. So, it's no wonder that the popular **Chicago Pizza Tour** is also headquartered here. From visiting restaurant kitchens, getting schooled on top ingredients, ovens, the physics of pizza-making, and digging into deep-dish pies (naturally!), this expedition is designed to showcase the true essence behind Chi-town's most notable food. During the warmer months, several farmer's markets cater to the downtown crowd. These may even include the ones stationed at Federal Plaza on Tuesdays or Daley Plaza on Thursdays. Though concession carts continue to dot the streets in nearby Millennium Park, home cooks are in for a serious treat at **Mariano's Fresh Market**. This gourmet emporium proffers everything from gluten-free lemon bars for stiletto-clad socialites to holiday gift spopular among local businesses. Moving on from food to wine, **Printers Row Wine Shop's** carefully curated wine selection and weekly wine tastings (every Friday at 5:00 PM.) make it the district's go-to wine stop—intent on equipping real folks with the right amount of information. Chicago, however, also sees its fair share of coffee connoisseurs, and tourists tired of sightseeing should be sure to stop in for a pick-me-up at **Intelligentsia Coffee**—a local coffee chain with an emphasis on direct trade. Locations can be found all over, but the **Millennium Park Coffeebar** is especially convenient and delicious.

TASTE OF CHICAGO

One of the Windy City's biggest events (and the second largest attraction in the state of Illinois) is **Taste of Chicago**—a five-day summer extravaganza in Grant Park. For the last 30 years, the festival's never-ending maze of real food booths and live music has attracted hordes of hungry diners from all over. It may be hot and crowded, but that's just part of the fun—or torture.

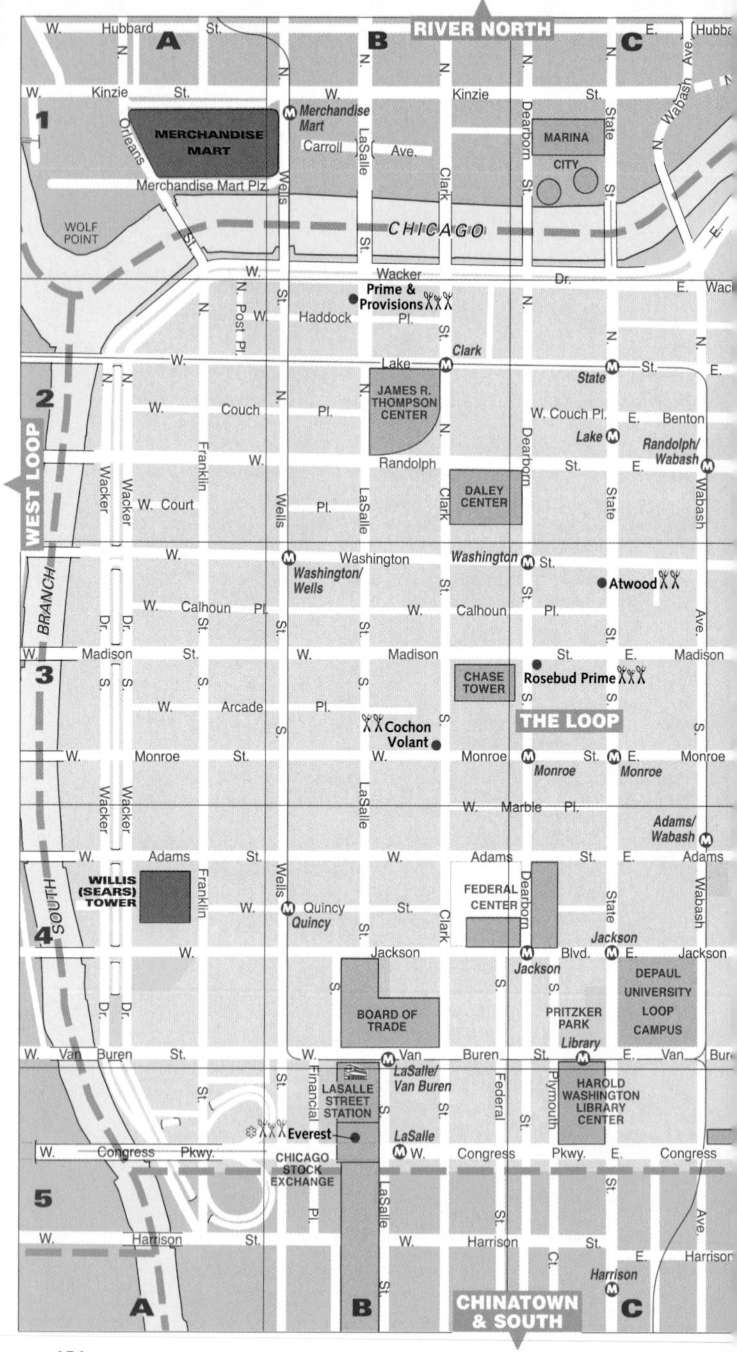
RIVER NORTH
WEST LOOP
THE LOOP
CHINATOWN & SOUTH
MERCHANDISE MART
MARINA CITY
WOLF POINT
CHICAGO
SOUTH BRANCH
JAMES R. THOMPSON CENTER
DALEY CENTER
CHASE TOWER
WILLIS (SEARS) TOWER
FEDERAL CENTER
BOARD OF TRADE
PRITZKER PARK
DEPAUL UNIVERSITY LOOP CAMPUS
HAROLD WASHINGTON LIBRARY CENTER
LASALLE STREET STATION
CHICAGO STOCK EXCHANGE
Prime & Provisions
Atwood
Rosebud Prime
Cochon Volant
Everest
Merchandise Mart
Clark
State
Lake
Randolph/Wabash
Washington/Wells
Washington
Monroe
Adams/Wabash
Quincy
Jackson
Library
LaSalle/Van Buren
LaSalle
Harrison

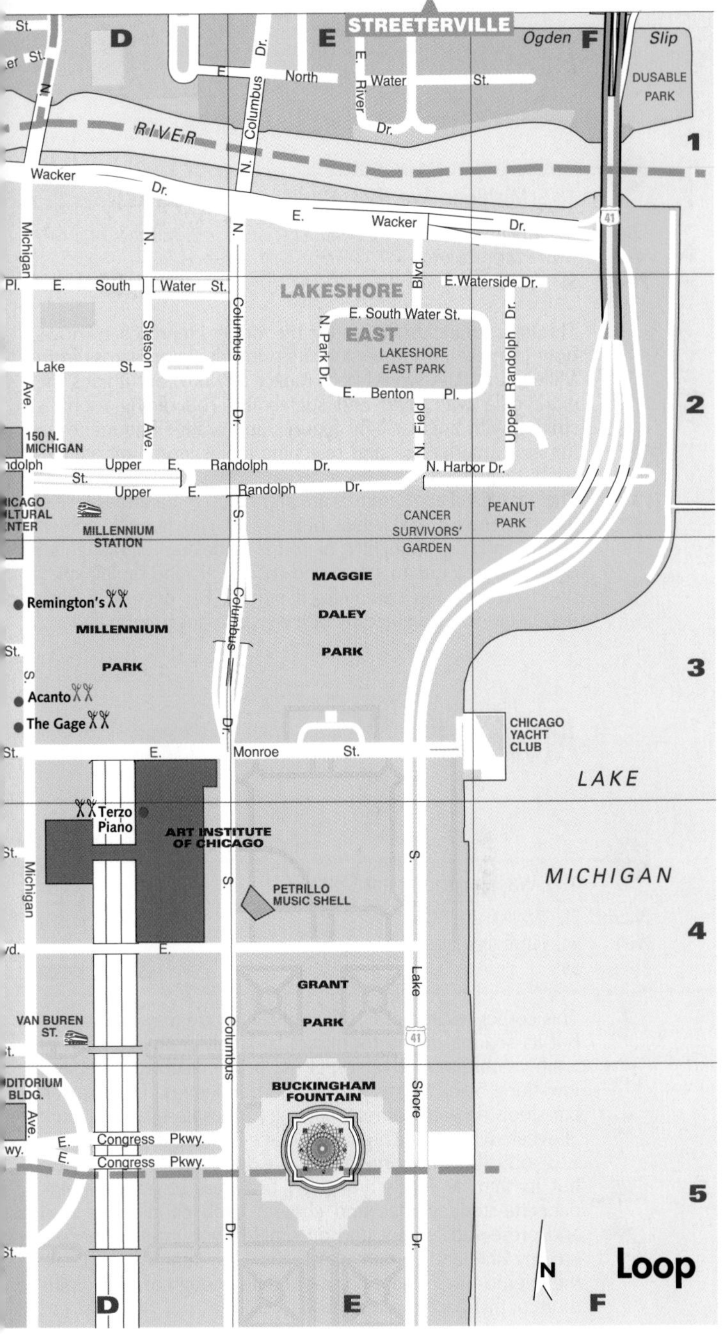
STREETERVILLE
D
E
F
Ogden
Slip
DUSABLE PARK
North
Water
St.
E. River Dr.
N. Columbus Dr.
RIVER
Wacker
Dr.
E.
Wacker
Dr.
1
LAKESHORE
EAST
E.Waterside Dr.
E. South Water St.
N. Park Dr.
LAKESHORE EAST PARK
E. Benton Pl.
N. Field Blvd.
Upper Randolph Dr.
2
E. South Water St.
Lake St.
Stetson Ave.
Michigan Ave.
150 N. MICHIGAN
Upper E. Randolph Dr.
N. Harbor Dr.
Upper E. Randolph Dr.
MILLENNIUM STATION
CANCER SURVIVORS' GARDEN
PEANUT PARK
MAGGIE DALEY PARK
Remington's
MILLENNIUM PARK
Acanto
The Gage
S. Columbus Dr.
3
CHICAGO YACHT CLUB
E. Monroe St.
LAKE
MICHIGAN
Terzo Piano
ART INSTITUTE OF CHICAGO
PETRILLO MUSIC SHELL
S. Lake Shore Dr.
4
GRANT PARK
VAN BUREN ST.
BUCKINGHAM FOUNTAIN
E. Congress Pkwy.
E. Congress Pkwy.
5
N
Loop

Acanto

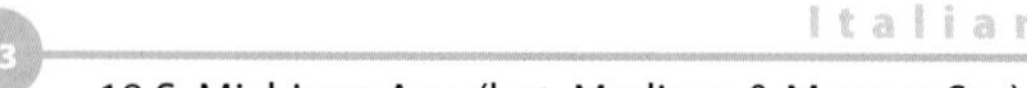

Italian XX

D3

18 S. Michigan Ave. (bet. Madison & Monroe Sts.)

Phone: 312-578-0763 Lunch & dinner daily
Web: www.acantochicago.com
Price: $$ Monroe

This Italian reincarnation set in the former Henri space knows how to make an impression: its prime location across from Millennium Park would be a looker any day, but it goes the extra mile with style and sociability. The dining room is striking with angular light fixtures and orange banquettes; a luminous marble bar and matching tables lend a masculine, sophisticated vibe.

The carte's Italian standards are amped up to luxurious levels, like the Treviso and white bean salad with fennel, golden raisins, and crispy pancetta; or house-made duck egg spaghetti drenched in a cream sauce and twirled around rapini, spicy pork sausage, and caramelized onions. For dessert, a fresh ricotta tart is highlighted by bittersweet orange marmalade.

Atwood

Contemporary XX

C3

1 W. Washington St. (at State St.)

Phone: 312-368-1900 Lunch & dinner daily
Web: www.atwoodrestaurant.com
Price: $$ Washington

This corner restaurant's 19th century façade may be historic, but its soaring dining room is a strikingly modern vision of white marble-topped tables, glossy beveled subway tiles, and low-slung black leather chairs and banquettes. The crimson bar stools fill with patrons meeting for business and pleasure all week, while brunch gets the place buzzing on weekends.

Atwood's brasserie menu isn't exactly full of surprises, but its familiar foods are given first-class upgrades—think pancetta-studded mac and cheese; lamb chops with basil and preserved lemon; and an omelet with crunchy bacon, creamy Brie, and verdant asparagus. For a real wake-up call, the Inferno Virgin Mary has more than enough of a kick (plus more of that bacon as a garnish).

Cochon Volant

French XX

100 W. Monroe St. (at Clark St.)

Phone: 312-754-6560 Lunch & dinner daily
Web: www.cochonvolantchicago.com
Price: $$ Monroe

Though it's attached to the Hyatt, Cochon Volant is quickly becoming a favorite with Loop locals and sightseers alike for its timeless warmth. Round bistro tables and bentwood chairs are clustered across the mosaic-tiled floor, while a broad, marble-topped bar is bustling with patrons from lunch to happy hour.

Brasserie favorites dominate the menu, ranging from rustic French onion soup to lavish raw seafood *plateaux*. Steak frites are juicy and flavorsome with a tender prime cut of bavette, offered with five sauce options like a classic béarnaise or rich Roquefort. Breakfast is delicious, but for those who don't have time to sit and stay a while, the café and takeaway bakery let commuters snag a pastry and coffee to go.

The Gage

Gastropub XX

24 S. Michigan Ave. (bet. Madison & Monroe Sts.)

Phone: 312-372-4243 Lunch & dinner daily
Web: www.thegagechicago.com
Price: $$

Monroe

For 10 years, this expansive, eclectic gastropub has catered to the Millennium Park crowds. Handsome banquettes and columns wrapped in celadon tiles lend a clubby allure, but the space's buzzy vibe never feels overwhelming. While a bar stretching half the length of the restaurant gets its fair share of happy-hour crowds, the rear dining rooms offer a more relaxed setting.

Pub classics with flair define the menu, like malt-battered cod with creamy tartar sauce and parsley-flecked thick-cut fries—a solid rendition of fish and chips. Keep it light with crunchy watercress and sugar snap pea salad with house-made burrata, or go all out with a plate of chocolate-toffee cream puffs garnished with tender cocoa-dusted marshmallows.

Everest ✿

French XXX

B5

440 S. LaSalle St. (bet. Congress Pkwy. & Van Buren St.)

Phone: 312-663-8920 Dinner Tue – Sat
Web: www.everestrestaurant.com
Price: $$$$ LaSalle/Van Buren

Summit the historic Chicago Stock Exchange building via a private elevator to reach the sophisticated—though not outdated—scene at Everest on the 40th floor. The sunken-level dining room stays dimly lit by contemporary circular metal light fixtures, all the better to gaze admiringly at the views from the windows framing the formal space. Heavy white linens and abstract bronze sculptures adorn each table, at which smartly dressed guests take it all in.

Alsatian Chef Jean Joho keeps to French tradition on his degustation and prix-fixe menus, with nods to local ingredients among the classical techniques and pairings presented nightly. Where other chefs may feel the need to update and tweak time-honored dishes, Everest celebrates the classics.

Subtle hints of ginger in a rich Gewürztraminer butter sauce complement succulent chunks of fresh Maine lobster. Two thick, bone-in lamb chops, ringed elegantly with flavorful fat, are tender but never too chewy—their richness amplified by delicate, silken spring garlic flan and a bed of crisp green beans that soak up the thyme jus. Cap it all off with tart and sweet pistachio vanilla *succès* dabbed with red rhubarb jam.

Prime & Provisions

Steakhouse

222 N. LaSalle St. (at Wacker Dr.)

Phone: 312-726-7777 — Lunch Mon – Sat
Web: www.primeandprovisions.com — Dinner nightly
Price: $$$ — Clark/Lake

Though it would also feel at home in Las Vegas, this glitzy oversized steakhouse fits right in with its swanky Chicago riverfront neighbors. The polished, masculine interior makes its priorities clear from the get-go, showcasing a two-story wine tower and a peek into the dry-aging room under bold, barrel-vaulted ceilings and chandeliers.

A starter of chewy rosemary-sea salt monkey bread whets the palate, while rosy pink slices of slow-roasted bone-in prime rib, rubbed with a crust of fragrant herbs, take a classic hoagie to new heights. When paired with house-cut fries and creamy horseradish dip, it's a meal to rival a Porterhouse. But save room for dessert: a single-serving banana cream pie with loads of whipped cream is a whimsical final bite.

Remington's

American

20 N. Michigan Ave. (bet. Madison & Washington Sts.)

Phone: 312-782-6000 — Lunch & dinner daily
Web: www.remingtonschicago.com
Price: $$ — Randolph/Wabash

This shiny restaurant is cavernous and versatile enough to impress anyone. Upon entry, guests can choose from a few great seating options in the enormous space: a table by the large windows up front, thrown open on temperate days for people-watching; the U-shaped bar, chockablock with televisions airing the latest games; or the intimate, glassed-in dining room lined with wine bottles at the back.

Remington's features an elevated roster of American classics including steaks, rotisserie chicken and seafood—not to mention a raw bar with Kansai-style box-pressed sushi. It's hard to go wrong here, but don't miss the No. 8 Tuna, which is a ruby-red slice of ahi wrapped in crispy nori and tempura, then paired with kimchi-studded rice.

Rosebud Prime

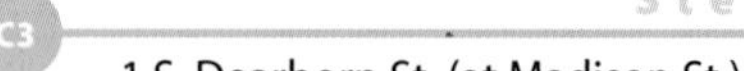

Steakhouse XXX

C3

1 S. Dearborn St. (at Madison St.)

Phone: 312-384-1900 — Lunch Mon – Sat
Web: www.rosebudrestaurants.com — Dinner nightly
Price: $$$ — Monroe

A member of Chicago's longstanding Rosebud Restaurants, this Loop darling plays the part of a throwback American steakhouse to the hilt. Crimson-hued, faux-alligator chairs and banquettes punctuate a sprawling wood-paneled dining room, where tuxedoed servers weave expertly among suited bankers. A winding staircase leads to a lofty mezzanine.

Classic cuts and chops abound, but Rosebud Prime does all of its dishes with panache. Double-cut bone-in lamb chops sport a plump ribbon of fat encircling their delicate, rich centers. Two strips of grilled skirt steak remain juicy and tender, complemented by a pile of caramelized Bermuda onions; and rich beef and veal ragù makes penne Bolognese a lovely surprise, finished with a dollop of fresh ricotta.

Terzo Piano

Italian XX

D4

159 E. Monroe St. (in the Art Institute of Chicago)

Phone: 312-443-8650 — Lunch daily
Web: www.terzopianochicago.com — Dinner Thu
Price: $$$ — Adams/Wabash

Whether you're taking in the modern masterpieces at The Art Institute or simply enjoying lunch and cocktails on the sculpture-filled garden terrace, Terzo Piano is a feast for all the senses. The windowed white room is mod and minimalist, allowing the artistry of the Mediterranean-influenced menu to shine brightly at each table.

With Tony Mantuano overseeing the kitchen, Italian influences find their way into many seasonal dishes. Charred tomato crème fraîche lends luxurious smokiness and a tart streak to tender chicken Milanese resting on roasted cipollini purée. And agnolotti bursting with a sweet pea-ricotta filling find savory balance with shards of crispy pancetta.

As an added bonus, museum members receive a 10 percent discount on the meal.

Pilsen, University Village & Bridgeport

This cluster of neighborhoods packs a perfect punch, both in terms of food and sheer vitality. It lives up to every expectation and reputation, so get ready for a tour packed with literal, acoustic, and visual flavor. The Little Italy moniker applies to a stretch of Taylor Street that abuts the University (of Illinois at Chicago) Village neighborhood, and it's bigger and more authentically Italian than it first appears. The streets are as stuffed with epicurean shops as an Italian beef is with meat. So, bring an appetite and try this iconic (and messy) Chicago specialty at **Al's No. 1 Italian Beef**. After combing through the supply at **Conte Di Savoia**, an Italian grocery and takeout spot, stop for lunch at **Fontano's Subs** (locally famous for their hearty subs) or old-school **Bacchanalia**.

Brunch your way through the day at **Pleasant House Bakery**; then save room for creative tamales (think crawfish etouffée) at **Dia De Los Tamales**, a great little spot replete with a funky décor. Speaking of south-of-the-border fun, don't miss out on the much-loved festival, **Mole de Mayo**, featuring an enticing lineup of Mexican cuisine mingled with cultural events. Parched after a long day on your feet? **Mario's Italian Lemonade** is where you can seal the deal over a frozen fruit slush. Later, consider

popping into **Scafuri Bakery** for a sugar refill, some biscotti, or *sfogliatelle*. This charming retreat has been delivering traditional Italian sweets to the community since opening its doors in 1904. Popular for fresh-baked breads, pastries, and cookies, wedding cakes and pies are also part of their ever-changing repertoire.

UNIVERSITY VILLAGE

Like any self-respecting college "town," University Village is home to a range of toasty coffee shops. Add to that the mélange of doctors, medical students, nurses, and others working in the neighborhood hospital, and you've got a perpetually bustling vibe with great people-watching potential. Take a break from the hustle to quench your thirst at one among a few select locations of **Lush Wine & Spirits**. On Sundays, follow the band of locals to **Maxwell**

Street Market. Having relocated to Desplaines Street in 2008, this sprawling bazaar welcomes over 500 vendors selling fresh produce, amazing Mexican eats, and other miscellanea. Watch celebrity chef, Rick Bayless, as he peruses these stalls for dried chiles or epazote, while lesser Gods can be seen gorging on tacos and tostadas.

PILSEN & BRIDGEPORT

Chicagoland's massive Mexican population (more than 650,000 according to the latest U.S. Census count) has built a patchwork of regional specialties, many of which are found in the south side's residential Pilsen and Little Village neighborhoods. Pilsen is also home to the free National Museum of Mexican Art, the only Latino museum accredited by the American Alliance of Museums, as well as countless taquerias and bakeries. **Birrieria Reyes de Ocotlan** is an authentic find for tender, delicious, and flavorful goat meat folded into juicy tacos. If that sounds too gamey, then **Pollo Express** oozing with the tantalizing aroma of whole char-grilled chicken, is always reliable. Join the line for Styrofoam containers filled with guacamole, adobo-rubbed chicken, and sweet empanadas. Everyone goes all out for Mexican Independence Day in September including area restaurants, while the Little Village Arts Festival packs 'em in every October. Just as the **Pilsen Community Market** held every Sunday in the Chicago Community Bank, with its assortment of fruits and vegetables, does much to replenish the soul, carb addicts get their fix on at **Sabinas Food Products**. And for a Mexican-themed evening at home, **La Casa del Pueblo** is an exceptional supermarket that offers all things imaginable, including household, health and beauty essentials. On the other hand, carnivores continue to gush over **Carnitas Uruapan's** pork carnitas paired with salty *chicharrónes*. Since 1950, **Taqueria El Milagro** has been proffering a unique taste with its cafeteria-style restaurant complete with a tamale-centric menu, as well as a store bursting with burritos and tortillas. But, lovers of all things "green" can't resist the siren call of **Simone's Bar**. This eco-friendly joint is hip and heavenly for a variety of sips. Over in Bridgeport, **Maria's Packaged Goods & Community Bar** has been a neighborhood institution in one form or another since 1939. Here, antique collectible beer cans line the space, and leftover beer bottle clusters are being constantly repurposed as chandeliers.

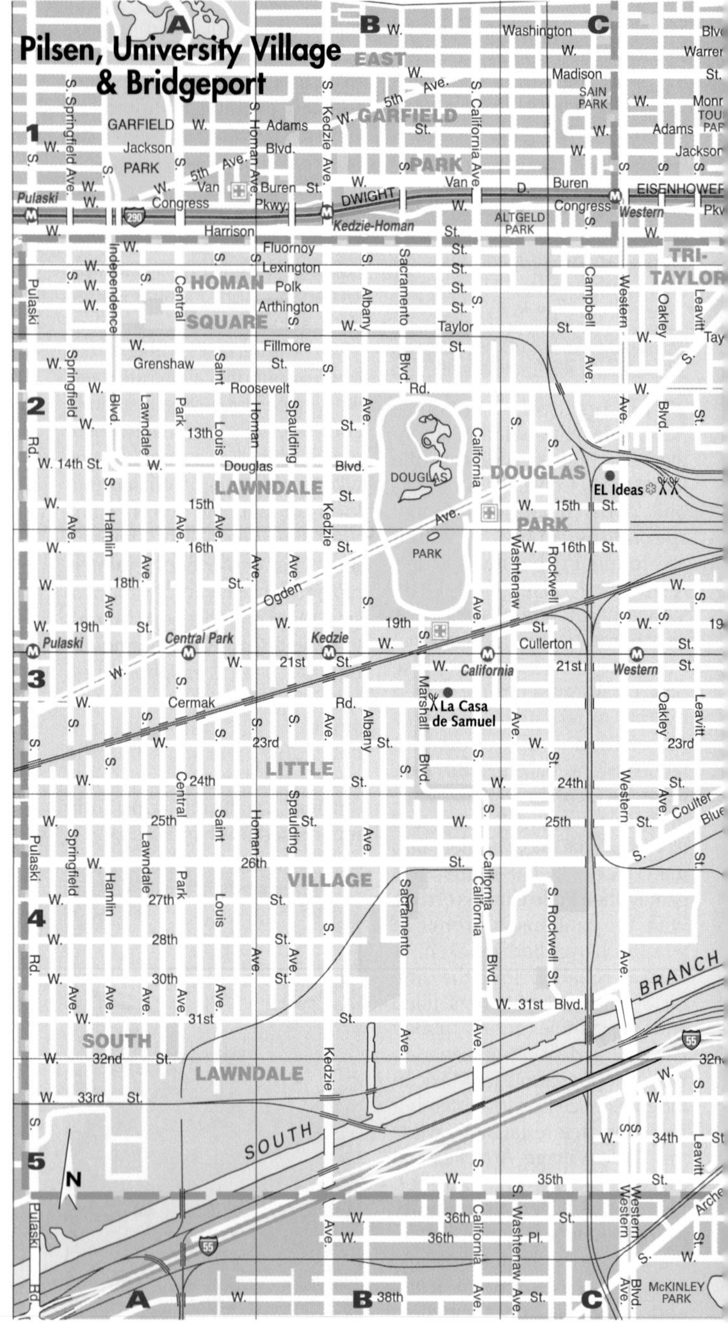
Pilsen, University Village & Bridgeport
A
B
C
1
2
3
4
5
N
EAST GARFIELD PARK
GARFIELD PARK
HOMAN SQUARE
LAWNDALE
DOUGLAS PARK
LITTLE VILLAGE
SOUTH LAWNDALE
ALTGELD PARK
SAIN PARK
TRI-TAYLOR
MCKINLEY PARK
EL Ideas
La Casa de Samuel
Pulaski
Central Park
Kedzie
California
Western
Kedzie-Homan
EISENHOWER
DWIGHT
290
55
SOUTH BRANCH
W. Washington
W. Madison
W. Adams
W. Jackson
W. Van Buren St.
W. Congress Pkwy.
W. Harrison St.
W. Fluornoy St.
W. Lexington St.
W. Polk St.
W. Arthington St.
W. Taylor St.
W. Fillmore St.
W. Grenshaw
W. Roosevelt Rd.
W. 13th
W. 14th St.
W. Douglas Blvd.
W. 15th St.
W. 16th St.
W. 18th St.
W. 19th St.
W. Cullerton St.
W. 21st St.
W. Cermak Rd.
W. 23rd St.
W. 24th St.
W. 25th St.
W. 26th St.
W. 27th St.
W. 28th St.
W. 30th St.
W. 31st St.
W. 31st Blvd.
W. 32nd St.
W. 33rd St.
W. 34th St.
W. 35th St.
W. 36th St.
W. 36th Pl.
W. 38th St.
Ogden Ave.
W. 5th Ave.
S. Pulaski Rd.
S. Springfield Ave.
S. Independence Blvd.
S. Hamlin Ave.
S. Lawndale Ave.
S. Central Park Ave.
S. Saint Louis Ave.
S. Homan Ave.
S. Spaulding Ave.
S. Kedzie Ave.
S. Albany Ave.
S. Sacramento Blvd.
S. Marshall Blvd.
S. California Ave.
S. Washtenaw Ave.
S. Rockwell St.
S. Campbell Ave.
S. Western Ave.
S. Oakley Blvd.
S. Leavitt St.
Coulter St.
Archer

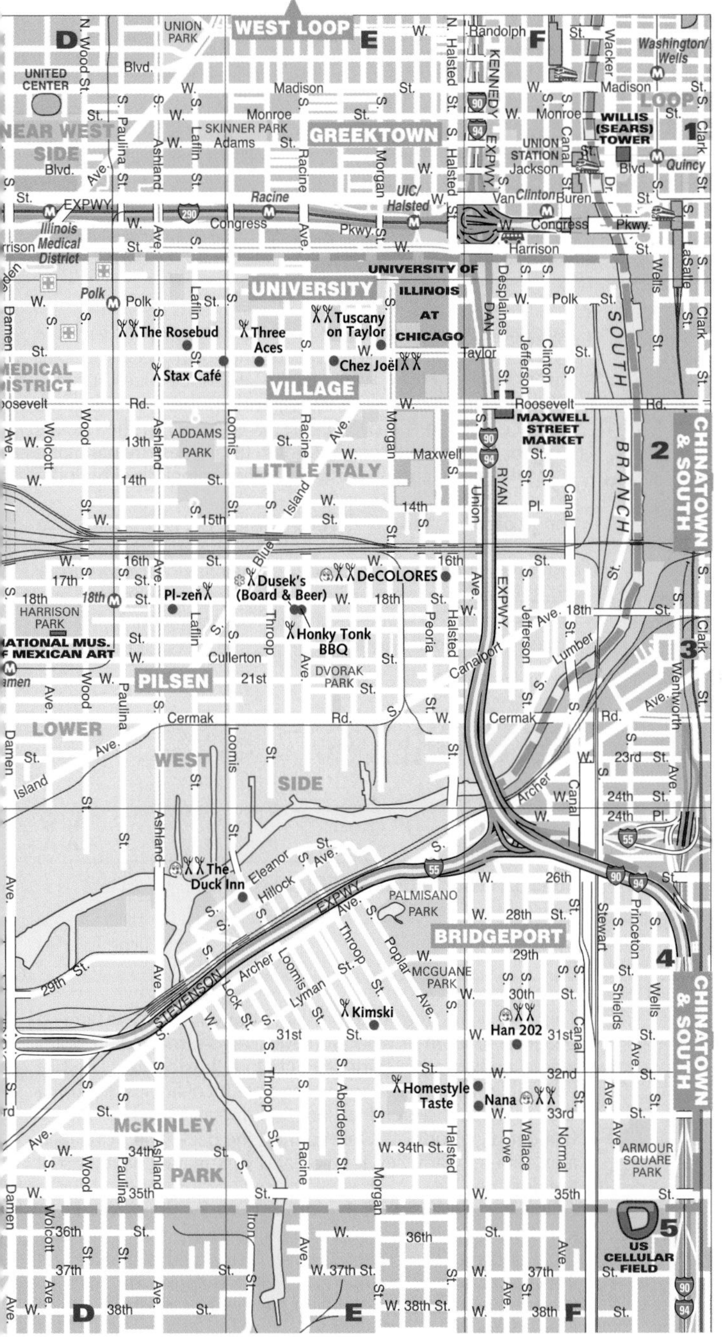
WEST LOOP
UNION PARK
UNITED CENTER
NEAR WEST SIDE
SKINNER PARK
GREEKTOWN
LOOP
WILLIS (SEARS) TOWER
UNION STATION
Washington/Wells
Quincy
Clinton
Racine
UIC/Halsted
Illinois Medical District
Polk
UNIVERSITY VILLAGE
UNIVERSITY OF ILLINOIS AT CHICAGO
The Rosebud
Three Aces
Tuscany on Taylor
Chez Joël
Stax Café
MEDICAL DISTRICT
ADDAMS PARK
LITTLE ITALY
MAXWELL STREET MARKET
SOUTH BRANCH
CHINATOWN & SOUTH
DeCOLORES
Dusek's (Board & Beer)
Pl-zeň
Honky Tonk BBQ
DVORAK PARK
HARRISON PARK
18th
NATIONAL MUS. OF MEXICAN ART
PILSEN
LOWER WEST SIDE
The Duck Inn
PALMISANO PARK
BRIDGEPORT
MCGUANE PARK
Kimski
Han 202
Homestyle Taste
Nana
McKINLEY PARK
ARMOUR SQUARE PARK
US CELLULAR FIELD
STEVENSON EXPWY.
DAN RYAN EXPWY.
KENNEDY EXPWY.
D
E
F
1
2
3
4
5

Chez Joël

French

E2

1119 W. Taylor St. (bet. Aberdeen & May Sts.)

Phone: 312-226-6479 — Lunch Tue – Sat
Web: www.chezjoelbistro.com — Dinner Tue – Sun
Price: $$

Bringing a bit of *je ne sais quoi* to Little Italy, Chez Joël is a stylish setting packed with expats and locals recalling their travel stories. Here walls gleam with ice-blue accents, windows are dressed with velvet, and art that is nothing less than ace adds to the overall lure. A cozy bar in the back is ideal for sipping, but then get down to business by partaking in this kitchen's cuisine—classic French mingled with global effects.

For a pleasing trio of flavors, *cuisses de grenouilles à la Provençale* or frogs legs are cooked with garlic, spinach and just the right dab of butter, just as *poulet aux champignons* or chicken breast is sautéed in a white wine- mushroom- and cream-sauce. Classic desserts round out the menu, but crème brûlée is not a bad way to go.

DeCOLORES

Mexican

E3

1626 S. Halsted St. (bet. 16th & 17th Sts.)

Phone: 312-226-9886 — Lunch Sat – Sun
Web: www.decolor.us — Dinner Tue – Sun
Price: $$

This Mexican restaurant's slate-colored walls feature a beautiful rotation of work from local artists, making the walls a great conversation starter even before the delicious fare hits your table. The lovely bar is yet another bit of artistry, featuring shelves tucked around a series of metal branches; and a wonderful, colorful flower motif on the back wall. A relaxed atmosphere, warm service staff and well-made cocktails seal the deal.

At this kitchen, many of the recipes have been passed down through the family for generations—and one taste of the silky *mole poblano,* laced over chicken and served with excellent refried beans and yellow rice, will transport you back to the motherland. Round out dinner with a wickedly good homemade cheesecake flan.

The Duck Inn

Gastropub

E4

2701 S. Eleanor St. (at Loomis St.)

Phone: 312-724-8811 Dinner nightly
Web: www.theduckinnchicago.com
Price: $$

Grab a taxi and head to the warehouses of Bridgeport, where this stylish, modern tavern—from neighborhood native Kevin Hickey—feels like a diamond in the rough. Through a set of French doors, the hubbub brought on by intricate cocktails in the retro globe-lit lounge leads to a decorous dining room with wide wooden tables and curvy midcentury seating.

Beyond the kitchen's signature rotisserie duck for two, the menu spreads its wings with a focused but diverse selection of small plates and entrées. Briny sea beans are the crowning touch to a winning dish of uni butter-slathered spot prawns and creamy risotto, while a duo of pickle- and beer-brined chicken thigh and drumstick glisten with a tableside finish of smoked paprika jus.

Han 202

Asian

F4

605 W. 31st St. (bet. Lowe Ave. & Wallace St.)

Phone: 312-949-1314 Dinner Tue – Sun
Web: www.han202.com
Price: $$

Near U.S. Cellular Field, this is the perfect spot to stop for an early meal before a White Sox game. The dining room feels polished and sophisticated, with leather-backed seats, large windows, and contemporary artwork.

The menu follows suit with food that is also an elegant departure from expectation, with cooking that is more Asian than specifically Chinese. The prix-fixe menu supplements may only be a few dollars more, but are well worth it. Diver scallops are wildly pristine and delicious, pan-seared and served with red beet and smoked yellow pepper purées over white chocolate sabayon jus. The plump bone-in rack of lamb is wonderful, as is its bonito plum sauce deeply flavored with lavender, mustard seeds, and Sichuan pepper.

Dusek's (Board & Beer) ✿

Gastropub 

E3

1227 W. 18th St. (at Allport St.)

Phone: 312-526-3851 Lunch & dinner daily
Web: www.dusekschicago.com
Price: $$ 18th

On the one hand, Dusek's is simply a great gastropub, serving food that is as tasty and down-to earth as one of their wood-roasted pretzels, tucked with gooey cheese and wickedly hot beer mustard. On the other hand, this is just *the* place to meet friends or grab a bite before heading to a concert at Thalia Music Hall, located next door. The fact that this spot is named for the man who founded the original venue back in 1892 shows the importance of this connection—those in-the-know are usually headed here before or after a show.

The space seems dark and moody, but everyone is having a rollicking good time. The front room feels more like a tavern; the back is a dining room warmed with wood-burning ovens. Yet both share that same friendly ambience and superb service.

Menu highlights include a beautiful dish of tortellini stuffed with braised veal heart, alongside crisp sweetbreads, purple huckleberries, and celery finished tableside with porcini and truffle broth. Every week, a new "ordinary" option pairs a different dish with a beer, like coral-colored *togarashi* prawns over edamame risotto, nori purée, trumpet mushrooms and "bottarga" bound with uni butter, all coated with dashi-air.

EL Ideas ✿

C2

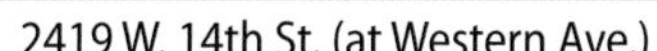

2419 W. 14th St. (at Western Ave.)

Phone: 312-226-8144 Dinner Tue – Sat
Web: www.elideas.com
Price: $$$$ Western (Pink)

BYO

Dining here feels like attending an underground dinner party prepared by a merry band of misfit cooks in Chef Phillip Foss's home (he lives right upstairs). There is one seating, everyone is served at the same time, and meals are prepaid so guests can linger or leave at their leisure. The fact that the restaurant resembles a test kitchen is heightened when guests are told to manage their BYO beverages themselves and cooks deliver dishes to your table. Don't worry—they turn the music down so you can hear each description. Yet this is all part of the show; it's a fun, friendly, totally unique experience.

The cuisine follows suit and works wonders by pushing—if not completely disregarding—the traditional boundaries of cooking. Outlandish surprises begin with *tosaka* (Japanese seaweed) accompanied by chopped raw scallop topped with creamy scrambled eggs, Ghost pepper-infused caviar, and shaved air-dried tuna. A humble sounding "ham and cheese" is actually intensely savory Bellota ham beneath a dome of fragrant black truffles and cheese fonduta over house-made potato bread.

Finish with a bowl of playful nostalgia that tastes better than childhood: chocolate cake batter with spatulas for licking it up.

Homestyle Taste

Chinese

F5

3205 S. Halsted St. (bet. 32nd & 33rd Sts.)

Phone: 312-949-9328 Lunch & dinner daily
Web: N/A
Price: ¢¢

BYO

For even more adventurous fare than spicy Sichuan lamb or dim sum, look no further than this family-run favorite. Though the lengthy menu offers plenty of usual suspects (think scallion pancakes and *mapo* tofu), it's also chock-full of Chinese dishes that will make any offal lover's day.

Thin slices of lamb kidney are dry stir-fried, their mild flavor boosted by copious amounts of cumin and red chilies. Then, a sweet and sour sauce offsets the funky flavor of quick-fried intestine, tripe, and liver; and pickled cabbage and pork meatball soup, boosted by tofu and noodles, is a welcome warmer on cold days. The service is friendly and amenable, so don't be afraid to specify your preferred meat or ask for chili oil to amplify the heat quotient.

Honky Tonk BBQ

Barbecue

E3

1800 S. Racine Ave. (at W. 18th St.)

Phone: 312-226-7427 Dinner Tue – Sun
Web: www.honkytonkbbqchicago.com
Price: $$ 18th

A rousing success since it opened in 2007, Honky Tonk BBQ serves up live music and award-winning Memphis-style treats on the southwest side of the city. Though the rollicking bar up front takes its cues from a swinging Wild West saloon, the rear dining room offers a more sedate—though still eclectic—setting for sipping house cocktails and chowing down on sensational smoked meats.

You'll need two hands to hold homemade empanadas stuffed with combinations like Manchego cheese and shiitake mushrooms, and extra cottony white bread to soak up the juices of bone-in, wood-smoked chicken. Brisket chili is even more robust with a scoop of creamy mac and cheese. And if you're still hungry, soda floats with Bridgeport-made Filbert's root beer are the cherry on top.

Kimski

E4

960 W. 31st St. (bet. Farrell & Keeley Sts.)

Phone: 773-890-0588 — Dinner Tue – Sat
Web: N/A
Price: ⊜

This long-awaited development in Bridgeport, connected to the popular Maria's Community Bar, serves up deliciousness and fun in equal parts. Think quirky Korean-Polish fusion menu; daily mish-mash specials; and T-shirts as well as fireball sauces to take home. All the food can be ordered at the counter to-go, but do yourself a favor and make your way to the open industrial dining space or large patio to enjoy the jamming bar and some live music with your food.

Everything at Kimski is delicious and truly unique. Try the homemade smoked sausage with *soju* mustard, *kraut-chi* (kimchi and kraut) and scallions tucked into a soft roll; or the *kopo wangs*, organic chicken wings slathered in a sweet--spicy AP sauce, laced with sesame seeds and scallions.

La Casa De Samuel

Mexican

B3

2834 W. Cermak Rd. (bet. California Ave. & Marshall Blvd.)

Phone: 773-376-7474 — Lunch & dinner daily
Web: www.lacasadesamuel.com
Price: ⊜ — California (Pink)

Going strong since 1989, La Casa de Samuel continues to be a great spot for a satisfying breakfast, lunch, or dinner. The spacious, immaculate, and comfortable room features exposed brick, large windows, and oil paintings depicting the Mexican landscape. Tables and booths are filled with families enjoying platters of fragrant cooking, presented by their affable servers.

A front section of the restaurant is dedicated to making outrageously good tortillas, warm and fresh to-order. The kitchen's pride and skill is clear in the chicken enchiladas, bathed in an outstanding *salsa roja*, served alongside refried black beans and rice studded with cubed potatoes and peas. The *cabrito* here is intensely tasty, perfectly seasoned, and slow-roasted with care.

Nana

American 

F5

3267 S. Halsted St. (at 33rd St.)

Phone: 312-929-2486 — Lunch daily
Web: www.nanaorganic.com — Dinner Wed – Sun
Price: $$

Nana Solis is the matriarch of this family-run Bridgeport favorite, whose visible kitchen and two dining rooms (one less formal) seem to be perpetually humming. A devoted breakfast crowd takes up residence at the coffee "bar" and butcher-block tables each day, often perusing the marvelous modern artwork—hung on the walls and usually for sale.

Locally sourced and organic are the guiding principles behind every ingredient here, which is given a bold Latin American bent. Avocado batons are tossed in panko, then flash-fried for a crispy exterior and creamy center. Another favorite among the "Nanadicts" is the eggs Benedict with chorizo, corn *pupusas*, and poblano cream. Sunday nights feature family-style fried chicken dinners fit for groups with larger appetites.

Pl-zeň

Gastropub 

D3

1519 W. 18th St. (bet. Ashland Ave. & Laflin St.)

Phone: 312-733-0248 — Lunch Sat – Sun
Web: www.pl-zen.com — Dinner nightly
Price: $$ —  18th

Don't be misguided by the name, which pays tribute to the area's Czech immigrants with rib-sticking Mexican(ish) cooking. Pl-zeň is both a reflection and a staple of this artsy, animated community thanks to an eclectic approach that can make it seem as though some items don't belong on a Mexican menu.

Bone marrow may be listed as an appetizer, but these Flintstone-sized bones topped with a smoky-spicy short rib "marmalade" of herbs and jalapeño purée on garlic toast are enough for a meal. Daily soups include chipotle chicken with crunchy ribbons of corn tortilla, roasted tomatillo, and chilies in rich chicken broth. Guacamole specials are enhanced with pomegranate arils and shredded *queso fresco*. Accompany everything with an excellent local craft beer.

The Rosebud

Italian

D2

1500 W. Taylor St. (at Laflin St.)

Phone: 312-942-1117 Lunch & dinner daily
Web: www.rosebudrestaurants.com
Price: $$ Polk

The Rosebud holds its own among the brass of University Village's Italian thoroughfare. The original location of what is now an extended family of restaurants throughout Chicagoland, it's nothing if not classic with its red neon sign, dark carved wood, and cool but accommodating all-male waitstaff.

Italian wedding soup brings comfort with moist, tiny meatballs, escarole, and *acini di pepe* simmered in broth; while sweet sausage chunks, caramelized onions, and a garlicky white wine sauce make chicken *giambotta* a satisfying choice. Loyal patrons crowd around white tablecloths for platters of their favorite chicken parmesan or linguine topped with a mountain of clams. Also, dessert is not to be missed: a single slice of carrot cake will gratify the whole table.

Stax Café

D2

1401 W. Taylor St. (at Loomis St.)

Phone: 312-733-9871 Lunch daily
Web: www.staxcafe.com
Price: Polk

With plenty of sunlight and swift service, Stax Café reminds us all that breakfast really is the most important meal of the day. Here, it can also be the heartiest. This food is all-American comfort, so begin your day with "the whole package" featuring the piping-hot and perfectly blended "Taylor Street" frittata gilded with cured ham, bacon, mushrooms, parmesan, and more. Decadent crêpes are folded with that wondrous combination of strawberries, bananas, and Nutella. Fresh juices make up for the fact that they do not serve alcohol. Be forewarned: desserts sell out early in the day (probably thanks to the takeout crowd).

A light-filled, airy and semi-industrial design makes the space feel crisp and clean enough to brighten any morning.

Three Aces

1321 W. Taylor St. (bet. Loomis & Throop Sts.)

Phone: 312-243-1577 — Lunch Sat – Sun
Web: www.threeaceschicago.com — Dinner nightly
Price: $$ — Polk

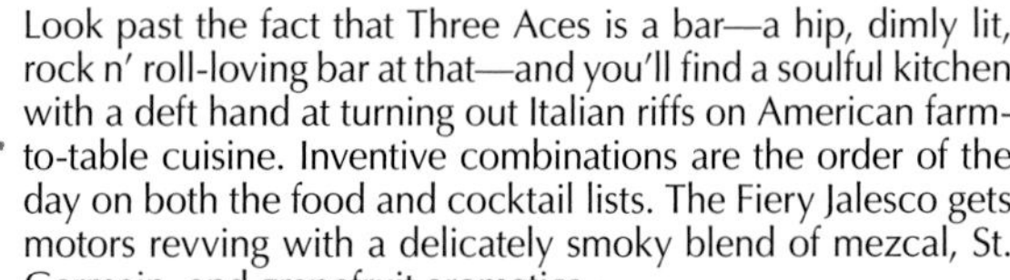

Look past the fact that Three Aces is a bar—a hip, dimly lit, rock n' roll-loving bar at that—and you'll find a soulful kitchen with a deft hand at turning out Italian riffs on American farm-to-table cuisine. Inventive combinations are the order of the day on both the food and cocktail lists. The Fiery Jalesco gets motors revving with a delicately smoky blend of mezcal, St. Germain, and grapefruit aromatics.

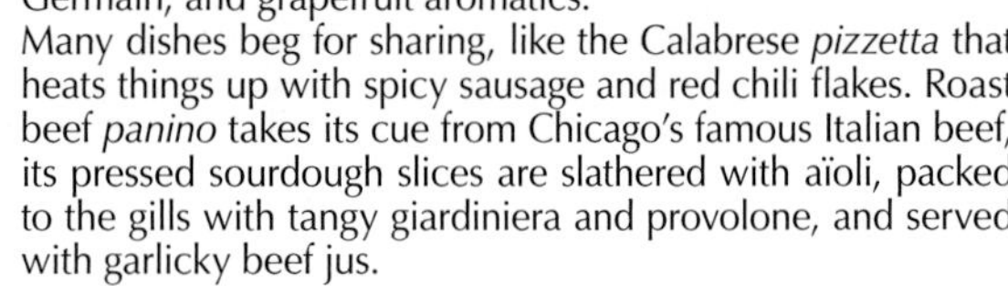

Many dishes beg for sharing, like the Calabrese *pizzetta* that heats things up with spicy sausage and red chili flakes. Roast beef *panino* takes its cue from Chicago's famous Italian beef, its pressed sourdough slices are slathered with aïoli, packed to the gills with tangy giardiniera and provolone, and served with garlicky beef jus.

Tuscany on Taylor

Italian

E2

1014 W. Taylor St. (bet. Miller & Morgan Sts.)

Phone: 312-829-1990 — Lunch Mon – Fri
Web: www.tuscanychicago.com — Dinner nightly
Price: $$ — UIC-Halsted

Italian and Chicago accents co-mingle at Tuscany on Taylor, where the classic cuisine and service are perfectly old-school (no pun intended—the university is a few blocks away). The formal staff tends to diners at white linen-topped tables in the terra cotta-tiled dining room. Chefs in puffy toques man the open kitchen amid shelves of polished copper pans.

A wide-ranging menu of modern Italian interpretations takes guests on a whirlwind tour of the boot. Tiny ravioli stuffed with roasted pears are set in a densely flavorful mascarpone cream sauce with toasted pine nuts and strips of sundried tomatoes. A simple caprese salad arrives as three stacks of thickly sliced heirloom tomatoes, buffalo mozzarella, and basil pesto drizzled with balsamic reduction.

River North

BEYOND THE ORDINARY

Urban, picture-perfect, and always-happening River North not only edges the Magnificent Mile, but is also set north of the Chicago River, just across the bridge from the Loop. Once packed with factories and warehouses, today this capital of commercialization is the ultimate landing place for art galleries, well-known restaurants, swanky shopping, and a hopping nightlife. Thanks to all this versatility, the area attracts literally everybody—from lunching ladies and entrepreneurs, to tour bus-style visitors. Tourists are sure to drop by, if only to admire how even mammoth chain restaurants ooze a particular charm here. Among them is **Rock 'n' Roll McDonald's**, a block-long, music-themed outpost of the ubiquitous burger chain. This is one of the world's busiest **MickeyD's** with an expanded menu, music memorabilia, and bragging rights to the first two-lane drive-through. Speaking of drive-throughs, River North is also home to the original **Portillo's**, a hot dog, burger, and beer favorite, whose giant exterior belies its efficient service and better-than-expected food. When it comes to size, few buildings can rival **Merchandise Mart** (so large it has its own ZIP code), known for its retail stores, drool-worthy kitchen showrooms, and two great food shops. **Artisan Cellar** is one such gem where in addition to boutique wines and cheeses, you can also purchase Katherine Anne Confections'

fresh cream caramels. Locals also adore and routinely frequent **The Chopping Block** for its expertly taught themed cooking courses; updated, well-edited wine selections; and sparkling knife collection.

From trends to legends, **Carson's** is a barbecue institution. This squat brick box has no windows, but is just the kind of place where wise guys like to do business, with a bib on of course! This old-school treasure features framed pictures of every local celebrity, who can also be seen gracing the walls at seafood superstar, **Shaw's Crab House**. Their nostalgic bar and dining den is dotted with stainless steel bowls to collect the shells from the multitude of bottom-dwellers on offer. Crab is always available of course, but selections spin with the season. For those who aren't down with seafood in any form, this kitchen turns out a few prime steaks as well. Combat the bitter-cold winters and warm your soul with hearty food and easy elegance at **Lawry's Prime Rib**, in the 1890's McCormick Mansion. Inside, the opulent dining room covers all bases from prime rib dinners to seafood signatures. But, true carnivores who like their meat and potatoes done in grand style will find deep comfort in **Smith & Wollensky's** elaborate carte. Another nationwide chain, **Fleming's Prime Steakhouse & Wine Bar** is as well-regarded and recognizable as the aromas wafting from **Bow Truss Coffee Roasters**, where busy commuters pop in for a robust espresso.

Further indulge your dessert dreams at **Firecakes Donuts** where coconut cream-filled buns are chased down by piping-hot chocolate bobbing with soft marshmallows. The Windy City's doughnut craze then carries on at **Doughnut Vault**, brought to you by restaurateur Brendan Sodikoff, who appears to have the Midas touch with this morning fried dough. Formerly the location for the infamous Cabrini-Green government housing, today **Chicago Lights: Urban Farm** showcases organic produce, nutritional education, and workforce training, thereby elevating the level of economic opportunities available to this vibrant community. On the other hand, **Eataly** is an impressive ode to Italian food, employing a massive workforce. This gourmet paradise may present the same delicacies as its NYC flagship, but the Nutella (counter) with its mouthwatering selection is sure to have folks returning for more.

DEEP-DISH DELIGHTS

Thanks to its diverse community, River North is also a great destination for myriad food genres, including the local phenomenon of deep-dish pizza. With a doughy crust cradling abundant cheese, flavorful sauce, and a host of other toppings, some may say this is closer to a casserole or "hot dish" than an Italian-style pizza. Either way, these pies take a while to craft, so be prepared to wait wherever you go. **Pizzeria Uno** (or sister **Pizzeria Due**), and **Giordano's** are some of the best-known pie makers in town. And if a little indigestion isn't a concern, chase these decadent delights with yet another local specialty—the Italian beef. At **Mr. Beef's**, these "parcels" resemble a messy, yet super-tasty French dip, wrapping thinly sliced beef with hot or sweet peppers on a hoagie. If you order it "wet," both the meat and bread will be dipped in pan juices. You could also add cheese, but hey, this isn't Philly! Distinguished by day, River North pumps up the volume at night with sleek cocktail lounges, night clubs, and Irish bars. Slip into **Three Dots and a Dash**, a retro, tiki-inspired bar featuring some of the city's most well-regarded mixologists. But, for a more rootin'-tootin' good time, stop by the electric **Underground Wonder Bar**, whose dangerously tenacious punchbowls and succinct pan-Asian menu make it a favorite for private parties. Meanwhile, happy hour is always hopping at **Green Door Tavern**, which gets its name from the fact that its colored front told Prohibition-era customers where to enter for a drink. To appreciate what all the fuss is about, order the "famous corned beef sandwich" or the "legend burger" and leave with a smile.

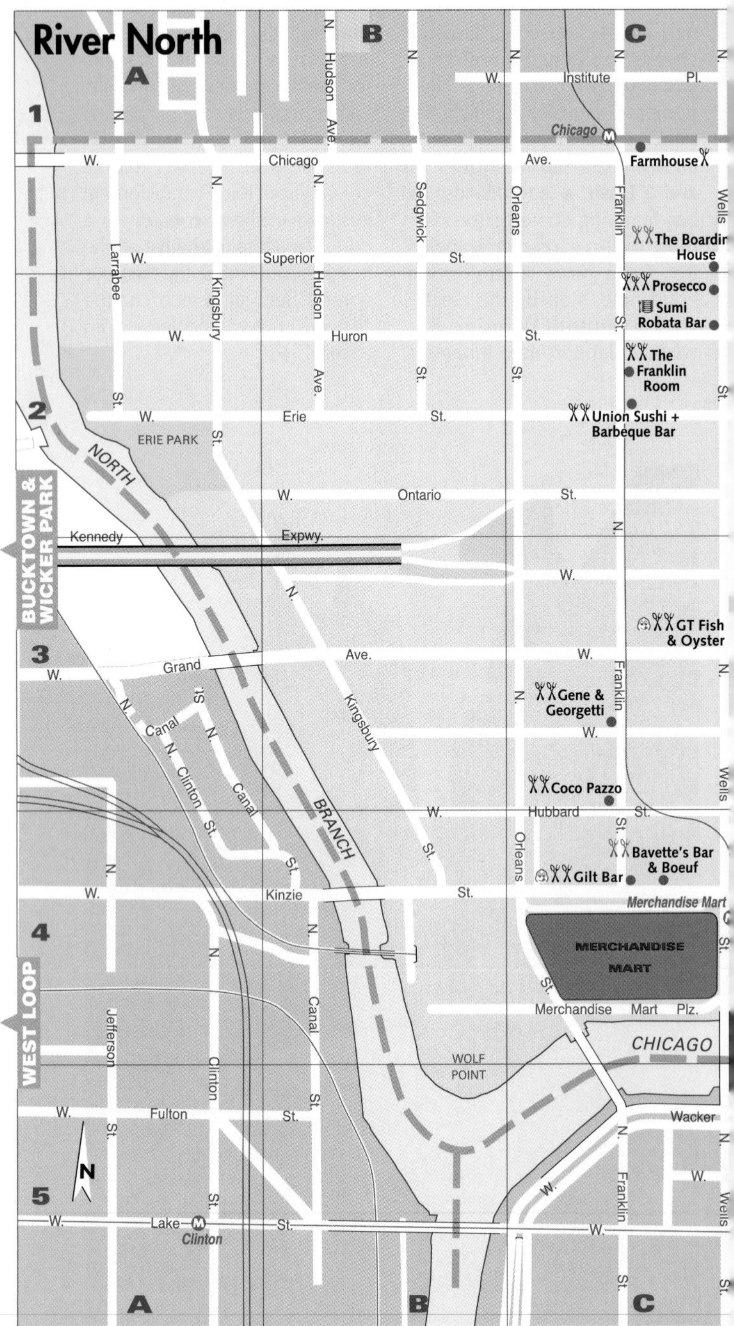
River North
Farmhouse
The Boarding House
Prosecco
Sumi Robata Bar
The Franklin Room
Union Sushi + Barbeque Bar
GT Fish & Oyster
Gene & Georgetti
Coco Pazzo
Bavette's Bar & Boeuf
Gilt Bar
Merchandise Mart
BUCKTOWN & WICKER PARK
WEST LOOP
W. Chicago Ave.
W. Superior St.
W. Huron St.
W. Erie St.
ERIE PARK
W. Ontario St.
Kennedy Expwy.
W. Grand Ave.
W. Hubbard St.
W. Kinzie St.
Merchandise Mart Plz.
W. Fulton St.
W. Lake St.
Clinton
Wacker
WOLF POINT
NORTH BRANCH
CHICAGO
W. Institute Pl.

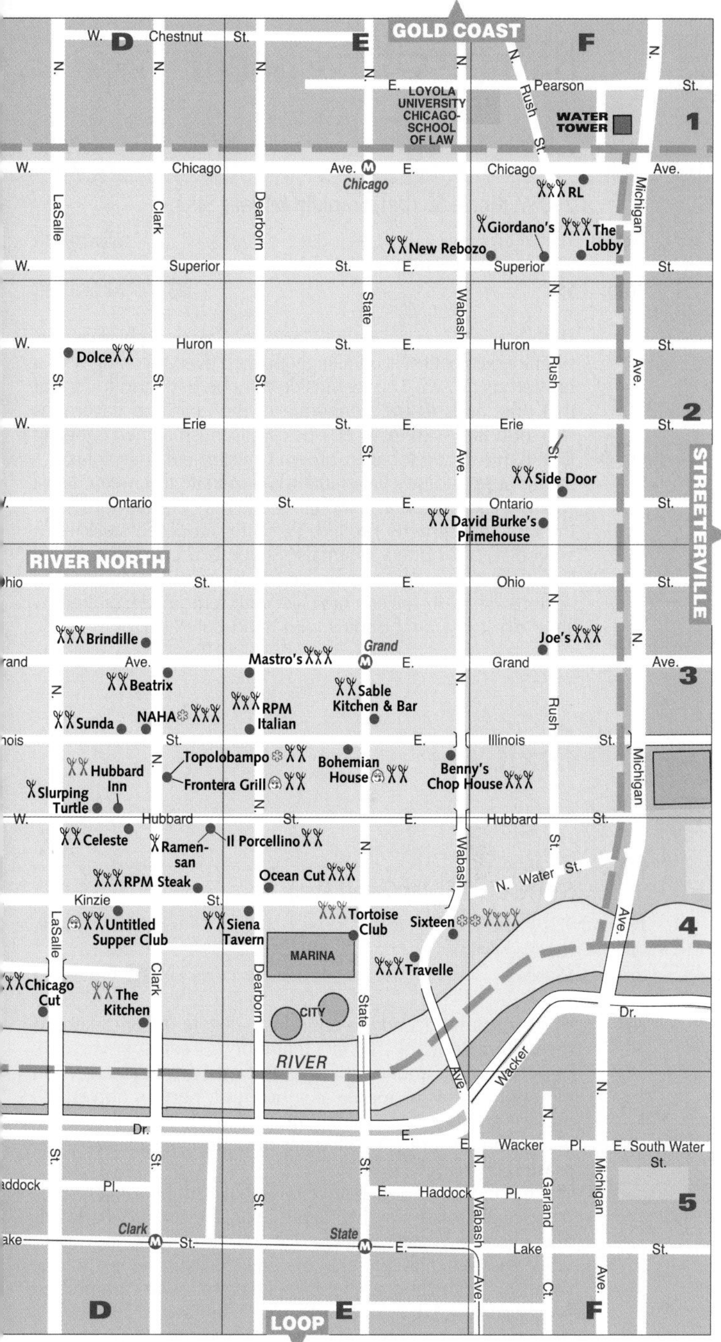
GOLD COAST
LOYOLA UNIVERSITY CHICAGO-SCHOOL OF LAW
WATER TOWER
RL
Giordano's
The Lobby
New Rebozo
Dolce
Side Door
David Burke's Primehouse
RIVER NORTH
STREETERVILLE
Brindille
Joe's
Mastro's
Beatrix
Sable Kitchen & Bar
RPM Italian
Sunda
NAHA
Topolobampo
Bohemian House
Benny's Chop House
Hubbard Inn
Slurping Turtle
Frontera Grill
Celeste
Ramen-san
Il Porcellino
Ocean Cut
RPM Steak
Tortoise Club
Sixteen
Untitled Supper Club
Siena Tavern
MARINA CITY
Travelle
Chicago Cut
The Kitchen
RIVER
LOOP

Bavette's Bar & Boeuf

Steakhouse XX

C4

218 W. Kinzie St. (bet. Franklin & Wells Sts.)

Phone: 312-624-8154 Dinner nightly
Web: www.bavetteschicago.com
Price: $$$ Merchandise Mart

With a sultry jazz soundtrack and speakeasy ambience, this swanky destination is unfailingly packed every evening with a boisterous crowd. The feel inside may be dark and loud, but that only adds to the bonhomie of the chic and cavernous den, outfitted with exposed brick walls, mismatched dangling light fixtures, and tobacco-brown Chesterfield-style sofas.
Steakhouse and raw bar standards dominate the menu. Most steaks are wet-aged and though some may prefer more funk, the cuts are expertly broiled. Perfectly rendered steak frites served with a buttery béarnaise sauce is a great way to go. But, the kitchen deserves praise for other, more unexpected options like fresh-baked crab cake with remoulade; or creamy short rib stroganoff bobbing with hand-cut pasta.

Beatrix

International XX

D3

519 N. Clark St. (at Grand Ave.)

Phone: 312-284-1377 Lunch & dinner daily
Web: www.beatrixchicago.com
Price: $$ Grand (Red)

From a Spartan façade to an industrial-style décor, Beatrix is the epitome of cool. The fact that it boasts eats for everyone, popular tunes, and trendy guests from the adjacent Aloft Hotel only seals its repute as a hot spot. Servers don stylish hairdos and tattoos to match the vibe while attending to the giant room featuring a coffee bar dispensing excellent locally roasted brews.
The menu veers from creative to global with pleasing results. A "special" salad may highlight flavor and texture via lentils and charred veggies enriched by coriander-kissed yogurt, while roasted chili- and chocolate-glazed salmon is a smoky surprise. For the end, apple strudel flavored with caramelized brown sugar is big in size and faultless in flavor.
An even more modern and larger sib is located in Streeterville.

Benny's Chop House

E3

444 N. Wabash Ave. (bet. Hubbard & Illinois Sts.)

Phone: 312-626-2444 — Lunch & dinner daily
Web: www.bennyschophouse.com
Price: $$$ — Grand (Red)

Old-school service meets modern elegance at Benny's Chop House. A far cry from the clubby, masculine steakhouses of yesteryear and just a stone's throw from the Magnificent Mile, this expansive but welcoming space goes for understated glamour, with tasteful inlaid wood and burgundy columns offset by natural stone walls, white birch branches, and a marble bar.

Though Benny's steaks are the draw, those prime cuts of filet mignon and ribeye are matched by fresh seafood like simply roasted bone-in halibut fillet and classic raw bar towers, along with a variety of pastas and salads. A trio of sliders featuring mini portions of Benny's burger, crab cake, and sliced filet with horseradish cream elevate the idea of bar snacks to new heights.

The Boarding House

American

C1

720 N. Wells St. (at Superior St.)

Phone: 312-280-0720 — Dinner Mon – Sat
Web: www.boardinghousechicago.com
Price: $$ — Chicago (Red)

This passion project, courtesy of master sommelier Alpana Singh, throws its doors open to four floors of grandeur. An alluring cellar leads to the first-floor bar, dangling with shimmering wine glass clusters. Then comes the kitchen; main dining room—donning mullioned windows and an installation made from over 4,000 green wine bottles; as well as another elevated mezzanine.

The space is dramatic, making it a favorite for weddings and celebratory events. However, the American food with global accents is a complete treat. Sharing is an appealing option, but you may also have the likes of Amish chicken with Calabrian chilies or wild king salmon with green curry all to yourself. Seal the deal over a bowl of brownies drizzled with merlot-chocolate chip ice cream.

Bohemian House

Eastern European 

E3

11 W. Illinois St. (bet. Dearborn & State Sts.)

Phone: 312-955-0439 Lunch & dinner daily
Web: www.bohochicago.com
Price: $$ Grand (Red)

This wickedly stylish "house" is exactly what River North needed to shake it up—a truly unique restaurant serving delicious Czech, Austrian, and Hungarian cuisines. The stunning beer hall-meets-art nouveau interior (think reclaimed wood beams, stunning tiles arching over a semi-open kitchen, sky-blue tufted leather couches, and Persian rugs) is worth a visit alone. No detail is overlooked.

Delightfully, the food is amazingly tasty and just as pretty to look at. Don't miss the open-faced schnitzel sandwich, highlighting juicy pork over apple and kohlrabi slaw, aged Gouda, a fried egg, and drizzle of coarse mustard. Also a must do? The warm blueberry *kolacky*, a traditional Czech cookie filled with blueberry coulis and served with lemon curd and blueberry-sour cream ice cream.

Brindille

French XXX

D3

534 N. Clark St. (bet. Grand Ave. & Ohio St.)

Phone: 312-595-1616 Dinner Mon – Sat
Web: www.brindille-chicago.com
Price: $$$$ Grand (Red)

This posh bistro is located just steps away from NAHA, it's impressive sister restaurant from cousins Carrie and Michael Nahabedian. Hushed and intimate, the dining room is awash with a palette of soothing greys and dressed up with herringbone floors along with black-and-white photography.

Brindille's menu isn't a sequel to NAHA's contemporary Mediterranean fare, but instead bears a strong Parisian accent influenced by the chef's love of French cuisine. Roasted chestnuts are whirled into a creamy soup and poured over compressed apple, wild mushrooms, and puffed rice. Spot-on Dover sole *meunière* is plated with a purée of watercress and golden-crisp *pommes rissolées*. And for dessert, preserved cherries are just one option to fill the baked-to-order almond clafoutis.

Celeste

American 

D4

111 W. Hubbard St. (bet. Clark & LaSalle Sts.)

Phone: 312-828-9000 — Dinner Tue – Sat
Web: www.celestechicago.com
Price: $$ — Merchandise Mart

Celeste celebrates the city's close relationship with that great American institution—the bar—and here it is a veritable palace of fun spread over three floors. On the first, find a bar—natch—with an abbreviated menu. On the second is the narrow and appropriately named Deco Room where the marble-topped tables face yet another bar, while the upstairs is reserved for private parties. The food is certainly more than a mere addendum to the terrific cocktail list and the kitchen is clearly a skilled one. Dishes are quite elaborate in their construction—order the chicken fried quail and you may find salty, crunchy pieces topped with *giardiniera* and tailed by buttermilk biscuits flavored with kimchi.
There is also a seasonal rooftop bar for outdoor libations.

Chicago Cut

Steakhouse 

D4

300 N. LaSalle St. (at Wacker Dr.)

Phone: 312-329-1800 — Lunch & dinner daily
Web: www.chicagocutsteakhouse.com
Price: $$$ — Merchandise Mart

Chicago Cut is a steakhouse perfectly suited for the City of the Big Shoulders. The finely tailored locale bustles day and night, thanks to being wrapped in windows along the riverfront, sumptuous red leather furnishings, warm wood trim, and a crackerjack service team cementing its steakhouse vibe.
Non-meat entrées include cedar-planked salmon with a *sriracha*-honey glaze, but make no mistake: beef is boss here. Prime steaks, butchered and dry-aged in-house for 35 days, get just the right amount of time under the flame, as is the case with the perfectly cooked-to-order Porterhouse—pre-sliced and plated for each guest. Sides are a must and should include the dome of hashbrowns, creamed spinach redolent of nutmeg, or tender stalks of grilled asparagus.

Coco Pazzo

C3

300 W. Hubbard St. (at Franklin St.)

Phone: 312-836-0900 — Lunch Mon – Fri
Web: www.cocopazzochicago.com — Dinner nightly
Price: $$ — Merchandise Mart

Vibrant blue-and-orange awnings help Coco Pazzo make its mark among the area's stellar restaurants, though their reputation for seasonal Tuscan cuisine has been going strong since 1992. Navy velvet curtains that hang in the wide, welcoming, high-ceilinged room may dampen the din, but not the enthusiasm from regulars ready for a delicious midday *tavolata* and bottle from the all-Italian wine list.

Business types fill every seat for the *piatti unici*, a chef-chosen lunch special that changes daily but is always made with expert care. Selections may include Rushing Waters trout over lentils and spinach paired with speck- and mushroom-studded risotto made with Carnaroli rice. Dinner options like pancetta-wrapped quail with taleggio fondue showcase the kitchen's ambitious side.

David Burke's Primehouse

Steakhouse

F2

616 N. Rush St. (bet. Ohio & Ontario Sts.)

Phone: 312-660-6000 — Lunch & dinner daily
Web: www.davidburkesprimehouse.com
Price: $$$ — Grand (Red)

Banish thoughts of musty wood-paneled rooms from your mind and unwind at this chic—and slightly tongue-in-cheek—steakhouse in the boutique James Hotel. Rawhide tablecloths and masculine wood-and-rope décor elements hint at the ranch and open range, though the cocktails and young, trendy clientele at the accompanying bar are strictly urban.

The all-American menu offers a wide selection of top-notch beef and hearty sides to match. Skewered cubes of maple syrup-smothered, black pepper-dusted bacon are a playful snack to share, a poppable prelude to the carnivorous courses to follow. Bone-in steaks like the 8-ounce filet are juicy and flavor-packed; many cuts are aged in-house in a Himalayan salt-tiled room for prime attention and coddling.

Dolce

Italian XX

127 W. Huron St. (at LaSalle St.)

Phone: 312-754-0700 Lunch & dinner daily
Web: www.dolceitalianrestaurant.com
Price: $$ Chicago (Red)

With locations in Miami and Atlanta, Dolce's newest outpost lands in Chicago's popular River North neighborhood, tucked into the lobby of the stunning, Cubist-influenced Godfrey boutique hotel. The spacious dining room features a sleek interior with dark wood grain tiles, orange leather furnishings, tweed-lined banquettes, and enormous windows.

Dolce offers a chic take on Italian dining, with a menu featuring pizzas, house-made pastas, and entrées like veal Milanese or fennel pollen-dusted roasted chicken. Try the cool watermelon salad studded with heirloom tomatoes, crumbled goat cheese, pea shoots, mint, and toasted pumpkin seeds. The *pappardelle alla Bolognese* arrives irresistibly silky and dressed in a wickedly good beef, pork, and veal ragù.

Farmhouse

Gastropub 

228 W. Chicago Ave. (bet. Franklin & Wells Sts.)

Phone: 312-280-4960 Lunch & dinner daily
Web: www.farmhousechicago.com
Price: $$ Chicago (Brown)

Like shaking the hand of your local farmer, grab the pitchfork door handles of Farmhouse and you'll be almost as close to the source of your food. Much of the décor is salvaged and much of the menu is procured right from the Midwest. From Indiana chicken to Michigan wine, local is more than a buzzword. Exposed brick, rough-hewn wood, and wire-encased filament bulbs make it the quintessential modern tavern.

Highlights of the harvest headline each course. Whole-grain mustard dresses up a vibrant (and requisite) beet salad. Nueske's bacon is the star in a rustic BLT, accompanied by Klug Farms peaches tossed with balsamic dressing. Cream cheese-frosted carrot bread pudding is fragrant from autumn spices, layered with a golden raisin purée and nutmeg crunch.

The Franklin Room

American

C2

675 N. Franklin St. (bet. Erie & Huron Sts.)

Phone: 312-445-4686 — Lunch Mon – Fri
Web: www.franklinroom.com — Dinner nightly
Price: $$ — Chicago (Brown)

With a motto like "Ladies and Gentlemen Welcome," it's no surprise that the subterranean space housing this modern-day tavern and whiskey bar is as inviting as they come. Surrounded by backlit bottles of top-notch spirits under wrought-iron latticework light panels, guests gather for convivial conversation and great drinks.

Fans of Bourbon will delight in the Derby Day Mule, which swaps out vodka for Buffalo Trace. Pair your libation with rib-sticking dishes like a sandwich of garlic- and balsamic vinegar-roasted portobello mushroom caps layered with a runny egg, grilled tomato, and blue cheese; or a steaming bowl of braised duck soup complete with thick and silky pappardelle. End on a high note—think Bourbon-infused milkshake with house-made ice cream.

Frontera Grill

Mexican

D3

445 N. Clark St. (bet. Hubbard & Illinois Sts.)

Phone: 312-661-1434 — Lunch & dinner Tue – Sat
Web: www.rickbayless.com
Price: $$ — Grand (Red)

The linchpin in Rick Bayless' empire, Frontera Grill is decidedly unique in its homage to regional Mexican cuisine and displays a near cult-like devotion to local product. The service at this dining room, psychedelic in its color scheme, can verge on vapid, but find a seat on the bar side for a warmer (and worthier) experience.

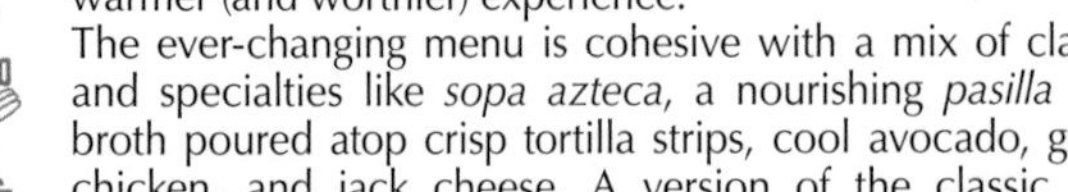

The ever-changing menu is cohesive with a mix of classics and specialties like *sopa azteca*, a nourishing *pasilla chile* broth poured atop crisp tortilla strips, cool avocado, grilled chicken, and jack cheese. A version of the classic from Morelia, *enchiladas a la plaza* are first flash-fried, then folded over seasoned cabbage, potatoes, and carrots. Pair this plate with a side of spinach in green chile and you won't be unhappy. Ever.

Gene & Georgetti

Steakhouse 

C3

500 N. Franklin St. (at Illinois St.)

Phone: 312-527-3718 Lunch & dinner Mon – Sat
Web: www.geneandgeorgetti.com
Price: $$$$ Merchandise Mart

No, it's not a Hollywood set. This Italian-American steak joint is the real thing, and those wiseguys at the bar have been clinking their ice cubes in this wood-paneled room for decades. The historic spot, founded in 1941, is boisterous downstairs with the aforementioned regulars and guys grabbing a bite; upstairs is more refined for local politico lunches and a bit of old-school romance at dinner.

Gene & Georgetti is a steakhouse with an Italian bloodline, prominently displayed in the heaping helping of fried *peperoncini* and bell peppers with the signature "chicken alla Joe." The cottage fries (oversized potato planks that come with most entrées) might necessitate a doggie bag, but all the better to leave room for a slice of classic carrot cake.

Gilt Bar

Gastropub XX

C4

230 W. Kinzie St. (at Franklin St.)

Phone: 312-464-9544 Dinner nightly
Web: www.giltbarchicago.com
Price: $$ Merchandise Mart

It's not easy to miss the revolving door entrance to Gilt Bar, a moody and imposing retreat. The bar up front mixes cocktails to a metronomic rhythm, while the back feels more intimate with studded leather banquettes and nostalgic lighting.

However make no mistake: this is no Bugsy Malone speakeasy, but a grown-up version for aficionados with astute palates. Snack on smoky Brussels sprouts finished with a Dijon vinaigrette and dusting of pecorino before savoring ricotta gnocchi tossed in nutty brown butter sauce with butternut squash, chives and parmesan. For the finale, diner-style pies are all the rage. Gorge on a coconut-cream rendition topped with pleasantly bitter coffee-infused ice cream and chocolate sauce—perhaps to the tunes of Bob Dylan? Bliss.

Giordano's

Pizza

F1

730 N. Rush St. (at Superior St.)

Phone: 312-951-0747 Lunch & dinner daily
Web: www.giordanos.com
Price: Chicago (Red)

Value, friendly service, and delicious deep-dish pizza make Giordano's a crowd sweetheart. With locations dotting the city and suburbs, this restaurant has been gratifying locals with comforting Chicago-style Italian-American fare for years. Come during the week—service picks up especially at dinner—to avoid the cacophony.

The menu includes your typical salads and pastas, but you'd do well to save room for the real star: the deep-dish. Bring backup because this pie could feed a small country. The spinach version arrives on a buttery pastry crust, filled with sautéed (or steamed) spinach with tomato sauce, and topped with mozzarella and parmesan. For those cold, windy nights, opt for delivery—their website sketches a detailed menu.

GT Fish & Oyster

Seafood

C3

531 N. Wells St. (at Grand Ave.)

Phone: 312-929-3501 Lunch & dinner daily
Web: www.gtoyster.com
Price: $$ Grand (Red)

Quaint seaside shacks have nothing on this nautical-chic urban spot. A boomerang-shaped communal table by the raw bar makes a perfect perch for slurping oysters. Lead fishing weights keep napkins in place on brass-edged tables, arranged beneath an enormous chalkboard mural of a jaunty swordfish skeleton.

Pescatarians savor the numerous seafood dishes meant for sharing, but those who forego fish are limited to three meat options. Start with fresh tuna poke dressed in soy sauce, sesame oil, and ginger with shaved cucumber. Then move on to plump deep-fried oysters topped with kimchi and served in a soft and delightfully squishy slider bun. Carrot cake with orange buttercream, pineapple purée, and a scoop of coconut ice cream is pure pleasure.

Hubbard Inn

American

110 W. Hubbard St. (bet. Clark & LaSalle Sts.)

Phone: 312-222-1331 Lunch & dinner daily
Web: www.hubbardinn.com
Price: $$ Merchandise Mart

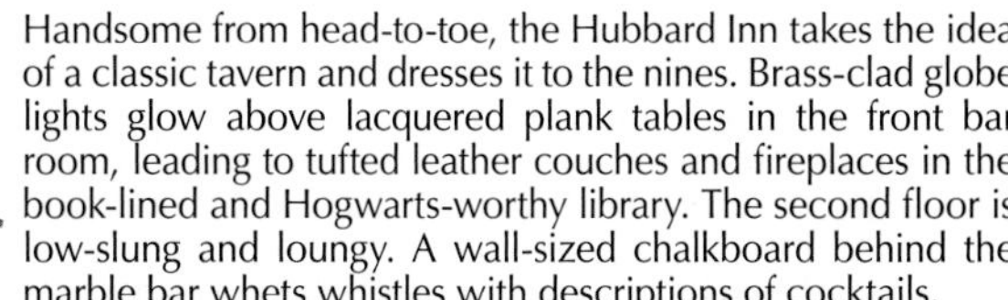

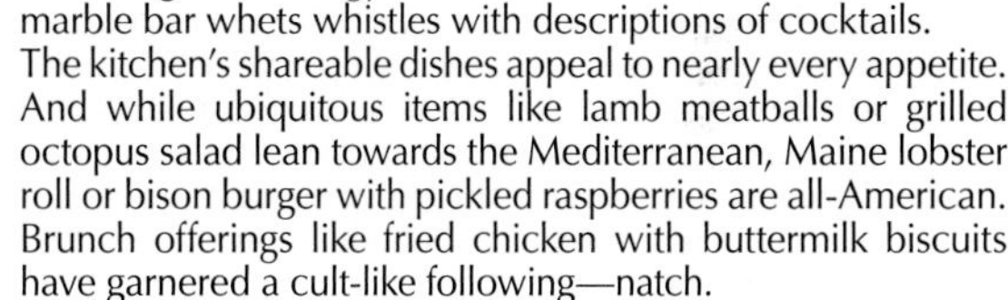

Handsome from head-to-toe, the Hubbard Inn takes the idea of a classic tavern and dresses it to the nines. Brass-clad globe lights glow above lacquered plank tables in the front bar room, leading to tufted leather couches and fireplaces in the book-lined and Hogwarts-worthy library. The second floor is low-slung and loungy. A wall-sized chalkboard behind the marble bar whets whistles with descriptions of cocktails.

The kitchen's shareable dishes appeal to nearly every appetite. And while ubiquitous items like lamb meatballs or grilled octopus salad lean towards the Mediterranean, Maine lobster roll or bison burger with pickled raspberries are all-American. Brunch offerings like fried chicken with buttermilk biscuits have garnered a cult-like following—natch.

Il Porcellino

Italian

59 W. Hubbard St. (bet. Clark & Dearborn Sts.)

Phone: 312-595-0800 Dinner nightly
Web: www.ilporcellinochicago.com
Price: $$ Grand (Red)

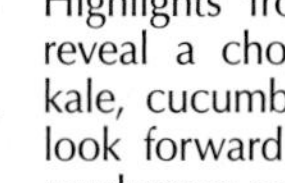
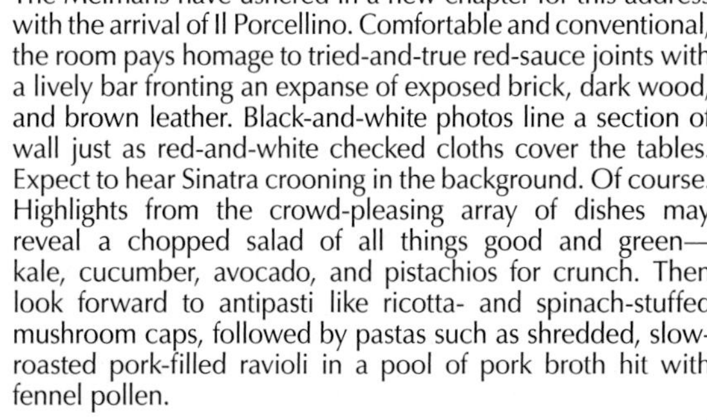

The Melmans have ushered in a new chapter for this address with the arrival of Il Porcellino. Comfortable and conventional, the room pays homage to tried-and-true red-sauce joints with a lively bar fronting an expanse of exposed brick, dark wood, and brown leather. Black-and-white photos line a section of wall just as red-and-white checked cloths cover the tables. Expect to hear Sinatra crooning in the background. Of course.

Highlights from the crowd-pleasing array of dishes may reveal a chopped salad of all things good and green—kale, cucumber, avocado, and pistachios for crunch. Then look forward to antipasti like ricotta- and spinach-stuffed mushroom caps, followed by pastas such as shredded, slow-roasted pork-filled ravioli in a pool of pork broth hit with fennel pollen.

Joe's

American XXX

F3

60 E. Grand Ave. (at Rush St.)

Phone: 312-379-5637 — Lunch & dinner daily
Web: www.joes.net
Price: $$$$ — Grand (Red)

Despite the ample neighborhood competition, this outpost of the original Miami seafood, steak, and stone crab palace does just fine up north. Clubby, masculine décor fashions a classic scene, while business diners and lively martini-toasting groups keep the leather booths full from lunch through dinner. Stone crab claws accompanied by signature mustard sauce are shared by nearly every table, followed by decadent dishes like a bone-in filet with their simple yet delicious coriander-spiked seasoning. Americana sides like Jennie's fontina and asiago mashed potatoes, or grilled tomatoes topped with cheesy spinach pesto, are ample enough to share. Joe's Key lime pie is rightly famous, but other retro sweets like coconut cream pie are worth a forkful.

The Kitchen

American XX

D4

316 N. Clark St. (bet. Kinzie St. & the Chicago River)

Phone: 312-836-1300 — Lunch & dinner daily
Web: www.thekitchen.com
Price: $$ — Merchandise Mart

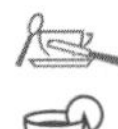

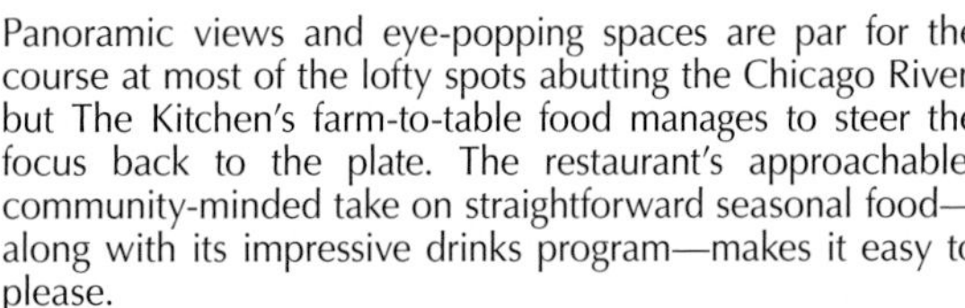

Panoramic views and eye-popping spaces are par for the course at most of the lofty spots abutting the Chicago River, but The Kitchen's farm-to-table food manages to steer the focus back to the plate. The restaurant's approachable, community-minded take on straightforward seasonal food—along with its impressive drinks program—makes it easy to please.

Even if you're not attending a Monday "Community Night" dinner alongside many of the purveyors whose ingredients appear on the plate, you'll find a fresh, flavorful mix of dishes. Crushed white bean bruschetta is topped with a sprightly herb and frisée salad, which is in turn dressed with a blood orange vinaigrette. And wild Bristol Bay salmon is poached with care, its silkiness punctuated by garlic-chive aïoli.

The Lobby

XxX

Contemporary

F1

108 E. Superior St. (at Michigan Ave.)

Phone: 312-573-6760 — Lunch & dinner daily
Web: chicago.peninsula.com
Price: $$$ — Chicago (Red)

You can't say you weren't warned. The Peninsula people sensibly realized that honesty was best when naming this vast space which looks remarkably like...a lobby. At least the friendly staff manages to wrestle back some control, and you know your conversation won't be overheard—because there aren't any tables near you.

So why the recommendation? Because the food is very good. The lunch menu doesn't really get past lobster rolls and chicken legs, but at night the kitchen's innate skill is very much in evidence. Dishes are good-looking, but also have depth, and ingredients are of irreproachable quality. Flavors marry well and there are intriguing touches of originality but never at the expense of the overall balance of the dish.

Mastro's

Steakhouse

E3

520 N. Dearborn St. (at Grand Ave.)

Phone: 312-521-5100 — Dinner nightly
Web: www.mastrosrestaurants.com
Price: $$$$ — Grand (Red)

Mastro's may be relatively young on the Windy City's steakhouse scene, but it shows up with the swagger of an old pro. Black SUVs unload VIPs in front of the revolving door, which leads to a gleaming wall of bottles at the gilded bar. Live lounge music may take the level of conversation up a notch, but sip on a shaken martini to blank out the surrounding din.

Steaks on screaming hot platters come unadorned unless otherwise listed, and servers will happily rattle off recommendations for toppings, sauces, and crusts. Salads like Mastro's house version, a local favorite stocked with chopped jumbo shrimp and a giant steamed prawn, are hearty (read: oversized), but smaller portions are on offer so you can leave room for the renowned butter cake.

NAHA 

American 

D3

500 N. Clark St. (at Illinois St.)

Phone: 312-321-6242
Web: www.naha-chicago.com
Price: $$$

Lunch Tue – Fri
Dinner Mon – Sat
Grand (Red)

After more than 15 years, NAHA is still strutting her stuff, remaining one of Chicago's most beloved dining destinations. Fans of Chef Carrie Nahabedian arrive expecting a creative, magnificent meal with exceptional service, and the kitchen consistently delivers it to a tee.

There's a quiet elegance to this dining room—a sleek, window-wrapped space with contemporary accents of concrete, wood and greenery. If your idea of relaxation starts with pre-dinner drinks, the sizable bar and smattering of tables in the front lounge are an open invitation to start slow and relish the evening. It's that kind of place.

Despite its understated setting, rest assured that the seasonally driven Mediterranean cuisine is anything but. Risotto arrives studded with braised oxtail, buttery Bietina greens, preserved black truffle, scallions, and parmesan. Next, sea scallops, seemingly plucked straight from the sea, are dusted with citrus, vanilla and spices, then laid on a bed of glazed Belgian endive, and finally accompanied by spearmint, celery fronds, pea shoots, and grapefruit. A Concord grape tart featuring dollops of pistachio-dusted meringue, tarragon, lemon rind and pistachio ice cream makes for a powerful finish.

New Rebozo

Mexican XX

F1

46 E. Superior St. (bet. Rush St. & Wabash Ave.)

Phone: 312-202-9141 — Lunch Sat – Sun
Web: www.newrebozo.com — Dinner Tue – Sun
Price: $$ — Chicago (Red)

This location is an offshoot of Chef Francisco Lopez's (known as Chef Paco) Oak Park original. Set on a leaf-lined stretch off Michigan Avenue, New Rebozo offers a particularly pretty sidewalk with umbrella-shaded tables for enjoying margaritas and excellent guacamole. Inside, the dining space features brick walls in red-and-white paint, and a small bar area.

The menu features impressive Mexican cuisine, with a notable lineup of *moles*: try the *fiesta mole*—a sampler platter of six enchiladas, each featuring a different version. Fajitas, tamales, and tacos round out the menu; as do delicious renditions of classics like tortilla soup bobbing with tortilla strips, tender shredded chicken, ripe avocado, and a dried pasilla chile drizzled with *crema*.

Ocean Cut

Seafood XXX

E4

20 W. Kinzie St. (at Dearborn St.)

Phone: 312-280-8882 — Lunch & dinner Mon – Sat
Web: www.cchicago.net
Price: $$$ — Merchandise Mart

A small tweaking, and *voila*—the short-lived C Chicago reemerges as Ocean Cut. Super conducive to schmoozing and celebrating, the elegant dining room features polished wood-and-leather seating; a grand staircase leading to a mezzanine area; and a sweet alfresco dining area come summer.

Given the moniker, it should come as no surprise that seafood is the focus here, though a delicious lineup of dry-aged steaks offers a tempting way to get your meat fix. The menu's modern spin on seafood includes "ocean charcuterie"—maybe barbecue eel and foie gras terrine—in addition to grilled or salt-crusted fish market selections, such as Faroe Island salmon. Plucked straight from the fish display in the dining room, it doesn't get much fresher than that.

Prosecco

Italian XXX

C2

710 N. Wells St. (bet. Huron & Superior Sts.)

Phone: 312-951-9500 Lunch Mon – Fri
Web: www.prosecco.us.com Dinner Mon – Sat
Price: $$ Chicago (Brown)

No matter the hour, it's always time for bubbly at Prosecco, where a complimentary flute of the namesake Italian sparkler starts each meal. This fizzy wine inspires the restaurant's elegant décor, from creamy pale walls and damask drapes to travertine floors. Sit at the long wooden bar or in one of the well-appointed dining rooms for a second glass chosen from the long list of *frizzante* and *spumante* wines.

Hearty dishes spanning the many regions of Italy cut through the heady bubbles. Carpaccio selections include the classic air-dried *bresaola* as well as whisper-thin seared rare duck breast. *Saltimbocca di vitello* marries tender veal medallions with crispy Prosciutto di Parma and creamy mozzarella, with hints of sage in the tomato-brandy sauce.

Ramen-san

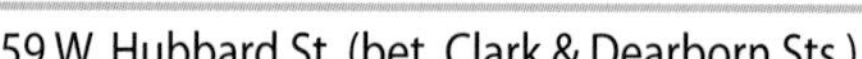

Asian X

D4

59 W. Hubbard St. (bet. Clark & Dearborn Sts.)

Phone: 312-377-9950 Lunch & dinner daily
Web: www.ramensan.com
Price: Grand (Red)

Lettuce Entertain You brings you bowlfuls of ingredient-driven noodle soups served up right next door to the restaurant group's Il Porcellino. The menu at this Asian concept revolves around a handful of tastefully crafted broths dancing with thin, wavy noodles produced by Sun Noodle. The *tonkotsu* ramen is a traditional pleasure afloat with sweet slices of *chashu*, *wakame*, and molten egg. Meanwhile, the kimchi and fried chicken ramen is a novel departure, defined by pungent fried garlic and buttered corn.

Ramen-san's loyal following is comprised of hipsters and suits alike, and they all seem to dig the salvaged look and booming playlist. Night owls take note: Japanese whiskies rule the bar and fried rice is served late into the night.

RL

American XxX

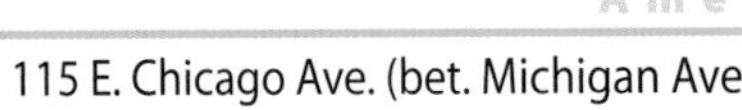

F1

115 E. Chicago Ave. (bet. Michigan Ave. & Rush St.)

Phone: 312-475-1100 Lunch & dinner daily
Web: www.rlrestaurant.com
Price: $$$ Chicago (Red)

If you swoon for tartan and pine for the posh life Ralph Lauren represents, head for the boîte attached to the flagship Michigan Avenue store. Like a stylish private club but without the centuries of stuffiness, RL offers options for a quick solo lunch, cocktail at the mahogany bar, or full dinner. The odd Blackhawks jersey here and there doesn't detract from the overall aura.

The menu is as classically American as the name, featuring bistro favorites like Waldorf salad and raw bar offerings alongside well-prepared dishes like sweet and plump pan-seared scallops with white balsamic-crème fraîche. The thin, flaky crust of a goat cheese and caramelized onion tart nearly steals the show from the rich atmosphere of the wood-paneled dining room.

RPM Italian

Italian XxX

E3

52 W. Illinois St. (at Dearborn St.)

Phone: 312-222-1888 Lunch Sun
Web: www.rpmitalian.com Dinner nightly
Price: $$ Grand (Red)

You'll want to bust out the Dolce & Gabbana for a sultry night at RPM. This see-and-be-seen scene starts at the wraparound Carrara marble bar and works its way to the mod black-and-white dining room, where sexy white leather chairs and booths don't detract from the pretty people on display. Even servers get into the spirit with white coats and skinny black ties.

If you can tune out the diversions, the poster-sized menu of modern Italian antipasti, snacks, and family-style plates won't disappoint. Classically prepared peppered beef carpaccio and shaved parmesan is garnished with crispy mushrooms, while a hearty entrée of gnocchi is tossed with mild Italian sausage and rapini. Save room to share a plate of freshly fried *bomboloni* oozing with Nutella.

RPM Steak

Steakhouse XXX

D4

66 W. Kinzie St. (bet. Clark & Dearborn Sts.)

Phone: 312-284-4990 — Lunch Mon – Fri
Web: www.rpmsteak.com — Dinner nightly
Price: $$$$ — Merchandise Mart

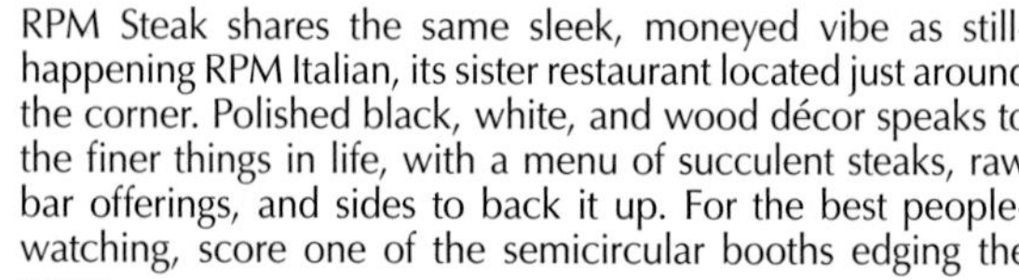

RPM Steak shares the same sleek, moneyed vibe as still-happening RPM Italian, its sister restaurant located just around the corner. Polished black, white, and wood décor speaks to the finer things in life, with a menu of succulent steaks, raw bar offerings, and sides to back it up. For the best people-watching, score one of the semicircular booths edging the room.

A massive single tiger prawn, served simply on ice with lemon, is a tasty, visually stunning starter. Steaks range from petite filets to dry-aged 24-ounce cowboy cuts with a list of big reds to match. Highlights include the classic, deeply satisfying steak frites, tender and pink inside, charred outside, and complemented by truffle béarnaise for the meat and Caesar dip for the fries.

Sable Kitchen & Bar

American XX

E3

505 N. State St. (at Illinois St.)

Phone: 312-755-9704 — Lunch & dinner daily
Web: www.sablechicago.com
Price: $$ — Grand (Red)

Tucked into the spacious and beautiful Hotel Palomar, Sable Kitchen & Bar is a sleek, sultry, and sophisticated number, fitted with different dining areas. There's the stunning 40-foot bar, tricked out in gorgeous dark paneling, soft leather seats, and unique light fixtures. The expansive dining room is equally elegant and urbane, attracting date-night duos looking for more intimacy or friends catching up over dinner.

An evening in this kitchen team's very capable hands might entail a decadently spicy and wonderfully complex starter of shrimp and roasted squash curry. Then diners may graduate to crispy, juicy adobo pork belly, served with sticky rice, and a pickled green papaya salad topped with a fried farm egg.

Side Door

Gastropub XX

F2

100 E. Ontario St. (at Rush St.)

Phone: 312-787-6768 Lunch & dinner daily
Web: www.sidedoorchicago.com
Price: $$ Grand (Red)

In a city with no shortage of steakhouses, Side Door dares to be different. It's the casual arm of Lawry's in the historic McCormick Mansion, offering the same quality and service without the power lunch vibe. Comfy leather banquettes and wide wooden tables are well spaced throughout the bi-level restaurant, offering a respite for shoppers to relax with a cheese plate and craft beer flight.

Share an order of prime rib poutine among friends—it's drenched in beef gravy and pepper jack cheese—or go whole hog with the prime rib sandwich, which is hand-carved to order and presented tableside with horseradish cream and *au jus*. For something lighter but just as pleasurable, try the kale Caesar, with white anchovies and a delicately creamy garlic dressing.

Siena Tavern

Italian XX

E4

51 W. Kinzie St. (at Dearborn St.)

Phone: 312-595-1322 Lunch & dinner daily
Web: www.sienatavern.com
Price: $$ Merchandise Mart

With a glitzy bar and cozy semicircular booths, this is where rustic Italian meets contemporary glam. The service and vibe are warmer than the pizza oven open to the room.

There is something for everyone on this menu, including an expansive selection of antipasti, salads, and pasta. Seasonal soups are excellent, like the smooth roasted butternut squash drizzled with truffle-chestnut gremolata. Pizzas arrive with a thin, fire-licked crust that is gently charred and puffed, perhaps creatively topped with a sauce-free mix of caramelized Brussels sprouts, roasted garlic, corn, gooey Taleggio, and white truffle oil. Brunch-time monkey bread is so sticky, sweet and oozing with caramel, candied hazelnuts, and whipped cream, that it must be eaten with a spoon.

Sixteen ✿✿

Contemporary

401 N. Wabash Ave. (bet. Hubbard St. & the Chicago River)

Phone: 312-588-8030
Web: www.trumpchicagohotel.com
Price: **$$$$**

Lunch daily
Dinner Tue – Sun
State/Lake

Dinner at Sixteen is many things: contemplative, memorable, delicious and, perhaps most importantly, fun. One thing it's not? Formulaic. And though Chef Thomas Lents' formidable talents are evident at first bite, each new dish begins to form a bigger picture until the chef's vision comes together to create an experience that's as fluid as it is sublime.

Nestled into the 16th floor of the Trump International Hotel & Tower, the space is dramatic and impressive. Guests walk through a glass-enclosed foyer lined with wine bottles to find a dining room centered around a striking Swarovski chandelier that hangs over a curved wall of African rosewood; and panoramic windows overlooking the city's twinkling skyline.

The nightly tasting menu is a showcase of thought-provoking flavor combinations, not to mention technical precision. The cuisine is contemporary American, but French techniques abound; courses are plated or finished tableside, offering guests a peek at the process. If Peking duck breast with chestnut, pear and citron; scallop blossom with sake cream and Espelette pepper; or roulade of hen and foie gras in cabbage with sunchoke duxelles and maitakes come to mind, you're on the right track.

Slurping Turtle

Japanese 

116 W. Hubbard St. (bet. Clark & LaSalle Sts.)

Phone: 312-464-0466 Lunch & dinner daily
Web: www.slurpingturtle.com
Price: ⇔ Merchandise Mart

Both turtles and noodles symbolize longevity, so a meal here should add a few years to your life (and warmth to your belly). Inside, diners sit elbow-to-elbow at sleek communal tables, but there are also a handful of booths along one wall as well as a glass mezzanine with a view of the dining room below. Boutique beverages like Hitachino Nest beer and Ramuné bubble-gum soda bring smiles to patrons in the know.

The menu of Japanese comfort food is compact, featuring a few ramen bowls, sashimi, maki, as well as hot and cold small plates for snacking and sharing. Then *bao* filled with smoky-glazed pork belly and pickled veggies arrive fluffy and piping hot, while deep-fried Brussels sprouts are crispy outside, tender inside, and finished with fried shallots.

Sumi Robata Bar

Japanese 

702 N. Wells St. (at Huron St.)

Phone: 312-988-7864 Lunch Sun – Fri
Web: www.sumirobatabar.com Dinner nightly
Price: $$ Chicago (Brown)

There's a degree of authenticity to this traditional *robata* bar and that includes the discreet entrance, although a spacious patio ultimately lets you know you're not in downtown Tokyo. Sit at the counter to best appreciate their specialty—the Japanese art of grilling. For a good value lunch look no further than the bento boxes, but come at night and you'll be able to try a variety of grilled items where the natural flavors shine through everything, from Wagyu beef to crab. You can also try more unusual cuts that you may hitherto have avoided, such as chicken heart or tail.

The service is smiley, helpful, and sincere. The guys behind the counter have a more serious countenance—well, good grilling is serious business.

Sunda

Fusion XX

110 W. Illinois St. (bet. Clark & LaSalle Sts.)

Phone: 312-644-0500 Lunch & dinner daily
Web: www.sundachicago.com
Price: $$ Grand (Red)

The Sunda shelf, an underwater outcropping that stretches along the coastline of Southeast Asia, connects the countries that provide culinary inspiration for this enormous River North lounge and restaurant. The beautiful people are naturally attracted to the clubby vibe Sunda radiates, complete with thumping music and a wide range of cocktail and sake selections.

The seafood is as fresh as the vibe is sultry, with numerous raw and cooked options like tempura rock shrimp tossed with candied walnuts in a creamy honey aïoli; or maki like the "tail of two tunas" pairing yellowfin and super white tuna with pickled jalapeños and fried shallots. Meat-eaters won't go hungry with creative plates like lemongrass beef lollipops and oxtail potstickers.

Tortoise Club

American XXX

E4

350 N. State St. (bet. Kinzie St. & the Chicago River)

Phone: 312-755-1700 Lunch Mon – Fri
Web: www.tortoiseclub.com Dinner nightly
Price: $$$ State/Lake

Every city needs a restaurant with the word "club" in the title—somewhere reassuringly old-school where you'd take your future father-in-law or anyone else you need to impress. Tortoise Club fits the bill perfectly. If it was just a few years older, it would be called an institution because it also harks back to more dissolute times; order a Negroni at lunchtime here and no one will bat an eyelid.

The place has an unapologetically masculine look thanks to the mahogany paneling and dark leather seating. It has a lounge bar with nightly live jazz and a familiar menu of American classics, from big plates of seafood to great steaks. Where it differs from many similar spots is that here the service is sprightly and sincere and the welcome is warm.

Topolobampo ✿

Mexican XX

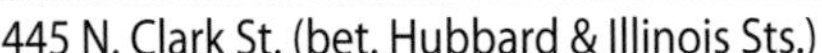

D3

445 N. Clark St. (bet. Hubbard & Illinois Sts.)

Phone: 312-661-1434 — Lunch Tue – Fri
Web: www.rickbayless.com — Dinner Tue – Sat
Price: **$$$$** — Grand (Red)

This jewel in the Bayless culinary crown welcomes a rush of serious eaters for original south-of-the-border food with an upscale twist. While it may share an entrance and bar with sibling Frontera Grill, that is where the likeness ends. This elegant, terra cotta-lined dining room feels worlds away from the fiesta upfront.

Lunches are more laid-back, while dinners feature multi-course tasting menus that demonstrate the full range of this kitchen's capabilities. The regional Mexican fare boasts a panoply of flavors, colors, and textures that are refined yet respect authenticity. The fish *a la Talla* is unbeatable, rubbed with spicy red chili adobo, grilled over a wood fire, and set in a pool of raw tomato and *chile de arbol* sauce that is a bright contrast to the spicy fish. Thin, eggy *crepas* arrive wrapped around crushed caramelized plantains and are drizzled with sticky-sweet homemade *cajeta* caramel, topped with a dollop of cream, *queso fresco* crumbles, and quenelle of *cajeta* ice cream.

It is no secret that cocktails here are noteworthy (margarita, anyone?), but teetotalers get equal attention with sweet and tangy *agua fresca* splashed with tropical juices that will be among the best you've had.

Travelle

330 N. Wabash Ave. (bet. Kinzie St. & the Chicago River)

Phone: 312-923-7705 — Lunch & dinner daily
Web: www.travellechicago.com
Price: $$$ — Grand (Red)

This contemporary Mediterranean dining room shares its home—a landmark Mies van der Rohe tower completed in 1972—with The Langham hotel. Floor-to-ceiling windows on the second floor space offer views of Marina City, but with its stunning kitchen displayed behind gradient glass panels, the scene inside is equally dramatic.

Creative add-ins bring flair and flavor to flawlessly executed and gorgeously composed dishes. A perfect, toothsome champagne risotto is enlivened by juicy, barely pickled grapes and toasted Marcona almonds, while a thick, creamy tranche of seared salmon rests on "healthy" fried green farro, finished with a tangy drizzle of spicy soy-mustard. Raspberry coulis and meringue shards are an ideal garnish for a fresh and zesty citrus tart.

Union Sushi + Barbeque Bar

Japanese

C2

230 W. Erie St. (at Franklin St.)

Phone: 312-662-4888 — Lunch Mon – Fri
Web: www.eatatunion.com — Dinner nightly
Price: $$ — Chicago (Brown)

The slogan of this big, bustling restaurant is "Uniting Japanese culinary tradition with a distinctly American persona," which roughly translates to "Japanese food with a party hat on." The cocktails are good, the noise levels are high, and there are more tattoos in the room than a Yakuza convention.

The menu will take forever to read so just go directly to their two specialties—the assorted sushi rolls, some of which use black rice, and meats and fish expertly cooked over an open flame on the seriously hot *robata*. The ingredients are good and the flavor combinations don't get silly. Just remember that sharing is the key to keeping that final check in check, especially as the T-shirted staff are masters of upselling with an iPad.

Untitled Supper Club

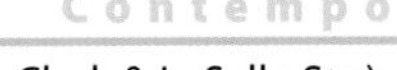

Contemporary XX

111 W. Kinzie St. (bet. Clark & LaSalle Sts.)

Phone: 312-880-1511 Dinner Mon – Sat
Web: www.untitledchicago.com
Price: $$ Merchandise Mart

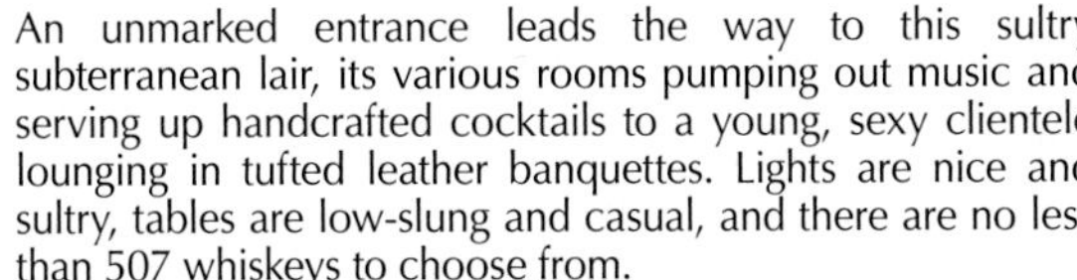

An unmarked entrance leads the way to this sultry subterranean lair, its various rooms pumping out music and serving up handcrafted cocktails to a young, sexy clientele lounging in tufted leather banquettes. Lights are nice and sultry, tables are low-slung and casual, and there are no less than 507 whiskeys to choose from.

A charcuterie board may offer up silky duck rillettes, shot through with foie gras; textured and spreadable liverwurst; as well as thin slices of prosciutto and *coppa* accompanied by a house-made *mostarda*. Overstuffed squash blossom *rellenos* are filled with creamy ricotta and served over Agave-spiked corn relish and chili-lime *crema*. Don't miss the scrumptious meatloaf sandwich, slathered with Korean-style ketchup, and laced with rosemary-infused aïoli.

Look for the symbol for a brilliant breakfast to start your day off right.

Streeterville

Bound by the strategically set Chicago River, swanky Magnificent Mile, and sparkling Lake Michigan, Streeterville is a precious quarter in the Windy City, housing hotels and high-rise residences alongside offices, universities, and museums. If that doesn't bespeak cultural diversity, the sights and smells at Water Tower Place's **Foodlife** offer indisputable proof. Located on the mezzanine floor of the shopping mall, this simple food court has been elevated to an art form. A veritable "United Nations of food courts," Foodlife draws a devoted following to its 14 different kitchens that whip up everything from Chinese potstickers and deep-dish pizza to crispy fried chicken. Unlike

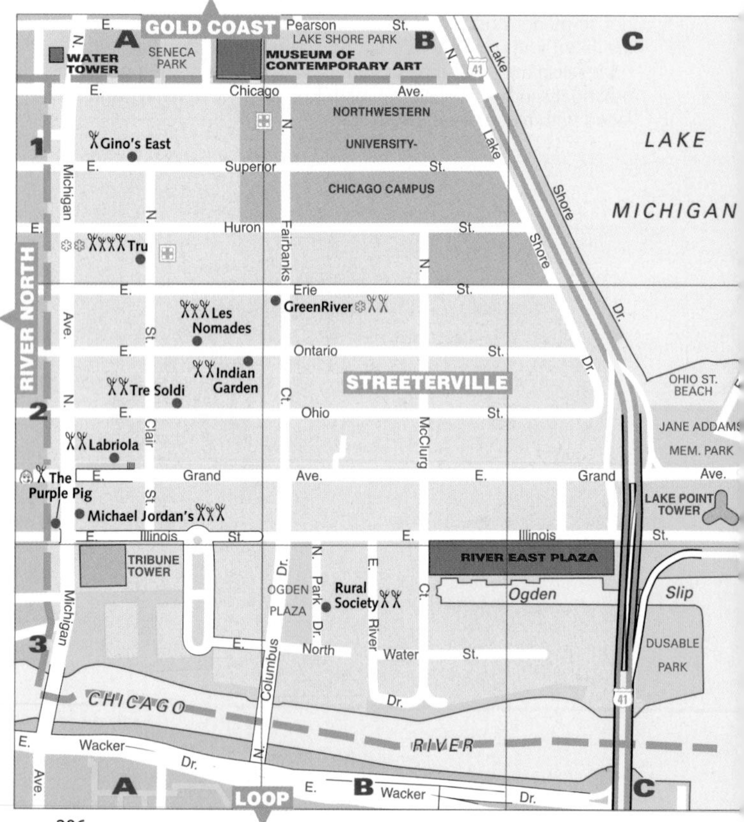

other food courts, you're given a card that can be swiped at as many stalls as you choose. Once you've had your fill, bring the card to the cash registers to receive your balance, and *voila*—a single bill to pay! Another notable tenant of Water Tower Place is **Wow Bao**, a spot known to dole out some of the best steamed veggie- and meat-filled buns in town. In fact, they were so popular that four locations sprouted downtown.

Hopping skyscrapers, the **John Hancock Center** is another iconic tower known to many as a "food lover's

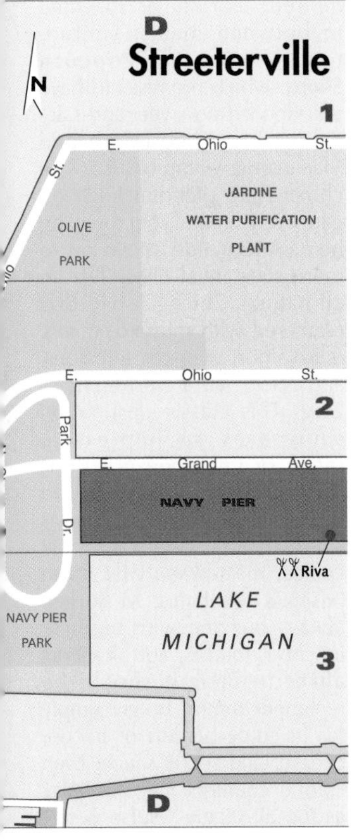

paradise." Here, lucky locals can choose to dine with fine wine at **Volare Ristorante Italiano**; while bachelors in business suits may shop for groceries with sky-high prices to match the staggering view at **Potash Brothers** (open to residents only). For those whose tastes run more toward champagne and cocktails than cheeseburgers and crinkle-cut fries, there's always the **Signature Lounge**, located on the 96th floor of the John Hancock Center. A sensational setting for delicious nightcaps, this sleek spot also proffers an incredible brunch, lunch, dinner, and dessert menu that employs some of the finest ingredients around town. While their creative cocktails may result in sticker shock, one peek at the sparkling cityscape will have you...at hello.

ART & CULTURE

The Museum of Contemporary Art is located next to Lake Shore Park, the city's outdoor recreational extravaganza. Well-known for housing the

world's leading collection of contemporary art, patrons here know to balance the gravitas of the setting with fresh nourishment at cute and casual **MCA Cafe**. But, it's also the peppers and potatoes that lure foodies to the farmer's market, held at the museum every Tuesday from June through October. Choose to bookend a home-cooked meal with some dark chocolate decadence at **Godiva Chocolatier**—a beautiful boutique carrying it all from chocolate-covered strawberries and truffles, to gourmet biscuits, chocolate bars, and snacks.

The world convenes at Chicago's lakefront **Navy Pier** for a day of exploration and eats. Showcasing lush gardens and parks in conjunction with shops and dining stalls, families usually flock to **Bubba Gump Shrimp Co.** for its convivial vibe and shrimp specials. But, locals looking for live music with their carnitas and margaritas may head to **Jimmy Buffett's Margaritaville Bar & Grill** (named after the rockstar himself). For stellar snacking in between meals, venture towards **Garrett Popcorn Shops**, which promises to have you hooked on sweet-and-salty flavors like CheeseCorn and Macadamia CaramelCrisp. The choices are plentiful and you can even create your own tin here. Afterwards, move on to more substantial chow like an all-natural Chicago-style dog (slathered with mustard, onion, relish, sport peppers, tomatoes, and celery salt) from **America's Dog**. This classic destination showcases an impressive range of city-style creations from Houston, New York, and Philadelphia, to Detroit, Kansas City, and San Francisco. Of course, meat-lovers who mean business never miss **M Burger**, always buzzing with business lunchers, tourists, and shoppers alike. In fact, it should be renamed "mmm" burger simply for its juicy parcels of bacon, cheese, and secret sauce. Even calorie counters may rest easy as the all-veggie "Nurse Betty" is nothing short of crave-worthy. For a bit more intimacy and a lot more fantasy, **Sayat Nova** is superb. Highlighting a range of *kibbee* alongside more exotic signatures like *sarma* or meat- and veggie-filled grape leaves bobbing in a light garlic sauce, this Middle Eastern marvel keeps its options limited but fan-base infinite.

Residents know that Chicago is big on breakfast—so big that they can even have it for dinner at Michigan Avenue's **West Egg**. This convivial café-cum-coffee corridor serves three meals a day, but it is their breakfast specials (choose between pancakes, waffles, or other "eggcellent" dishes) that keep the joint jumping at all times. Finally, the Northwestern Memorial Hospital complex is another esteemed establishment that dominates the local scene. Besides its top medical services, a parade of dining gems (think coffee shops, lounges, and ethnic canteens) catering to their staff, students, and visitors looms large over this neighborhood—and lake.

Gino's East

162 E. Superior St. (bet. Michigan Ave. & St. Clair St.)

Phone: 312-266-3337 Lunch & dinner daily
Web: www.ginoseast.com
Price: $$ Chicago (Red)

Pizza pilgrims continue to make the trek to the original location of this renowned local deep-dish chain, where a 45 minute wait is the norm. However, solo diners may rest easy as they can order personal pies from a walk-up counter. The walls, scribbled with years of graffiti, are nearly as iconic as the high-walled pies themselves, whose crusts get their signature crunch from cornmeal and searing-hot metal pans with two inch-high sides.

Filled with heaps of mozzarella and toppings like the "Meaty Legend" lineup of spicy pepperoni, Italian sausage, and both Canadian and regular bacon before getting sauced, it's hard for some to eat more than two wedges here. Nonconformists can of course opt for thin-crust pies, gussied-up by add-ons like roasted red peppers.

Indian Garden

Indian 

A2

247 E. Ontario St. (bet. Fairbanks Ct. & St. Clair St.)

Phone: 312-280-4910 Lunch & dinner daily
Web: www.indiangardenchicago.com
Price: $$ Grand (Red)

Frequent diners know it as "The IG," but first-timers will appreciate the copious lunch buffet as much as the doctors, med students, and locals. These faithful droves routinely make the trip up a few flights of stairs to get their *pakora* and tandoori fix, among kitschy but ornate touches like richly colored fabrics and wafting incense.

Though the à la carte menu offers Northern Indian dishes brought to the table in shiny copper vessels, the lunch buffet covers all bases with vegetarian, chicken, and lamb items. Staples like *saag, dal,* naan, and basmati rice are freshly made. *Bhuna gosht* mixes succulent lamb with tomatoes, onions, and spices; while *lassi* or masala tea provides refreshment along with a decent selection of wine, beer, and cocktails.

GreenRiver 

American XX

259 E. Erie St., 18th fl. (at Fairbanks Ct.)

Phone: 312-337-0101
Web: www.greenriverchi.com
Price: $$$

Lunch daily
Dinner Mon – Sat
Grand (Red)

When a cocktail carte is arranged by grains (corn, rye, agave) rather than the spirits made from them, a serious focus on drinking is immediately clear—and we should expect no less from the mixology gurus behind New York City's The Dead Rabbit. Your cocktails, wines, and green cardamom sodas are going to be masterpieces, yet the cuisine is anything but an afterthought.

Whether you make it to a table or just end up staying at the bar, be sure to order some of the city's most luscious beef tartare, topped with shaved horseradish, quail egg yolk, and judiciously dressed with capers, anchovies, and onion. If you prefer your meat perfectly cooked, try the Slagel Farm ribeye, carved tableside and set in a pool of rich bone marrow jus and draped atop cippollini, mushrooms, and a potato purée. Desserts are refreshing and none-too-sweet, like the wintery citrus *chiboust* garnished with sugared cranberries, fennel fronds, and red-veined sorrel leaves—surrounded by a nest of crisp-baked pastry threads.

And even though lunch may seem corporate, the 18th-floor location commands panoramic views of the city and is ideal at all times of day. In fine weather, the wraparound terrace is unbeatable.

Labriola

Italian XX

A2

535 N. Michigan Ave. (at Grand Ave.)

Phone: 312-955-3100 Lunch & dinner daily
Web: www.labriolacafe.com
Price: $$ Grand (Red)

Supersizing his popular Oak Brook café, baker Rich Labriola expands his eponymous empire just off Michigan Avenue. The hangar-sized space is three operations in one: a café for pastries and casual bites; a bar; and a full-scale restaurant. Though the décor takes cues from French brasseries, the menus have a decidedly Italian focus.

No matter where you're seated, you can sample the quality imported *salumi* and *formaggio* selections like Parma ham and Granduca pecorino, accompanied by charred bread and sharp chutney. Neopolitan pizzas, *fritto misto*, and house-made pastas like *bucatini all'Amatriciana* don't disappoint. Tiramisù gets a new twist in a mélange of velvety smooth chocolate mousse, espresso-infused mascarpone, and coffee-soaked cake cubes.

Les Nomades

French XXX

A2

222 E. Ontario St. (bet. Fairbanks Ct. & St. Clair St.)

Phone: 312-649-9010 Dinner Tue – Sat
Web: www.lesnomades.net
Price: $$$$ Grand (Red)

A giddy excitement bubbles through the air at Les Nomades, and with good reason: this intimate, charming restaurant feels like a secret hideaway within a gated Streeterville brownstone. Owner Mary Beth Liccioni welcomes all as if they were old friends, seating guests among the graciously arranged fresh flowers, framed artwork, and linen-topped tables.

Though the fragrant herb-loaded lavash presented at each table is good enough to make an entire meal out of, save room for entrées like grilled Scottish salmon, served medium-rare with a colorful, flavorful blend of beets, cucumber, and black olive tapenade. A single translucent langoustine *raviolo* duets on a plate with tempura soft shell crab, both enhanced by harissa- and saffron-spiked rouille.

Michael Jordan's

Steakhouse

505 N. Michigan Ave. (bet. Grand Ave. & Illinois St.)

Phone: 312-321-8823 Lunch & dinner daily
Web: www.mjshchicago.com
Price: $$$ Grand (Red)

Leave your dated 1993 Bulls jersey in the closet for a meal at this swanky steakhouse, tucked just off the lobby of the InterContinental Hotel. Leather and velvet accents telegraph an upscale vibe, and references to His Airness are subtle—from oversized sepia photographs of basketball netting to a 23-layer chocolate cake for dessert.

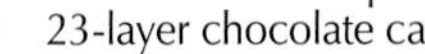

A glass of Amarone with a dry-aged Porterhouse is always a slam-dunk, but the kitchen also turns out pleasing modern twists on steakhouse classics. Chicago's famous Italian beef gets an upgrade with smoked ribeye and aged provolone. Similarly, the traditional wedge salad is presented as a halved small head of baby romaine, layered here with creamy Wisconsin blue cheese and thick slabs of crispy bacon.

The Purple Pig

Mediterranean

500 N. Michigan Ave. (at Illinois St.)

Phone: 312-464-1744 Lunch & dinner daily
Web: www.thepurplepigchicago.com
Price: $$ Chicago (Red)

No matter the time of day, this is a fave among groups craving first-rate Mediterranean cooking with drinks and a setting to match. Everything is tasty, fun, and great for sharing, so go with a posse and get a communal table all to yourselves. The bar is just as nice for solo dining, thanks to the chatty staff.

The menu covers a range of specialties from the Med, from panini to *a la plancha*. But, don't miss starting with the incredibly smart take on *cannolo* filled with whipped burrata, mixed with candied, puréed and ground pistachios, as well as a minty herb salsa and butternut squash. Also try tender and nicely charred octopus with green beans, fingerling potatoes, and salsa verde. Finally, delve into their selection of top-notch cheese and charcuterie.

Riva

D2 — Seafood XX

700 E. Grand Ave. (on Navy Pier)

Phone: 312-644-7482 — Lunch & dinner daily
Web: www.rivanavypier.com
Price: $$

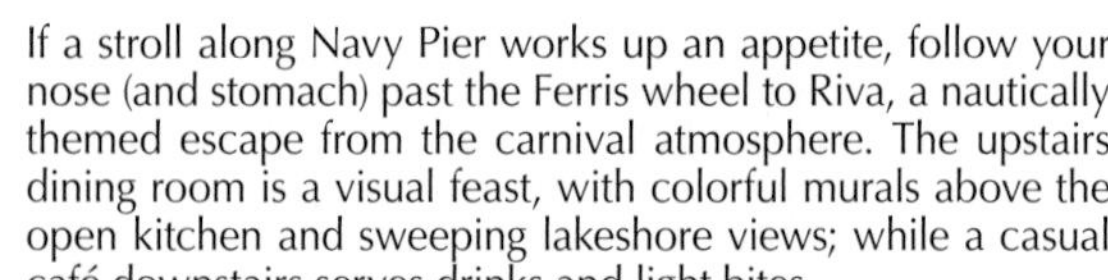

If a stroll along Navy Pier works up an appetite, follow your nose (and stomach) past the Ferris wheel to Riva, a nautically themed escape from the carnival atmosphere. The upstairs dining room is a visual feast, with colorful murals above the open kitchen and sweeping lakeshore views; while a casual café downstairs serves drinks and light bites.

Though the menu swims with seafood, Prime steaks and Italian-inspired dishes like pear-and-cheese agnolotti offer variety. Caper-studded Louis sauce augments a single plump cake of jumbo lump crab with a crisp side of Asian slaw. A fillet of Atlantic salmon is placed atop a vibrant plate and paired with cherry tomato fondue, a handful of quartered Brussels sprouts, and bite-sized potato *gnocchetti*.

Rural Society

B3 — Steakhouse XX

455 N. Park Dr. (bet. Illinois & North Water Sts.)

Phone: 312-840-6605 — Dinner nightly
Web: www.ruralsocietyrestaurant.com
Price: $$$ — Grand (Red)

This buzzy Argentinean steakhouse from prolific Chef Jose Garces brings a touch of international flair to Chicago's already meat-heavy roster. The ranch-inspired space is smart and upscale, with oversized iron chandeliers, framed photos of show cattle, and a painted wood kitchen from which a wood-fired oven and grill fill the air with a smoky aroma.

In addition to excellent cuts of beef, Rural Society grills up stellar Maine lobster, chicken, and chops, while the oven produces mouthwatering Argentinean pizzas and homemade-spiced sausages. Be sure to try the *plana di hierro* and *fritas*, a South American version of traditional steak frites that boasts a subtly smoky flavor and a creamy, chili-spiced butter dip for those crispy chips.

Tru ✿✿

Contemporary XXXX

676 N. St. Clair St. (bet. Erie & Huron Sts.)

Phone: 312-202-0001 Dinner Tue – Sat
Web: www.trurestaurant.com
Price: **$$$$** Chicago (Red)

Fine dining at Tru has an air of formality that extends from the service team to the moneyed and well-dressed clientele. Beyond the discreet exterior, find an intimate lounge with a vivid blue spotlit sculpture. Decorative branches and net curtains divide the cavernous space, while white walls adorned with Warhol lithographs lend a luxe-gallery feel. Leather and velvet banquettes surrounding well-spaced tables are popular for quiet gatherings or romantic interludes.

Chef Anthony Martin has been leading this kitchen for several years, but his cuisine remains fresh, exciting, and a perfect reflection of contemporary American cooking. His six- and eight-course fixed menus may highlight a classically French yet soigné sweet onion tart draped with thick shavings of black truffle, or a presentation of crisp golden pork belly with a dollop of rich stone-ground grits that allude to the American South. Don't be surprised if some of the best dishes here also happen to be the simplest, as in the incredibly supple Jidori chicken breast set in jus enriched with foie gras, alongside crisped oyster mushrooms and nutty wheatberries.

Conversely, the caviar offerings are wonderful and worth the price!

Tre Soldi

Italian XX

A2

212 E. Ohio St. (bet. Fairbanks Ct. & St. Clair St.)

Phone: 312-664-0212 Lunch & dinner daily
Web: www.tresoldichicago.com
Price: $$ Grand (Red)

Set a few steps above street level, Tre Soldi's tomato-red awning and floor-to-ceiling windows beckon Michigan Avenue shoppers and business lunchers. Inside, splashes of red-and-white refer subtly to those classic red-sauce joints complete with checkered tablecloths, but glossy ceramic-tiled columns and Italian stone floors up the ante.

Rome and its surroundings inspire the menu and all-Italian wine list. Local Slagel Family Farm's beef becomes carpaccio, shingled on the plate and drizzled with tangy mustard aïoli, fresh parsley, and celery leaves. Thin-crust pizzas strewn with quality ingredients like *cavolo nero*, featuring caramelized onions and pecorino, are large enough to share. Finish with dark chocolate-hazelnut tarts, perfectly balanced by apricot jam.

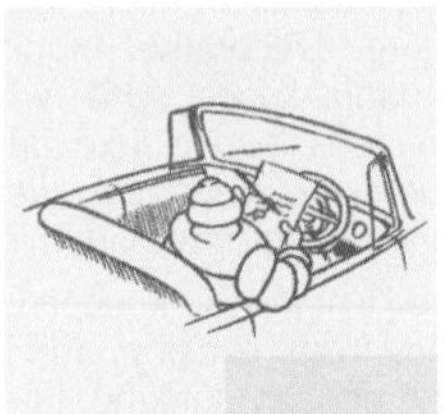

Avoid the search for parking. Look for .

West Loop

Once home to scores of warehouses and smoke-spewing factories, the West Loop today is arguably the most booming part of the Windy City, whirring with sleek art galleries, attractive lofts, hopping nightclubs, and cool, cutting-edge restaurants. Young residents may have replaced the struggling immigrants of yore; nevertheless, traces of ethnic flavor can still be found along these vibrant blocks. They certainly aren't as dominant as before—what a difference a century or two can make—but nearby Taylor Street continues to charm passersby, tourists, and residents alike with that timeless-turned-slightly kitschy feel. Imagine the likes of delis, groceries, and food stops galore and you will start to get the picture.

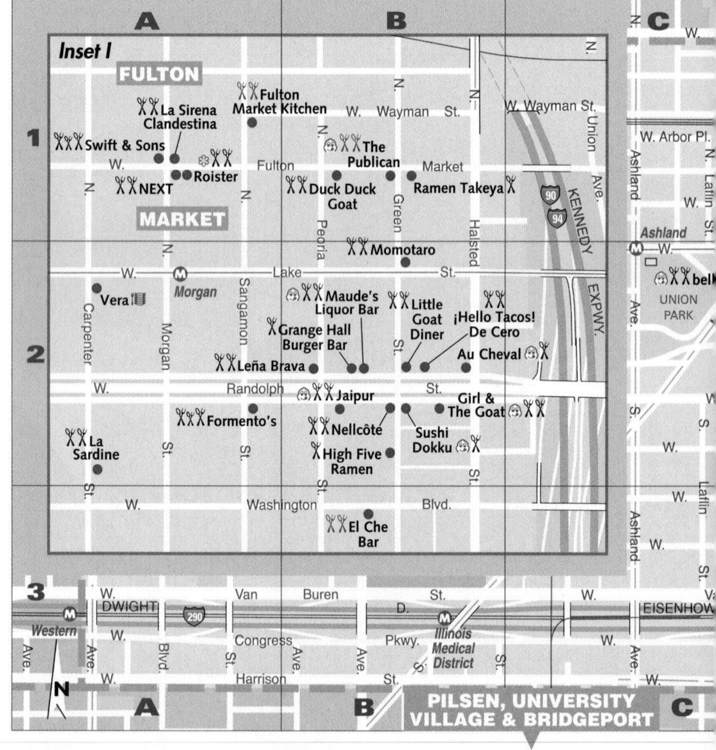

A MEDITERRANEAN MARVEL

For tasty, Mediterranean-inspired munching, make your way to Greektown where everybody's Greek, even if it's just for the day. Shout "opa" at the **Taste of Greece** festival held each August, or while away an afternoon at the always-packed **Parthenon**. Its moniker may not signal ingenuity, but the menu is groaning with gyros, signature lamb dishes, and even flaming *saganaki*, displaying serious showmanship. Sound all too Greek to you? Venture beyond the Mediterranean and into "Restaurant Row" along Randolph Street, where culinary treasures hide among beautiful, fine dining establishments. Whet your appetite with everything from sushi to subs—this mile-long sandwich breed is a best seller bursting with salty meats at **J.P. Graziano's**. Don't let their long lines deter you; instead, take your smoky temptation to **West Loop Salumi** and let their platters of glistening cured treats do the trick.

If all else fails, round-up say 1,000 of your closest friends for meze at one of the Moroccan spots nearby. Wash down West Randolph's exquisite eats with intricately crafted sips at **The**

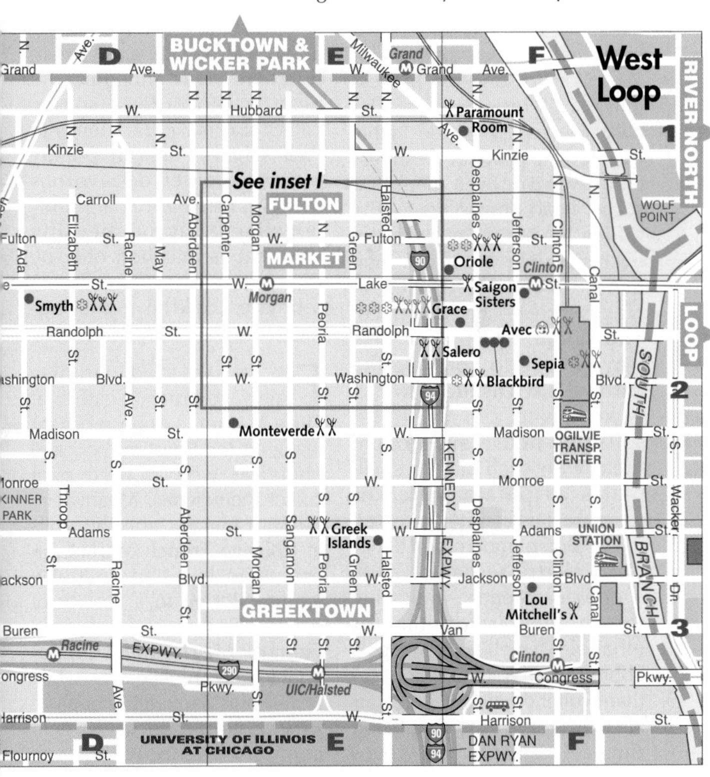

Aviary. This bar in West Fulton Market is the brainchild of Chef Grant Achatz, and boy is it a charmer. Noted as much for its expert bartenders and their spherical concoctions as for its tedious reservation process (this is a Kokonas business, after all!), The Aviary is also highly devoted to product freshness and flavor. For even more of a scene, head downstairs to **The Office**, a super secret and super exclusive bar, before settling in for an intimate dinner at Next's private dining space, **The Room**. Some carousers may choose to continue the party at **CH Distillery**, which is known to cull the finest spirits in-house and couple them with such simple small plates as potato pancakes to more lavish bites like red caviar atop pumpernickel blinis. Nerd alert: the name CH is a double entendre indicating the molecular formula for ethanol as well as Chicago's abbreviation. Rather whip it up than wolf it down? Beef up your kitchen skills at the **Calphalon Culinary Center**, where groups can arrange for private hands-on instruction. After mastering the bœuf Bourguignon, get in line at **Olympia Meat Packers** (also known as Olympia Meats), or stroll into **Peoria Packing**, a veritable meat cooler where butchers slice and dice the best cuts to order. Aspiring cooks also make the rounds to Paul Kahan's **Publican Quality Meats**, another carnivorous mecca, filled with a mind-boggling array of specialty eats that is matched only by the spectacular setting. Think: intimate cocktail gathering-meets-extravagant dinner party.

For artisan food paradise savvy gourmands gather at **Dose Market**, a pop-up bazaar featuring the finest in food and chefs (as well as their own secret ingredients). Meanwhile, treasure hunters troll the stalls at **Chicago French Market**, an epicurean hub and multi-use arena catering to a variety of palates. Red meat fiends love **Fumaré Meats and Deli** for traditionally smoked cuts, while health-nuts can't get enough of **Raw**, a grab-n-go vegan gem committed to providing the healthiest food money can buy.

Moving beyond the market, even the most die-hard dieters need a lil' sugar and nearby **Glazed and Infused**, an early member of the current donut craze, is sublime. Then, spice things up at the flagrantly sexy **RM Champagne Salon**.

BEER & THE BALLGAME

Hoops fans whoop it up at Bulls games at the United Center, also home to the Blackhawks. Depending on the score, the most exciting part of the night is post-game, binging with buddies over beer and bar food. **The Aberdeen Tap**, for instance, is a neighborhood hangout where everybody knows your name as well as the exceptional selection of beers on tap—they boast over 65 brews. But, be sure to also take your more finicky pals to **Rhine Hall**, a boutique brandy distillery run by father-and-daughter duo. Finally, those who prefer a little brawl with their beer will fall for **Twisted Spoke**, a proverbial biker bar with tattoos and 'tudes to match. The music is loud and drinks are plentiful, but it's all in good testosterone- and alcohol-fueled fun.

Au Cheval

American

B2

800 W. Randolph St. (at Halsted St.)

Phone: 312-929-4580 — Lunch & dinner daily
Web: www.auchevalchicago.com
Price: $$ — Morgan

This corner bar on Randolph Street's restaurant row may be dim, but it's got a few glittering edges. The reel-to-reel in the doorway lends a retro feel, but the rest is decidedly cushy. Late-night revelers prefer to sit at tufted leather booths or savor beers at the zinc-topped bar, rather than endure a wait for a table in the raucous space. Bartenders work just as hard as line cooks until the wee hours.

The kitchen puts a highfalutin spin on simple bar eats. In-house butchers craft 32-ounce pork Porterhouses for sharing; foie gras for folding into fluffy scrambled eggs; and house-made sausages for bologna sandwiches that go well beyond a kid's wildest dreams. Thin griddled cheeseburger patties are perked up by maple syrup-glazed peppered bacon.

Avec

Mediterranean

F2

615 W. Randolph St. (bet. Desplaines & Jefferson Sts.)

Phone: 312-377-2002 — Lunch Sun
Web: www.avecrestaurant.com — Dinner nightly
Price: $$ — Clinton (Green/Pink)

Fans have been clamoring for the dinner plates at this West Randolph mainstay for more than a decade—and now that lunch is on the menu, it's official: Avec is a non-stop hangout. It's a fun vibe, as diners are tightly packed at a long counter and communal seating in the chic wood plank encased room; servers do a good job attending to the crowd.

Mediterranean flavors factor prominently in the kitchen's stimulating creations, like a kale and carrot salad dressed with delightfully herbaceous and spicy green harissa as well as sunflower seeds for crunch. A thick slice of excellent whole grain bread spread with walnut-beet *muhamarra* is the foundation of an open-faced roasted salmon sandwich. Other delights—there are many—come and go with the seasons.

bellyQ

Asian XX

C2

1400 W. Randolph St. (at Ogden Ave.)

Phone: 312-563-1010
Web: www.bellyqchicago.com
Price: $$

Lunch Sun
Dinner nightly
Ashland (Green/Pink)

This end of West Randolph Street might be quiet, but it's always a party inside bellyQ. The volume and energy are high throughout the lofty, concrete-heavy space with tabletop hibachi booths and industrial metal seating. A wall-length horse-themed screen separates the restaurant from casual sister spot Urban Belly, which shares the open kitchen.

As imagined by prolific Chef/owner Bill Kim, the Asian barbecue experience at bellyQ takes its form in a number of genre-melding shareable plates. A side of *bibimbap*-style sticky rice is crunchy and tender, tossed with glistening slices of Chinese sausage and generously sprinkled with *togarashi*. Chewy chunks of brownie in vanilla soft-serve are drizzled with caramel-balsamic-soy "Seoul sauce" for a savory twist.

Duck Duck Goat

Chinese XX

B1

857 W. Fulton Market (bet. Green & Peoria Sts.)

Phone: 312-902-3825
Web: www.duckduckgoatchicago.com
Price: $$

Dinner nightly
Morgan

The latest in hometown hero Stephanie Izard's foodie empire is a runaway hit. Duck Duck Goat isn't by-the-books authentic, but one bite and you might think her creative, fun, and mouthwatering version of Chinese fare deserves its own category. The space is an attractive take on Chinoiserie—numerous seating areas, like a dramatic red alcove and an intimate lounge with green tile and lacquered walls, come together to form a terrific, eclectic space.

The regional Chinese menu is ample, offering upwards of 50 items, including dim sum like wood-fired *char siu* ribs; cold dishes like pickled vegetables; or creative noodles like goat belly *lo mein*. Don't miss the spot-on seafood rice or even the Peking duck, offered as a family-style large plate.

Blackbird ✿

F2 Contemporary XX

619 W. Randolph St. (bet. Desplaines & Jefferson Sts.)

Phone: 312-715-0708 Lunch Mon – Fri
Web: www.blackbirdrestaurant.com Dinner nightly
Price: **$$$** Clinton (Green/Pink)

In many ways, an acclaimed restaurant that opened in 1997 may seem like old news, but Chef/owner Paul Kahan continues to enliven this Chicago original with fresh talent and new flavor.

The space is small but packed, right down to the last lunchtime bar stool. Everything feels glossy and white, accented with high-back leather banquettes and orange place mats at the bar that pop with color. Service is sharp, busy, and handling it all very well. Meals may begin with a symphony of flavors in what appears to be a breakfast sausage patty. However, this golden-brown rabbit sausage is coarsely ground and intensely savory, fragrant with sage and pepper, set over gnocchi dressed in creamed parsley root topped with a bit of "bread and butter" pickled fennel. Slightly crisped grilled monkfish has an almost Californian sensibility, with puntarelle, shaved persimmon, sunchoke, and a dollop of green basil foam. Inspired by the yeasty baked doughnuts of the Czech Republic, Blackbird's version of *kolache* is light, sweet, and filled with what tastes like a perfect slice of cheesecake.

Dinner may be served as a ten-course tasting menu that shows just what this capable kitchen can do. Lunch is an astounding bargain.

El Che Bar

Latin American

845 W. Washington Blvd. (bet. Green & Peoria Sts.)

Phone: 312-265-1130 — Dinner nightly
Web: www.elchebarchicago.com
Price: $$$ — Morgan

This love letter to Argentine cooking arrives courtesy of Chef John Manion (of La Sirena Clandestina), who spent much of his childhood in Sao Paulo, Brazil and traveling through South America. Look beyond the obvious Checker Taxi signage to find El Che Bar hidden in plain sight. Its long, narrow space is lined with black brick, white mortar, wood slats and leads to an enormous blazing open-hearth oven in the rear. Tiny votives and hanging tropical plants warm the room.

Big knives are a must for any good Argentinian meal, and El Che Bar is no exception. Meat plays a big role on this menu, so try the tender, braised lamb ribs, their edges charred to a beautiful crisp in the hearth, then paired with fennel salad and yogurt-mint relish.

Formento's

Italian

925 W. Randolph St. (at Sangamon St.)

Phone: 312-690-7295 — Lunch Sun
Web: www.formentos.com — Dinner nightly
Price: $$$ — Morgan

This fresh venue is an old soul at heart, a retro-cool den where you half expect to see Frank, Dean, and Sammy downing martinis in a corner booth. Appointed with tanned leather banquettes, crisply dressed tables, and terra-cotta-tiled floors, the scene is an enticing one in which to sup on remarkable red-sauced food.

Proving that throwback doesn't equate tired, the menu is an inspired collection of renovated favorites. Crab-and-artichoke dip arrives with house-made "Ritz" crackers; while eggplant parmesan is a fine-tuned layering of fried eggplant slices and house-pulled mozzarella that's accompanied by spaghetti draped with delicious pomodoro sauce. A refreshing spin on saltimbocca reveals pancetta-wrapped quail and leaves nothing to be desired.

Fulton Market Kitchen

Contemporary XX

A1

311 N. Sangamon St. (at Wayman St.)

Phone: 312-733-6900 Dinner Mon – Sat
Web: www.fultonmarketkitchen.com
Price: $$$ Morgan

Fulton Market Kitchen epitomizes the term "feast for the eyes." The interior explodes with colorful graffiti murals and quirky wood-and-steel assemblages. Fixtures like paint-dripped tables repurposed from bowling alleys and old barn doors complement the eye-catching display.

A cocktail list with sections like "Oldies but Goodies" and "The Art of the Old Fashioned" shines with an array of Kentucky whiskeys served in frosty rocks glasses with hand-cut ice. In addition to small plates, pasta, and main dishes, the menu offers items "for the table" such as an earthen *cazuela* filled with a combination of creamy beans, thick strips of bacon, and grilled ciabatta. Playful desserts include freshly fried doughnut holes and vanilla ice cream splashed with coffee.

Girl & The Goat

Contemporary XX

B2

809 W. Randolph St. (bet. Green & Halsted Sts.)

Phone: 312-492-6262 Dinner nightly
Web: www.girlandthegoat.com
Price: $$ Morgan

The revolving door never stops turning as Girl & The Goat's party keeps going. Even on a Monday night, guests linger for hours, shouting over the din at this sceney but always friendly stunner. Appropriately rustic wooden pillars and beams connect a warren of seating areas, from elevated platforms to banquettes to dim private corner nooks.

A pick-your-own-protein adventure, the menu is organized by ingredient with a dedicated section for goat. Start with freshly baked ham bread with smoked Swiss-cheese butter seasoned with coarse mustard and olive tapenade, then end with an almost pudding-like "all leches" cake with a scoop of strawberry-rhubarb sorbet. The kitchen will even send out mini portions of menu items for solo diners—a truly thoughtful touch.

Grace ✿✿✿

652 W. Randolph St. (bet. Desplaines & Halsted Sts.)

Phone: 312-234-9494 Dinner Tue – Sat
Web: www.grace-restaurant.com
Price: $$$$ Clinton (Green/Pink)

Ask a passing foodie to name one of Chicago's most elegant and sophisticated restaurants and they'll probably say Grace. This room is as handsome as it is urbane and provides a supremely comfortable environment for those spending an evening discovering the culinary wizardry of Curtis Duffy.

You'll be presented with a choice between two seasonally changing menus: "Fauna" or, for vegetarians, "Flora." Opt for the wine pairings and you're done on the decision making for the night. Trying to keep track of the ingredients of each dish will nullify the benefit of the wine, so instead just marvel at the clever presentation and dig in—because taste is what this food is all about. The dishes are intricate and elaborately constructed, with herbs playing an integral part rather than merely being a garnish. Occasionally your taste buds will get a little slap, perhaps with the odd Thai or Vietnamese flavor, and the courses will fly by.

This style of cooking is very labor-intensive and if you want to learn more, then take advantage of their offer of a postprandial kitchen tour.

Grange Hall Burger Bar

B2

844 W. Randolph St. (bet. Green & Peoria Sts.)

Phone: 312-491-0844 — Lunch Tue – Sun
Web: www.grangehallburgerbar.com — Dinner Tue – Sat
Price: $$ — Morgan

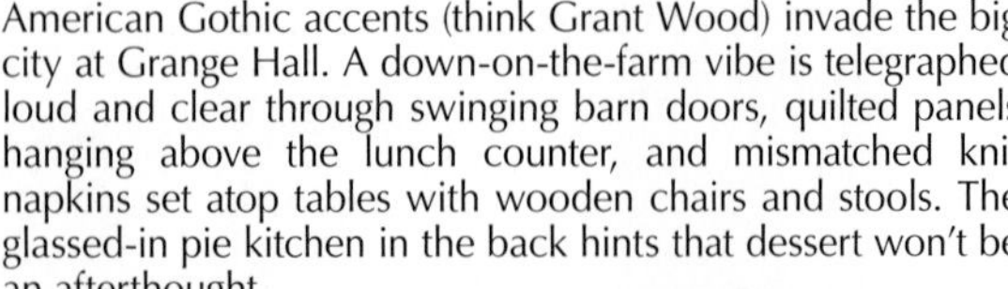

American Gothic accents (think Grant Wood) invade the big city at Grange Hall. A down-on-the-farm vibe is telegraphed loud and clear through swinging barn doors, quilted panels hanging above the lunch counter, and mismatched knit napkins set atop tables with wooden chairs and stools. The glassed-in pie kitchen in the back hints that dessert won't be an afterthought.

Choose your own adventure when building a burger, starting with a six- or nine-ounce grass-fed beef patty and adding toppings like Midwestern cheeses, smoked bacon, jalapeños, or homemade pickles. If a wedge of strawberry rhubarb pie or Bourbon-spiked milkshake is calling your name (especially when freshly churned ice cream is involved), go easy on those hand-cut farmhouse chili fries.

Greek Islands

Greek

E3

200 S. Halsted St. (at Adams St.)

Phone: 312-782-9855 — Lunch & dinner daily
Web: www.greekislands.net
Price: $$ — UIC-Halsted

This Greektown retreat sports multiple dining areas as well as a perpetually bustling bar. Diners sup among a Disneyfied décor of faux terraces and balconies, overhangs topped by terra-cotta tiles, and a trellised ceiling entwined with artificial greenery. The chance of a courteous someone whose name ends in "os" attending to you is good, but it's the food that has kept the joint hopping for more than 40 years.

Salads are crisp and refreshing, pan-seared cheese is flambéed tableside, and the fresh seafood doesn't disappoint: fish are grilled whole, filleted, and dressed simply with herbs, a few glugs of olive oil, and squeeze of lemon. Specialties include *spetsofai*, house-made sausage sautéed with onions and peppers in a red wine- and tomato-sauce.

¡Hello Tacos! De Cero

Mexican XX

816 W. Randolph St. (at Halsted St.)

Phone: 312-455-8114 Lunch & dinner Tue – Sat
Web: www.hellotacos.com
Price: $$ Morgan

As a *muy* popular member of restaurant row, this spot takes the traditional taqueria and turns it on its head...with spice! Lively music keeps the energy level high, though low lighting lends a cozy vibe to the sleek wood-dominated space. Two rooms, each equipped with a bar, make it easy to get started with a strawberry-mint margarita or Mexican beer.

Don't let the quirky name fool you; ¡Hello Tacos! is still everything you've come to love about De Cero over the years. Tacos are made with hand-pressed corn tortillas and ordered individually, letting diners sample a range of fillings including rich duck confit and spicy corn salsa. Ample chunks of carnitas with habanero salsa and julienned radish is another fave, while jalapeño-marinated skirt steak tortas are pressed to order and ooze with melting *Chihuahua*.

High Five Ramen

Japanese 

112 N. Green St. (bet. Randolph St. & Washington Blvd.)

Phone: N/A Dinner nightly
Web: www.highfiveramen.com
Price: ⊜ Morgan

This re-purposed industrial setting is a hipster dining hall serving two hot foodie trends under one roof. The bulk of the sprawling space is devoted to Green Street Smoked Meats, a barbecue joint where crowds of cool kids sit side-by-side downing beers and heaps of pulled pork, brisket, and Frito pie.

More worthy of attention, however, is High Five Ramen, a downstairs nook where the queue for one of its 16 seats starts early. Once inside, slurp a bowl of the signature, crazy-spicy broth. Loaded with thin alkaline noodles, a slow-cooked egg, roasted pork belly, locally grown sprouts, and black garlic oil, this unique rendition is worth the burn. For sweet, icy relief, sip on a slushy tiki cocktail—then wipe your brow and dig back in.

Jaipur

Indian XX

B2

847 W. Randolph St. (bet. Green & Peoria Sts.)

Phone: 312-526-3655 Lunch & dinner daily
Web: www.jaipurchicago.com
Price: $$ Morgan

Business execs expecting the ubiquitous lunch buffet will be sorely disappointed by Jaipur—that is until they realize this popular weekday spot serves an affordable full-service lunch special that brings the buffet to your table in a parade of hammered copper *katoris*. In the evening, locals fill every sleek, nail-studded chair in the refined dining room as they await plates of boldly flavored Indian cooking.

The broad menu features a lengthy selection of fresh and authentically treated favorites, most of which are available as part of the bountiful lunch special. Staples on the vast à la carte menu may include *aloo papdi chaat;* a rich and creamy chicken korma; spiced carrot soup; and scarlet-red tandoori chicken, served with garlic naan.

La Sardine

French 

A2

111 N. Carpenter St. (bet. Randolph St. & Washington Blvd.)

Phone: 312-421-2800 Lunch Mon – Fri
Web: www.lasardine.com Dinner Mon – Sat
Price: $$ Morgan

In a neighborhood packed to the gills with gastronomic innovation, La Sardine may be the most daring option of all, flaunting hearty French bistro food in a warm and rustic setting. The time-tested combination of wheezing accordion music, white linens, tile floors, and pastoral murals makes it all the rage among diners craving the familiar—and a $30 lunch prix-fixe doesn't hurt either.

From escargots and steak tartare to bouillabaisse and steak frites, the adept kitchen nails the classic bistro dishes. Don't miss the steak haché, a patty of excellent ground beef seared to perfection, then topped with smoked goat cheese and plated with truffle-laced Bibb lettuce, a thick slice of maple bacon, and crunchy fried onion rings.

La Sirena Clandestina

Latin American XX

A1

954 W. Fulton Market (at Morgan St.)

Phone: 312-226-5300 — Lunch Sun – Fri
Web: www.lasirenachicago.com — Dinner nightly
Price: $$ — Morgan

Chef John Manion may be splitting his time between El Che Bar and his first baby, La Sirena Clandestina, but he hasn't missed a beat. The decor reflects the location's warehouse roots through drafting stools at the bar, well-tread wood plank floors, and rugged wood tables edged in steel. Silvery pressed tin ceilings echo the happy din of conversation below.

Be sure to try the wonderful Brazilian bowl, filled with *bomba* rice, *chimichurri,* and *malagueta* salsa, topped with juicy grilled hangar steak (as well as avocado, grilled chicken or shrimp). Even kale salad deserves top billing, dressed with a creamy roasted poblano vinaigrette. Desserts feature a buttermilk *tres leches*, tender lemon-poppy seed cakes set over plum marinade and sliced market peaches.

Leña Brava

Mexican XX

B2

900 W. Randolph St. (at Peoria St.)

Phone: 312-733-1975 — Dinner Tue – Sun
Web: www.rickbayless.com
Price: $$$ — 

This prime Randolph Street corner is home to a one-two punch of Rick Bayless-ness—an excellent taqueria and brewery named Cruz Blanza as well as this sophisticated cantina. An open kitchen displaying open-fire cooking is Leña Brava's stimulating focal point, while a buzzing bar pouring an encyclopedic range of agave spirits, brews from next door, and rare Mexican wines enhances the two-floor scene.

The kitchen's Northern Mexican-influenced menu combines the bounty of the sea with the primal joy of wood-fired cooking. Be tempted by icy seafood preparations like an *aquachile* of sashimi-grade diver scallops in spiced cucumber juice. Then consider hearth-roasted black cod *al pastor* with sweet and sour pineapple, coupled with heirloom corn tortillas.

Little Goat Diner

American XX

B2

820 W. Randolph St. (at Green St.)

Phone: 312-888-3455 — Lunch & dinner daily
Web: www.littlegoatchicago.com
Price: $$ — Morgan

Every neighborhood needs a good diner and in the booming West Loop, this enthusiastic homage to the reliable road trip stopover fits in perfectly. The décor gives a wink and a nod to classic design with retro booths, spinning chrome barstools, and blue-rimmed plates, but the top-quality materials keep it on the modern side. An all-day menu of amped-up faves can be had no matter the hour. Craving a shrimp cocktail at 7:00 A.M.? Five jumbo fried shrimp wrapped in *somen* noodles are ready to go. The Goat Almighty burger lives up to its name with fatty beef brisket, saucy pulled pork, and a ground goat patty.

Ease the pain of waiting for a table here by cooling your heals at the adjacent LG Bakery with a cup of Stumptown, s'mores cookie, or Bloody Mary at the bar.

Lou Mitchell's

American X

F3

565 W. Jackson Blvd. (bet. Clinton & Jefferson Sts.)

Phone: 312-939-3111 — Lunch daily
Web: www.loumitchellsrestaurant.com
Price: ⊗ — Clinton (Blue)

At the top of Chicago's list of beloved names is Lou Mitchell. This eponymous diner is by no means an elegant affair, but thanks to its delicious omelets and iconic crowd, it has been on the Windy City's must-eat list since 1923. Don't panic at the length of the lines: they are long but move fast, and free doughnut holes (one of the restaurant's signature baked goods) make the wait go faster.

Back to those omelets: they may be made with mere eggs, like everyone else's, but somehow these are lighter and fluffier, almost like a soufflé, stuffed with feta, spinach, onions, or any other ingredients of your choice. They arrive in skillets with an Idaho-sized helping of potatoes. The best part? Everyone gets a swirl of soft-serve at the meal's end.

Maude's Liquor Bar

French XX

840 W. Randolph St. (bet. Green & Peoria Sts.)

Phone: 312-243-9712 Dinner nightly
Web: www.maudesliquorbar.com
Price: $$ Morgan

It's impossible not to love this place. The overstuffed curio cabinet and blue French metal chairs aren't true antiques, for this gorgeously disheveled and rather classy French brasserie isn't as old as the mirror's arful patina would have you believe. A handsome bar mixing contemporary and classic cocktails adds to the vintage atmosphere.

Fill up on French comfort food under the glow of mismatched crystal chandeliers, or head to the second-floor bar to snack on oysters and frites. The Lyonnaise salad is downright beautiful, tossing escarole, frisée, and baby romaine in chive vinaigrette beneath a soft boiled egg and chunks of grilled pork belly. Steak tartare satisfies from beginning to end, and the crème brûlée is a deliciously textbook finish.

Momotaro

Japanese 

820 W. Lake St. (at Green St.)

Phone: 312-733-4818 Dinner nightly
Web: www.momotarochicago.com
Price: $$ Morgan

Boka Restaurant Group's stunning West Loop canteen embraces a fantastical view of Japanese dining. An impressive selection of imported whiskies is listed on a retro-style departure board; a private dining room upstairs is styled to resemble a mid-century corporate boardroom; and a traditional *izakaya* beckons diners downstairs. Consistently packed, the impeccably designed space boasts numerous kitchens churning out a wide range of dishes.

Creative bites abound in the chef's omakase featuring torched baby squid wrapped in nori. Then a Hawaiian seaweed salad with diced nopales may be followed by *robata*-grilled Wagyu skirt steak with foie gras, shisito pepper, and *yuzu kosho*. The steamed yuzu pudding cake is just one example of the surprisingly strong dessert roster.

Monteverde

Italian XX

E2

1020 W. Madison St. (at Carpenter St.)

Phone: 312-888-3041 — Dinner Tue – Sun
Web: www.monteverdechicago.com
Price: $$ — Morgan

Chef Sarah Grueneberg is something of a local celeb, so expect this newcomer to be packed to the last dining counter stool by 5:30P.M. Then again this is prime seating, because behind that wood-grain bar lies the pasta station where sheets are rolled, cut, and hung to dry before appearing on your plate. Her signature Italian cooking—or *cucina tipica* as the menu lists it—is what draws crowds.

That said, this menu is about more than pasta, beginning with an extraordinary yet humble vessel displaying neat little bundles of cabbage leaves stuffed with herbed breadcrumbs and mushrooms, served in an inky-dark porcini Bolognese. "Wok-fried" orecchiette are pleasantly toothsome, slicked with spicy tomato sauce, and topped with gorgeously fresh head-on shrimp.

Nellcôte

Italian XX

B2

833 W. Randolph St. (at Green St.)

Phone: 312-432-0500 — Dinner nightly
Web: www.nellcoterestaurant.com
Price: $$ — Morgan

The orange canopy above Nellcôte's entrance and stylish plaque would look at home on the Côte d'Azur. Named after the villa where the Rolling Stones recorded their iconic Exile on Main Street, this West Loop rock star—decked out with a lacquered ivory bar, marble staircase, and antique chandeliers—feels like a playground for the glam.

Vases of dried lavender evoke scents of the Mediterranean, as do the kitchen's creations, beginning with bread and pasta made in-house from hand-milled flour. Vegetable dishes are a consistent highlight, especially wood-roasted cauliflower florets with slivers of chili, mint, local honey, and mustard. Finish on a sweet note with classic opera cake, sliced to reveal genoise, chocolate ganache, and espresso buttercream.

NEXT

Contemporary XX

A1

953 W. Fulton Market (at Morgan St.)

Phone: N/A- Dinner Wed – Sun
Web: www.nextrestaurant.com
Price: $$$$ Morgan

Welcome to dinner as theater, where the only thing more radical than each new theme is the success (or failure) of the cuisine. Next's conceit is reinvention. It may begin the year as, say, a culinary homage to "bistro" cooking with hit-or-miss fare that does little to underscore the kitchen's strengths. The motif of the windowless room reflects the current concept.

Some themes may be rooted in regional innovation, offering a Tour of South America with stops in Peru, Chile, and Argentina depending on the week. Innovation can be replaced by nostalgia, as in a year-ending menu devised to simulate Chef Grant Achatz's inspirational first meal at The French Laundry. This is a unique place with an adept and dexterous kitchen, but the experience just isn't for everyone.

Paramount Room

Gastropub X

F1

415 N. Milwaukee Ave. (bet. Hubbard & Kinzie Sts.)

Phone: 312-829-6300 Lunch Thu – Sun
Web: www.paramountroom.com Dinner nightly
Price: $$ Grand (Blue)

Though a few blocks north of the hot-and-heavy Fulton Market food scene, this edgy joint, equal parts gastropub and dive bar, more than holds its own. To start, make like the cool kids and order something from the well-stocked bar: Moscow Mules are presented properly in frosty copper mugs, killer Bloody Marys are fortified by skewers of huge olives and blocks of dill Havarti, and the beer list boasts there's "no crap on tap."

Paramount's menu features dishes that make the most of top-quality ingredients, like a plump burger crafted from 100 percent Wagyu beef on a toasted brioche bun. Daily specials have featured a trio of sweet and zesty pulled pork sliders sided by a heap of crisp and crunchy tempura-style green beans.

Oriole ✿✿

F1 Contemporary

661 W. Walnut St. (at Union Ave.)

Phone: 312-877-5339 Dinner Tue – Sat
Web: www.oriolechicago.com
Price: $$$$ Clinton (Green/Pink)

Welcome to Chicago's next great restaurant. The interior is mod yet industrial, with an open kitchen—filled with jovial professionals who look like they're cooking for a dinner party—that takes up a good deal of the space. The fact that nothing feels stuffy should not surprise since Oriole is something of a family business. Crisp attention to detail is clear in every member of the team, who are thoroughly versed in the intricacies of this rather complex menu.

Laying aside his previous gluten-free cooking at Senza, Chef Noah Sandoval embraces all ingredients with contemporary edge and global flavors. Expect *binchotan* grilling, fresh pasta, frozen foam, and recurring flourishes like gastriques or Spanish cheeses.

The kitchen's opening salvo may feature a warm Scottish langoustine with slivers of white asparagus, a dollop of Kristal caviar, and torched *lardo*. This may be followed by *jamón Ibérico de Bellota,* served as a sort of "salad" with black walnut, bits of Campo de Montalban, and drizzle of black pepper gastrique. Superb desserts courtesy of Pastry Chef/partner Genie Kwon pay homage to NOLA, like chicory custard with frozen whiskey foam, orange zest, and cinnamon-dusted vanilla ice cream.

The Publican

Gastropub

837 W. Fulton Market (at Green St.)

Phone: 312-733-9555 — Lunch Sat – Sun
Web: www.thepublicanrestaurant.com — Dinner nightly
Price: $$ — Morgan

This Fulton Market stalwart is something of a local legend and the flagship of Paul Kahan's restaurant empire. Inspired by century-old public houses where political conversations and beer flowed with equal fervor, The Publican remains true to its roots with cloistered wood booths, a brass bar, and background music that cannot be heard over the patrons' happy din.

As expected from the portraits of pigs displayed throughout the room, pork takes precedence here with spicy rinds, potted rillettes, or grilled Berkshire pork collar with watermelon, tomatoes, burnt chili, and dill. No matter what you order, pair it with one of their worldly or local brews—the glassware alone makes for a superlative experience.
Weekend brunch is farm-fresh and just as popular.

Ramen Takeya

Japanese

819 W. Fulton Market (bet. Green & Halsted Sts.)

Phone: 312-666-7710 — Lunch & dinner Tue – Sun
Web: www.ramentakeya.com
Price: — Morgan

Dining at Fulton Market is now even hotter (literally and metaphorically) thanks to these steaming bowls of noodles served in a cool setting. While a variety of soups at this *ramen-ya* are thoroughly rewarding, the signature broth made from gently simmered organic Jidori chicken proves not only the kitchen's skill but its dedication to authenticity. This is used as the pleasantly refined base for a hearty bowl of curly noodles, pork *char sui, hijiki,* and slow-cooked Jidori egg, garnished with bits of white onion for heat and crunch.
That delectable chicken appears again, *char siu*-style, along with shredded romaine lettuce and a bit of mayo stuffed into tender steamed buns. Stop at the bar for a Japanese whiskey to start or end your night.

Roister ✿

Contemporary XX

A1

951 W. Fulton Market (bet. Morgan & Sangamon Sts.)

Phone: N/A — Lunch & dinner Wed – Sun
Web: www.roisterrestaurant.com
Price: **$$$** — Morgan

Unapologetically loud, laid-back, and lively, Roister is the instant success from the Alinea Group. Even the ambient design reminds you of its sibling restaurants, though the cooking here, courtesy of Chef Andrew Brochu, is far more rustic.

The kitchen is boldly incorporated into the dining room and serves as its main focal point, adding to the synergy between front and back of house. Even service is a collaboration. The best seats are along the counter, before the kitchen's blazing hearth.

As expected, the food is creative and modern, but it is also soulful in incorporating its wood-fired hearth (don't miss the lasagna). Items may be served as small plates, family-style, or a tasting menu, culled from the à la carte offerings. Start with snacks like crisp-fried Yukon potato wedges dusted with soy and presented in a bowl with creamy tofu purée and rice vinegar. Mains include a whole chicken served as sweet-tea brined breast and crisp-skinned dark meat marinated in buttermilk and chamomile with creamy gravy and sunchoke hot sauce. For dessert, the poached apricot with sour cherry sorbet, fried almond crumble, and almond ice may sound straightforward, but is in fact beguilingly complex.

Saigon Sisters

F2

567 W. Lake St. (bet. Clinton & Jefferson Sts.)

Phone: 312-496-0090 — Lunch Mon – Fri
Web: www.saigonsisters.com — Dinner Tue – Sat
Price: ⇔ — Clinton (Green/Pink)

The sign of a great restaurant is when the owner is on-site. Such is the case at Saigon Sisters, where the warm staff and familial vibe keep things ultra-pleasant. Named after Mary and sister, Theresa Nguyen, the lofty room belies its compact size with glass windows and high ceilings. Simple banquettes and wood tables are a perfect canvas for the quality Vietnamese cuisine that comes speeding out of the kitchen. Lunch is notable, with businessmen ordering a fragrant and satisfying *pho* floating with noodles, bean sprouts, jalapeños, and cilantro. Then sliced hoisin-glazed pork, char-grilled red pepper, and cool avocado stir-fried with noodles make for yet another dream team of flavor and texture.

Their casual sib, Bang Chop Thai Kitchen, continues to serve the classics.

Salero

F2

621 W. Randolph St. (bet. Desplaines St. & Jefferson St.)

Phone: 312-466-1000 — Dinner nightly
Web: www.salerochicago.com
Price: $$ — Clinton (Green/Pink)

Nestled among neighboring Randolph Street hangouts, this upscale Spaniard holds its own. Accented by wood details set aglow with pillar candles and a turquoise wall hung with steer horns, the space boasts a chic front bar area for cocktails and a dining room that welcomes guests in for a meal.

A contemporary vision of Spanish cuisine turns out *pintxos* to start—try the Gilda, a single bite skewer featuring a brown anchovy, pickled guindilla pepper, and a manzanilla olive. Follow this up with a slick risotto-paella hybrid; or boneless roasted quail stuffed with chorizo and set over wilted spinach with toasted pine nuts. For dessert, order the *manzana* to receive a miniature apple cake dressed with rosemary crumble, cider reduction, and goat cheese ice cream.

Sepia ✿

F2 — American XX

123 N. Jefferson St. (bet. Randolph St. & Washington Blvd.)

Phone: 312-441-1920
Web: www.sepiachicago.com
Price: $$$

Lunch Mon – Fri
Dinner nightly
Clinton (Green/Pink)

When a restaurant's excellence is this consistent, it should come as no surprise that the First Lady names it as one of her favorites. Set inside a 19th-century print shop, the historic dining room does a fine job mixing original details with modern touches. Muted tones in the exposed brick walls and custom tile floors complement newer elements like floor-to-ceiling wine storage and dramatic smoke-shaded chandeliers that drip with crystals. Though the décor may tip its hat to yesteryear, Chef Andrew Zimmerman's cuisine is firmly grounded in the 21st century.

Meals here deliciously reflect the amalgam of American cuisine, with hints of Southeast Asian, Korean, and Mediterranean tastes. But, it is at dinner when this kitchen truly comes to life. Gnocchi may seem commonplace, but this version is memorable thanks to the flawless components and rich flavors of lamb sugo with ciabatta breadcrumbs. Chicken here is downright exciting, served tender and crisp-skinned with a supremely buttery Albufera sauce, crumbly chestnuts, caramelized fennel, and sausage.

Simple-sounding desserts keep the bar high until the very end, by way of offerings like toffee-coconut cake with chocolate ganache and burnt caramel.

Smyth 

Contemporary 

D2

177 N. Ada St. (bet. Lake & Randolph Sts.)

Phone: 773-913-3773 Dinner Tue – Sat
Web: www.smythandtheloyalist.com
Price: $$$$ Ashland (Green/Pink)

Find this remarkable home to fine-dining in an ivy-covered building just upstairs from The Loyalist bar and lounge, though it almost feels like the posh studio apartment of a culinary geek with a trust fund. The look is stark, stylish, and masculine to match the smart, come-as-you-are crowd.

The open kitchen is led by Chefs John Shields and Karen Urie Shields who met while working at Charlie Trotter's—you'll meet the back-of-house staff as they are often the ones presenting dishes.

The cuisine is unique and inventive, but not experimental. This is a restaurant with a vision that keeps the guests' pleasure and kitchen's near-flawless execution at the heart of each combination. Subtle seafood notes finesse nearly every plate, with wild but wonderful surprises like the deep bowl of aromatic green herbs with duck tongues that are tempura fried to be as airy as popcorn, and braised as tender as an oyster, served with roasted squid jus. Desserts are equal parts grace and skill, which is abundantly clear in the whipped tomato mousse. Garnished with vanilla-candied tomatoes, tangy peach wedges, cape gooseberries, and tiny nasturtium petals, it makes for a light, bright, and delicious finale indeed.

Sushi Dokku

Japanese

823 W. Randolph St. (at Green St.)

Phone: 312-455-8238 — Lunch Fri
Web: www.sushidokku.com — Dinner Tue – Sat
Price: $$ — Morgan

Creatively adorned nigiri is the featured attraction at this hip sushi-ya that's all wood planks, stainless steel, chunky tables, and hefty benches.

Just one piece of Sushi Dokku's supple cuts showcasing quality and technique is not enough—thankfully each nigiri order is served as pairs. Among the terrific selection, enjoy the likes of hamachi sporting a spicy mix of shredded Napa cabbage, daikon, and red chili; or salmon dressed with a sweet ginger-soy sauce and fried ginger chips. South Pacific sea bream is deliciously embellished with a drizzle of smoky tomato and black sea salt. Those who wish to branch out from sushi should go for *takoyaki* (crispy fried octopus croquettes), grilled hamachi collar, or a brownie-crusted green tea-cheesecake.

Swift & Sons

Steakhouse

1000 W. Fulton Market (at Morgan St.)

Phone: 312-733-9420 — Dinner nightly
Web: www.swiftandsonschicago.com
Price: $$$$ — Morgan

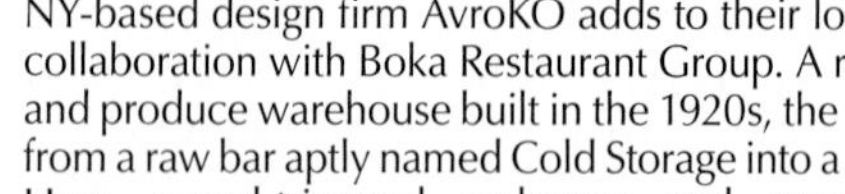

With the inception of this massive steakhouse at 1 K Fulton, NY-based design firm AvroKO adds to their local portfolio in collaboration with Boka Restaurant Group. A renovated meat and produce warehouse built in the 1920s, the space unwinds from a raw bar aptly named Cold Storage into a plush hangout. Here, wood-trimmed archways and concrete columns modulate the scale of the rooms. The kitchen's contemporary take on steak serves up USDA Prime beef seared at high heat and presented with a trio of sauces. It's the kind of place where gluttony is rewarded (even their wine program features Coravin selections in three- or six-ounce pours. Extras like King crab Oscar and dessert (Boston cream pie?) are worth the calories.

Lunch is offered on weekdays at Cold Storage.

Vera

Spanish

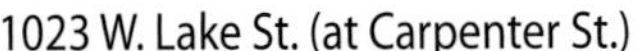

A2

1023 W. Lake St. (at Carpenter St.)

Phone: 312-243-9770 — Dinner Mon – Sat
Web: www.verachicago.com
Price: $$ — Morgan

Pimentón de la Vera, one of the most powerful spices in Spanish cuisine, also provides partial inspiration for this first-come, first-served wine bar. (The other homage? Chef/owner Mark Mendez's grandmother.) The exposed brick walls and walnut floors are lovely, but do little to soften the din of a happy hour crowd after a few glasses from their very impressive sherry list.

The menu is comprised of classic tapas as well as larger plates like a piled-high paella with rabbit, duck, and chorizo, though the Serrano ham is sure to steal the thunder. Shell out a few extra dollars for crusty bread to sop up the garlicky, lemony olive oil that bathes their plump head-on shrimp. Grilled rounds of octopus are sweet and smoky thanks to a liberal dose of *pimentón.*

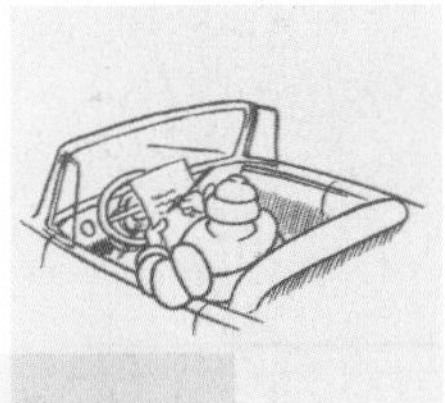

Avoid the search for parking. Look for .

MICHELIN

Tires wear more quickly on short urban journeys.

TRUE!

You tend to accelerate and brake more often when driving around town so your tires work harder!
If you are stuck in traffic, keep calm and drive slowly.

Tire pressure only affects your car's safety.

FALSE!

Driving with underinflated tires (0.5 below recommended pressure) doesn't just impact handling and fuel consumption, it will take 8,000 km off tire lifespan.
Make sure you check tire pressure about once a month and before you go on vacation or a long journey.

If you only encounter **winter weather from time to time** - sudden showers, snowfall or black ice - **one type of tire** will do the job.
?
TRUE!
The revolutionary **MICHELIN CrossClimate** - the very first summer tire with winter certification - is a practical solution to keep you on the road whatever the weather.

Fitting **2 winter tires** on my car guarantees maximum safety.
?
FALSE!
In the winter, especially when temperatures drop below 44.5°F, to ensure better road grip, all four tires should be identical and fitted at the same time.
2 WINTER TIRES ONLY = risk of compromised road grip.
4 WINTER TIRES = safer handling when cornering, driving downhill and braking.
If you regularly encounter rain, snow or black ice, choose a **MICHELIN Alpin tire**. This range offers you sharp handling plus a comfortable ride to safely face the challenge of winter driving.
MICHELIN

MICHELIN IS COMMITTED

► *MICHELIN IS THE **GLOBAL LEADER IN FUEL-EFFICIENT TIRES** FOR LIGHT VEHICLES.*

► ***EDUCATING YOUNGSTERS ON ROAD SAFETY FOR BIKES,** NOT FORGETTING TWO-WHEELERS. LOCAL ROAD SAFETY CAMPAIGNS WERE RUN IN **16 COUNTRIES** IN 2015.*

QUIZ

1 TIRES ARE BLACK SO WHY IS THE MICHELIN MAN WHITE?

Back in 1898 when the Michelin Man was first created from a stack of tires, they were made of natural rubber, cotton and sulphur and were therefore light-colored. The composition of tires did not change until after the First World War when carbon black was introduced. But the Michelin Man kept his color!

2 HOW LONG HAS MICHELIN BEEN GUIDING TRAVELERS?

Since 1900. When the MICHELIN guide was published at the turn of the century, it was claimed that it would last for a hundred years. It's still around today and remains a reference with new editions and online restaurant listings in a number of countries.

3 WHEN WAS THE "BIB GOURMAND" INTRODUCED IN THE MICHELIN GUIDE?

The symbol was created in 1997 but as early as 1954 the MICHELIN guide was recommending "exceptional good food at moderate prices." Today, it features on the MICHELIN Restaurants website and app.

If you want to enjoy a fun day out and find out more about Michelin, why not visit the l'Aventure Michelin museum and shop in Clermont-Ferrand, France:

www.laventuremichelin.com

Indexes

Where to **Eat**

Alphabetical List of Restaurants

K

L

M

N

O

P

Restaurants by Cuisine

Contemporary

Deli

Eastern European

Ethiopian

Filipino

French

Fusion

Jamaican

Japanese

Korean

Latin American

Macanese

Mediterranean

Mexican

Middle Eastern

Moroccan

Persian

Peruvian

Pizza

Polish

Puerto Rican

Seafood

Southern

Spanish

Steakhouse

Thai

Vegan

Vegetarian

Vietnamese

Bib Gourmand

This symbol indicates our inspectors' favorites for good value. For $40 or less, you can enjoy two courses and a glass of wine or a dessert (not including tax or gratuity).

Cuisines by Neighborhood

Gold Coast

Humboldt Park & Logan Square

Lakeview & Wrigleyville

Lincoln Park & Old Town

Loop

Pilsen, University Village & Bridgeport

River North

Starred Restaurants

Within the selection we offer you, some restaurants deserve to be highlighted for their particularly good cuisine. When giving one, two, or three Michelin stars, there are a number of elements that we consider including the quality of the ingredients, the technical skill and flair that goes into their preparation, the blend and clarity of flavors, and the balance of the menu. Just as important is the ability to produce excellent cooking time and again. We make as many visits as we need, so that our readers may be assured of quality and consistency.

A two or three-star restaurant has to offer something very special in its cuisine; a real element of creativity, originality, or "personality" that sets it apart from the rest. Three stars – our highest award – are given to the choicest restaurants, where the whole dining experience is superb.

Cuisine in any style, modern or traditional, may be eligible for a star. Due to the fact we apply the same independent standards everywhere, the awards have become benchmarks of reliability and excellence in over 20 countries in Europe and Asia, particularly in France, where we have awarded stars for 100 years, and where the phrase "Now that's real three-star quality!" has entered into the language.

The awarding of a star is based solely on the quality of the cuisine.

Exceptional cuisine, worth a special journey

One always eats here extremely well, sometimes superbly. Distinctive dishes are precisely executed, using superlative ingredients.

Alinea	XxxX	139
Grace	XxxX	227

Excellent cuisine, worth a detour

Skillfully and carefully crafted dishes of outstanding quality.

Acadia	XxX	72
42 Grams	XX	27
Oriole	XxX	236
Sixteen	XxxX	200
Tru	XxxX	215

A very good restaurant in its category

A place offering cuisine prepared to a consistently high standard.

Band of Bohemia	XX	23
Blackbird	XX	224
Boka	XxX	141
Dusek's (Board & Beer)	X	168
EL Ideas	XX	169
Elizabeth	XX	26
Everest	XxX	158
Goosefoot	XX	29
GreenRiver	XX	211
Longman & Eagle	X	106
NAHA	XxX	194
North Pond	XX	145
Parachute	X	109
Roister	XX	238
Schwa	X	64
Sepia	XX	240
Smyth	XxX	241
Spiaggia	XxX	92
Topolobampo	XX	203

Under $25

Credits

Page 4: AS - **Page 5**: Peter L. Wrenn - **Page 9**: H. Soto
Pages 12-13: Peter L. Wrenn - **Page 15:** AS
Page 16: Maralayna - **Page 17:** Rich B. - **Page 23:** Maralayna
Page 26: H. Soto - **Page 27:** Neil Burger - **Page 29:** Neil Burger - **Pages 40-41:** RAA - **Page 44:** Rich B. - **Page 45:** AS
Page 64: Neil Burger - **Page 68**: Rich B. - **Page 70**: RAA
Page 71: MR - **Page 72**: Neil Burger - **Page 79**: Rich B.
Page 81: RAA - **Page 92**: Neil Burger - **Page 93**: Rich B.
Page 94: MR - P**ages 96-97:** MR - **Page 106**: MR -
Page 109: Neil Burger - **Page 116**: JEM - **Page 117**: M. Chan
Page 118: Rich B. - **Page 119**: SS - **Page 132**: AS
Pages 133-134: MR - **Page 135**: RAA - **Page 139**: Neil Burger
Page 141: Neil Burger - **Page 145**: Neil Burger - **Page 150**: SS
Pages 151-152: Rich B. - **Page 153**: Peter L. Wrenn
Page 158: Neil Burger - **Page 161**: Peter L. Wrenn
Page 162: JEM - **Page 163**: SS - **Pages 168-169**: Neil Burger
Page 175: Rich B **Page 176**: Rich B. - **Page 177**: Peter L. Wrenn **Page 178**: Rich B. - **Page 179**: Peter L. Wrenn - **Page 194**: MR **Page 200**: Neil Burger - **Page 203**: Neil Burger
Page 207: Peter L. Wrenn - **Page 208**: SS - **Page 209**: Peter L. Wrenn - **Page 211**: H. Soto - **Page 215**: MR - **Page 217**: Rich B. **Page 220**: SS - **Page 221**: Rich B.; Maralayna - **Page 224**: AS **Page 227**: Neil Burger - **Page 236**: AS - **Page 238**: AS
Page 240: Neil Burger - **Page 241:** SS - **Page 273**: Rich B.

SYMBOLS

Awards

✿✿✿	Three stars • Exceptional cuisine, worth a special journey
✿✿	Two Stars • Excellent cooking, worth a detour
✿	One Star • High quality cooking, worth a stop
☺	Bib Gourmand • Inspectors' favorites for good value

Facilities & Services

- Cash only
- Wheelchair accessible
- Outdoor dining
- Breakfast
- Brunch
- Dim sum
- Notable wine list
- Notable sake list
- Notable cocktail list
- Notable beer list
- Valet parking
- BYO Bring your own
- Private dining room
- El station

Classification

More pleasant if in red.

	Small plates
X	Comfortable
XX	Quite comfortable
XXX	Very comfortable
XXXX	Top class comfortable
XXXXX	Luxury in the traditional style

Average Prices

	Under $25
$$	$25 to $50
$$$	$50 to $75
$$$$	Over $75

Map Legend

- ● Restaurant
- Hospital
- Ⓜ *Clark* El station
-  Main bus station
-  Train station
- 

Adjacent neighborhood